Mass Atrocity Crimes

Mass Atrocity Crimes

Preventing Future Outrages

Robert I. Rotberg

Editor

World Peace Foundation
Cambridge, Massachusetts

Harvard Kennedy School Program on Intrastate Conflict
Cambridge, Massachusetts

Brookings Institution Press
Washington, D.C.

Mass Atrocity Crimes: Preventing Future Outrages may be ordered from:
Brookings Institution Press, 1775 Massachusetts Avenue, N.W., Washington, D.C. 20036
Telephone: 1-800/537-5487 or 410/516-6956
E-mail: hfscustserv@press.jhu.edu; www.brookings.edu

Library of Congress Cataloging-in-Publication data

Mass atrocity crimes : preventing future outrages / Robert I. Rotberg, editor.
p. cm.
Sponsored by the World Peace Foundation and the Harvard Kennedy School Program on Intrastate Conflict.
Includes bibliographical references and index.
ISBN 978-0-8157-0471-3
1. Genocide—Prevention. 2. Crimes against humanity—Prevention. I. Rotberg, Robert I. II. World Peace Foundation. III. John F. Kennedy School of Government. Program on Intrastate Conflict. IV. Title.
HV6322.7.M374 2010
364.4—dc22 2010013690

9 8 7 6 5 4 3 2 1

Printed on acid-free paper

Typeset in Minion

Composition by Cynthia Stock
Silver Spring, Maryland

Printed by R. R. Donnelley
Harrisonburg, Virginia

Contents

Preface

Two broad-ranging conferences at Harvard Kennedy School on how best to end the scourge of crimes against humanity—from the Cambodian and Rwandan genocides to ethnic cleansing in Bosnia, Croatia, and Kosovo, and on to another genocidal crisis in Darfur and thence to the brutal wars of the Congo—preceded and fueled this volume of fresh essays on how best to deter renewed mass atrocity crimes. This book thus examines the emerging norm: "responsibility to protect" (R2P), the use of international humanitarian law to prevent all manner of war crimes, the role and efficacy of the International Criminal Court and special judicial tribunals, and new approaches to amassing information about anticipating zones of catastrophic risk.

Both conferences, in 2008, were jointly organized and sponsored by the Kennedy School's Program on Intrastate Conflict, the Mass Atrocity Response Operations (MARO) project of the Kennedy School's Carr Center for Human Rights Policy, and the World Peace Foundation. Sarah Sewall, then Acting Director of the Carr Center, also supervised the MARO project. Her collaboration made a difficult epistemological journey much easier and more successful than expected.

In addition to the chapter authors of this book, participants in the two meetings contributed tellingly to the eventual shape and contents of this book. Those participants included Patrick Ball, Rachel Davis, Gareth Evans, Helen Fein, Ben Heineman, Diane Orentlicher, John Packer, Sheri Rosenberg, Andrea Rossi, David Scheffer, Taylor Seybolt, John Shattuck, Scott Straus, Horacio Trujillo, Lawrence Woocher, and Micah Zenko. Evans provided a keynote address on R2P at the second meeting.

This volume's various parts could not have been assembled coherently without the dedicated editorial oversight of Emily Wood. The contributors and I remain truly grateful for her imaginative and thorough editing and for her coordinating of a long and taxing process. I am also very appreciative of the research assistance of Emily Turner and Julia Mensah.

The support of the World Peace Foundation, chaired by Philip Khoury, was once again essential to the completion and publication of this volume. I remain grateful for the Foundation's backing.

Robert I. Rotberg
March 2010

ROBERT I. ROTBERG

1 Deterring Mass Atrocity Crimes: The Cause of Our Era

Nation-states persist in killing their own citizens. In 2010, Congolese in their millions were still facing death in the cross-fire of continuing civil warfare between the national army and diverse rebel militias, from starvation and disease, and because of violence against women and children. Zimbabwe's ruling Zimbabwe African National Union–Patriotic Front (ZANU-PF) Party and the military and police apparatus of the state were continuing to attack, maim, and kill, in hundreds, members of the Movement for Democratic Change (MDC), their supposed partners in a year-old joint government. The strong arm of the Sudanese state continued to foster inter-ethnic violence in its western (Darfur) and southern reaches, and even in supposedly autonomous South Sudan. Yemenis still kill Yemenis, Thai kill Muslim Thai, Colombians kill Colombians, and throughout the ungoverned space of Somalia clans seek to extirpate each other and Islamist movements seek hegemony through aggression. Innocent civilians and non-combatants are no less at risk than they were in previous years and decades. For them, danger is the default setting.[1]

Many of the contemporary intrastate conflicts that embroil the globe may not reach in common parlance the level of mass atrocity crimes. Only recent experiences in the Congo (5? million) and the Sudan (2 million north-south, .3 million in Darfur) fully echo the terrible genocidal losses in Rwanda (.8 million Tutsi) and Cambodia (2 million citizens), Turkey's wiping out of 1.5 million Armenians in 1915–1916, the depredations of Charles Taylor's regime in Liberia and Sierra Leone (1.3 million), Serbian attempts to ethnic cleanse Muslims in Bosnia and Kosovo (8,000 in just one calamitous incident and a total of 200,000 in both territories), the killing of 500,000, mostly Chinese, allegedly communist Indonesians during Sukarno's presidency,

Japan's extirpation of 300,000 Chinese in Nanking, Syria's elimination of 40,000 Sunni Muslims in Hama, the 40,000 "disappearances" in Argentina and Chile, the killing of 150,000 Mayans in Guatemala, or the massive losses during Nazi Germany's horrific Holocaust (6 million Jews).[2] Nevertheless, it is obvious that rulers or ruling groups in nation-states continue to prey upon inhabitants within their own borders. Globally, the era of ethnic cleansing is not over. Nor are genocide and genocidal-like affronts to human existence confined to twentieth century events, as the Darfurian experience shows and the massacres in the eastern Congo imply. Desperate or despotic rulers continue to kill their fellow countrymen, harm and destroy opponents, target less favored ethnic groups simply because of their ethnicity, attack persons from regions that are unpopular or threatening to the status quo (as in Côte d'Ivoire, Iraq, Syria, Tajikistan, and Uzbekistan), or arouse one kind or class of citizen to attack another for political or nationalistic gain.

These are not new arousals of enmity. Nor do they represent novel approaches to our shared humanity or advances in political and ruler avarice. Even in the pre-Westphalian world, and certainly in post-Westphalian times well before the twentieth century and since, rulers have targeted their enemies by religion, ethnicity, language, and race. Ethnic cleansing is a hoary phenomenon.

Crimes against Humanity Defined

What has and is occurring in the Congo and the Sudan, and what enormities transpired in Cambodia and Rwanda, and in dozens of other places, offends world order and is presumptively wrong according to the United Nations' (UN) Charter, international conventions, and current interpretations of crimes against humanity. But such enormities persist. Despite significant advances since the end of the Cold War, mass atrocity crimes are still not unthinkable; nor has world order created a legal architecture capable of deterring despots and other authoritarian leaders who are among the main perpetrators of contemporary crimes against humanity.

Politicians, diplomats, theologians, and lawyers have long tried to define how wars should be fought. Prohibitions against war-time atrocities can be found in most religious and political traditions. In the modern era the components of international humanitarian law have emerged from the elaborate conclusions of The Hague Conventions of 1899 and 1907, the statute of the Nuremburg Tribunal, the 1948 Genocide Convention, the Geneva Conventions of 1949, the additional protocols to the Geneva Conventions in

1977, the statutes of the International Tribunals for Former Yugoslavia and Rwanda, and, most recently, the Rome Statute of the International Criminal Court (ICC). These critical affirmations of the international regulation of human conduct during war forbid a range of odious behavior: genocide, ethnic cleansing, enumerated other crimes against humanity, and all manner of atrocity crimes, mass or otherwise. But their prohibitions are not necessarily precise, given different interpretive traditions. Collectively, as the contributors to this book attest, they compose an overarching norm that should be sufficient to prevent renewed attacks on civilians or particularized groups. But converting that norm into a series of effective preventive measures is still a work very much in progress, and tentative in its advances.

Genocide and Ethnic Cleansing

Genocide should be the most heinous of war crimes, and the easiest to prevent and prosecute. But whether acts are classified and persecuted as genocidal depends upon a careful parsing of Articles II and III of the 1948 Convention on the Prevention and Punishment of Genocide. Article II describes two elements of the crime of genocide: 1) the *mental element*, meaning the "intent to destroy, in whole or in part, a national, ethnical, racial or religious group, as such," and 2) the *physical element*, including killing members of a group, causing serious bodily or mental harm to members of a group, deliberately inflicting on a group conditions of life calculated to bring about its physical destruction in whole or part, imposing measures intended to prevent births within a group, and forcibly transferring children of one group to another.

A war crime must include both 1 and 2 to be called "genocide." Article III of the Genocide Convention describes five punishable forms of the crime of genocide: genocide; conspiracy to commit genocide; direct and public incitement to commit genocide; any attempt to commit the act; and complicity in genocidal acts. The Genocide Convention protects national, ethnical, racial, and religious groups, with each group being listed in the Convention. Intent to engage in genocidal acts may be inferred from a pattern of coordinated acts, however difficult to prove. Moreover, intent is construed as being not necessarily the same as motivation. It is the *intent* to commit the acts and the *commission* of the acts that are critical.[3]

Admittedly, "intent" is difficult to prove. Indeed, the UN's International Commission of Inquiry on Darfur found it taxing, unlike the lawyers of the Bush administration and the U.S. Congress, to demonstrate "intent" in

Darfur and thus to sustain a probable indictment of genocide. Likewise, if Pol Pot were merely killing fellow Cambodians with little interest in their ancestries, perhaps the horrific killing fields there technically did not breach the Genocide Convention because no specific internal group was being targeted for destruction.

Although the Genocide Convention imposes no right of or duty for nation-states to intervene to end genocidal acts, it does obligate those same nation-states and, by extension, world order (the UN), to take action "to prevent and to suppress acts of genocide." It is that obligation, Dan Kuwali contends in his chapter, in this volume, that compelled many nation-states to "play down" the scale of the Rwandan killings and to dither over Darfur. Admittedly, he agrees, it can be hard to demonstrate that victims in situations such as in Darfur constitute the cohesive group(s) that the Genocide Convention protects. He urges an evolution of domestic law to expand the terms of the Convention, particularly to include groups defined by political views and economic and social status and not only by ethnicity, etc. "The mass destruction of any human collective . . ." ought to be sufficient, he says.[4] Because time is always of the essence in cases of unfolding genocide and other mass atrocities, if world order cannot respond effectively and if there is no effective Responsibility to Protect mechanism, Kuwali advocates shifting potential African cases to the African Court of Human and Peoples' Rights, where a more rapid adjudication of gross human rights violations might be possible.

Ethnic cleansing (as commonly believed to have been perpetrated in Bosnia, Croatia, and Kosovo; in Darfur; and in the Congo) has no accepted legal definition but is widely regarded both as a war crime and a crime against humanity. Large-scale massacres of a group or a classification of individuals constitute ethnic cleansing. So do acts of terror intended to encourage flight, rape when systematically engaged in to alter the ethnic makeup of a group, outright expulsions and even agreed upon population exchanges (as in post-World War I Greece, Turkey, and Bulgaria).[5] Ethnic cleansing is the elimination of an unwanted group from a society, the use of force to remove people of a certain ethnic or religious group from a section of a territory, and the rendering of an area to be ethnically homogeneous by force or intimidation. Whereas genocide is a legally defined criminal offence, ethnic cleansing is not a self-standing crime, but an expression describing events that might be criminal. Whereas the intent of genocide is to destroy a group, the purpose of ethnic cleansing is to rid an area of a group that is being discriminated against by the state or powerful elements within the state.[6] In practice, however, ethnic cleansing efforts may well be or become genocidal or crimes against humanity.

The Rome Statute

The 1998 Rome Statute of the ICC further defines war crimes and crimes against humanity. The Statute says that a "crime against humanity" is any of the following acts when committed as part of a widespread or systematic attack directed against any civilian population: murder; extermination; enslavement; deportation or forcible transfer of a population; imprisonment or other severe deprivation of physical liberty in violation of fundamental rules of international law; torture; rape; and sexual slavery. The term "crimes against humanity" has also come to encompass any atrocious war crimes that are committed on a large scale. This is not, however, the original meaning nor the technical one. The term originated in the preamble to the 1907 Hague Convention, which codified the customary law of interstate armed conflict.[7] This codification was based on existing state practices that derived from those values and principles deemed to constitute the "laws of humanity," as reflected throughout history in different cultures. Today the ICC, as per the Statute, is interested in war crimes, such as murder, torture, and attacking civilians, "in particular when committed as part of a plan or policy or as part of a large-scale commission of such crimes."[8] Indeed, Kuwali suggests that war crimes must be premeditated and be a result of willful intent, high thresholds when taken together with the requirement to establish their "widespread" and "systematic" nature, as well as the large-scale character of attacks.

As compared to the laws controlling behavior in interstate wars, the protocols of the Rome Statute as they apply strictly to intrastate conflicts are less extensive. They do not cover situations of internal disturbances and tensions such as riots, isolated and sporadic acts of violence, or other acts of a similar limited or sporadic nature. But when protracted armed conflicts take place in the territory of a state between governmental authorities and organized armed groups or between such groups, the provisions of the Statute and the jurisdiction of the ICC fully apply.[9]

At the heart of the concept of war crimes is the idea that an individual can be held responsible for the actions of a country or that nation's soldiers. Genocide, crimes against humanity, and the mistreatment of civilians or combatants during civil hostilities all fall under the category of war crimes. The body of laws that define war crimes are the Geneva Conventions, a broader and older area of laws referred to as the Laws and Customs of War, and, in the case of the former Yugoslavia, the statutes of the International Criminal Tribunal in The Hague (ICTY). Article 147 of the Fourth Geneva Convention defines a war crime as "Willful killing, torture or inhuman treatment, including . . . willfully causing great suffering or serious injury to body or health, unlawful deportation or transfer or unlawful confinement of a protected person, compelling a protected person to serve in the forces of a hostile power, or willfully depriving a protected person of the rights of fair and regular trial . . . [and the] taking of hostages and extensive destruction and appropriation of property, not justified by military necessity and carried out unlawfully and wantonly."[10]

These legal prohibitions are mostly clear, powerful, and capable theoretically of being employed to prevent or at least reduce state-organized intercommunal carnage. Yet, although these and other key international legal conventions outlaw crimes against humanity; mass atrocity crimes; genocide; and violations of the civil, political, and physical rights of citizens everywhere, few effective mechanisms have been devised to hinder, to prevent, or to halt conflicts within states that are—at the very minimum—atrocity crimes. There are no internationally accepted ways, for example, of enforcing the provisions of the Genocide Convention. The UN Security Council can in theory (but rarely does) authorize preemptive strikes or intervention to halt atrocity crimes under Chapter VII of the UN Charter. But even when it does, it must then wait at the best of times for member states to fund and then supply troops for any intervention—nowadays a laborious and prolonged process with less than invigorating results. So can regional organizations or coalitions of the willing, again in theory, send troops to halt atrocity crimes? The African Union physically intervened in the Comoros and threatened successfully to do so in Guinea, Mauritania, Niger, and Togo, but the larger country cases of Madagascar and Somalia have been and are apparently too tough or insufficiently malleable. The Economic Community of West African States (ECOWAS), led by the Nigerian military, effectively slowed warfare in Liberia and Sierra Leone in the 1990s, but has not otherwise intervened in places such as Côte d'Ivoire. Nor has it considered attempting to act forcibly to moderate the inhumane actions of despotisms such as in Equatorial Guinea.[11] The Southern African Development Community (SADC), led by South Africa, was able to enter tiny Lesotho, but SADC has refused in this century to intervene in Zimbabwe's mayhem even though Zimbabwe is, at the very least, in breach of rulings on land tenure cases by SADC's own regional court.

Even when it may be obvious to credible observers, local and distant, there are no internationally conclusive agreements on what constitutes an atrocity crime or a breach of international law. When, exactly, are national governments unable or unwilling to protect their citizens? That is, President Ian Khama of Botswana may declare (as he has on several occasions) that President Robert Mugabe's thugs are breaching the human rights of Zimbabwe's citizens in impermissible ways without being able to trigger even a sub-regional agreement that Mugabe's legions have been behaving illegally and need to be stopped.[12] Khama could point to international statutes and to evidence that Zimbabwean human rights organizations have compiled, or to the reports of international bodies such as Amnesty International. He could demonstrate the efficacy of his assertions. But in terms of removing the yoke of despotism from the heads of the people of Zimbabwe, nothing has occurred or will occur.

Intrinsic Sovereignty

Zimbabwe, and other contemporary tyrannies, is, except in very special cases, protected from UN or regional intervention by the Westphalian notion of intrinsic sovereignty. The sanctity of a nation-state's ability to do nearly whatever it wants within its own borders is generally well-accepted internationally.[13] Indeed, the UN Security Council is often powerless to mobilize any kind of intervening action, sometimes even a verbal one, against countries that harm their own citizens unless the violations of international norms are wildly egregious and (usually) when the state in question (like Guinea) is distinctly small and powerless. If Russia's or China's vote is required in the Security Council to sanction a possible miscreant—a gross violator of UN conventions, say—Russia and China worry about setting precedents. They fear that someday world order will overlook sovereignty and attempt to chasten Russia or China for breaches of international law.

When world order was a somewhat simpler proposition than it is in the twenty-first century—when the tentacles of empire stretched across the globe and public consciences and public opinion could be aroused in powerful capitals by supposed outrages in distant regions—sovereignty was indeed often overlooked or ignored. As Don Hubert reminds us, in his chapter, when the UN Charter was signed in 1945 intervention by one state in the affairs of another, whether for humanitarian reasons or not (and except in self-defense), was deemed illegal except in extraordinary circumstances under Article II. Despite breaches of this prohibition against intervention by India in East Pakistan (Bangladesh) in 1971, by Vietnam in Cambodia in 1978, and by Tanzania in Uganda in 1979, there were no repercussions and few complaints. In each case the humanitarian justification for the intervention was well understood.

Those "successes" on behalf of world order, but not at the initiative of world order, were followed by the massacres at Srebrenica in Bosnia and the genocide in Rwanda, both testifying officially and dramatically to the failure of world order to respond in a timely and decisive manner to threats to peace within a territory. The UN then decided that it had an obligation to act to protect civilians, which superseded existing principles of peacekeeping and non-interference. There could be "no impartiality in the face of a campaign to exterminate part of a population."[14]

The International Criminal Court and the Tribunals

The Rome Statute of 1998 was a response to the events in Rwanda and Serbia, and an attempt to create a judicial mechanism that would be more enduring and more global in its jurisdiction than the two special *ad hoc* tribunals. As Richard J. Goldstone, distinguished jurist and the chief prosecutor for the Yugoslav special court, writes in his chapter in this volume, when the ICC was officially constituted in 2002 it transformed for all time the way in which perpetrators of war and atrocity crimes would be regarded by world order. (As of early 2010, only 110 nation-states have ratified the Statute and thus put themselves under the ICC.) Foremost, it ended impunity (hitherto almost guaranteed for most post-Nuremberg and post-Tokyo leaders) and provided a broad accountability globally. The ICC could now at least indict egregious offenders, such as Sudanese President Omar al-Bashir, even if it had no policing arm capable of bringing him and others to The Hague, where the ICC sits. Yet it successfully indicted Congolese miscreants and induced several to place themselves before the court. Its ability to indict has also put presumed war criminals such as President Mugabe on notice that they, too, could be indicted. Albeit the ICC has as of late June 2010 jailed no one after a successful prosecution, the court and prosecutorial team's mere existence has, as Goldstone suggests, significantly curtailed the prospect of impunity.

The ICC's presence has also enabled victims of atrocity crimes to obtain implicit acknowledgment of their suffering. Truth and Reconciliation commissions (nearly fifty have met or are meeting in a variety of countries), if they are run well and their proceedings are open, provide an even more pronounced capability to acknowledge the suffering of putative victims. But, if its judgments are forceful and compassionate, the reach and moral authority of a global tribunal, such as the ICC, permits victims even more conclusive forms of psychological redress. "The common factor," as Goldstone writes, ". . . is to ensure that the truth be exposed for the benefit of the victims and to provide a basis for peace in the future."[15]

The establishment of the ICC can bring fabricated denials of the very existence of war crimes to a halt. Goldstone suggests that the testimony of innumerable witnesses before the Yugoslav tribunal banished the notion forever that war crimes had not proliferated in Bosnia, Croatia, and Kosovo between 1991 and 1994. The Arusha tribunal for Rwanda did the same for the history of genocide in that country. The piling up of details of complicity and atrocity ended forever claims that no genocide had been perpetrated.

"When law is not used," Goldstone declares, "it stagnates and does not develop."[16] He says that positive international humanitarian legal principles previously existed, as set out in The Hague and Geneva Conventions. However, those strictures were hardly ever applied before the Yugoslav and Rwandan courts were created and the Rome Statute drafted. The ICC now has the opportunity and the challenge of strengthening and deepening international law through its identification of atrocity crimes and its effective prosecution of war criminals. The Rome Statute has usefully eased prosecutorial limits by refusing to link a war crime necessarily to an "armed conflict." Severe deprivation of "physical liberty" becomes criminal, too. However, such crimes must be part of widespread and systematic attacks against civilians; further, the Rome Statute requires that "knowledge of the attack" must be present. More broadly, in the special realm of abusive gender crimes, such as rape, sexual assault, and forced prostitution, the ICC can expand international jurisprudence in this area even beyond the advances that the special tribunals have made. The Rome Statute, after all, has declared a host of gender offences, even forced pregnancy, one of the "crimes against humanity."

The Rome Statute and the functioning of the ICC, together with the acts of the special tribunals and the new "mixed" tribunals for Sierra Leone, Cambodia, Timor Leste, and Lebanon, are intended to deter renewed atrocity crimes globally. Neither Goldstone nor David M. Crane, chief prosecutor of the Sierra Leonean court and the author of another chapter in this book, are persuaded that the ICC and the special courts have as yet necessarily prevented atrocity crimes. Proving the negative is almost impossible.[17] Nevertheless, Goldstone suggests that the loss of impunity and the greater vigilance that has now been created "must" deter the commission of at least some crimes. He detects a moderation of the language of tyrants about prospective war crimes, and attributes that alteration in the tenor of abuse to the new jurisprudential possibilities posed by the ICC's oversight. That may be so, but Mugabe's rhetoric and behavior has not altered. Nor has that of Presidents Muammar Qaddafi of Libya or Teodoro Obiang Nguema of Equatorial Guinea. Bashir continues as before, as well, albeit with his travels curtailed.

The Sierra Leonean Special Court was created in 2002 not by the UN, as were the Yugoslav and Rwandan special tribunals, but by a treaty agreement between the UN Security Council and the Government of Sierra Leone. It was the world's first hybrid international war crimes accountability mechanism, with jurisdiction over atrocities that were committed against Sierra Leoneans during the country's recently concluded ten-year civil war and with mixed local and international judges and prosecutors. Crane was responsible for prosecuting those who were most culpable for crimes against humanity, i.e., those who had attacked civilians in a widespread and systematic manner and knowingly understood the broader context in which their acts were committed. Systematic meant that the crime occurred as part of a "preconceived" plan or policy.

Before he could prosecute effectively, even in the aftermath of the clear carnage of the Sierra Leonean civil war, Crane believed that he could best discharge his duties if he took testimony informally on the ground from victims and witnesses. He toured towns and villages for four months, gathering a deep sense of Sierra Leone's trauma. Victims, in turn, obtained a sense that they would not be forgotten. Their suffering was acknowledged, even before the tribunal heard cases. Crane came away from his immersion in the countryside conversations with an appreciation of the magnitude of the overall atrocity and the anguish of the survivors. He touched, smelled, and tasted it all. "When drafting indictments, I only had to close my eyes to relive the perpetration of the crimes . . . ," he writes.[18]

Crane avers that prosecutors in situations similar to Sierra Leone must understand the political and diplomatic context in which their mixed courts operate. Whom to indict was a key question in Sierra Leone since not all offenders could be brought before a court, which had funding for only a few years. Thus, Crane chose to indict former President Charles Taylor of Liberia, who then hunkered down in eastern Nigeria, for his grand part in funding and sponsoring the Sierra Leonean mayhem, and chose not to indict similarly Presidents Blasé Compare of Burkina Faso and Muammar Qaddafi of Libya, whom Crane believed were equally culpable. He also brought the senior leaders of the warring factions to book. In early 2010, the Special Court largely has ended its work after a number of successful prosecutions and imprisonments. But the trial of Taylor, moved to The Hague for security reasons, continues with a spirited battle between the prosecutors and the defense. Again, whether his trial and the imprisonments in Sierra Leone have effectively prevented future crimes may never be known. But, at the very least, the suffering of victims and the suffering of one country has been acknowledged.

The Responsibility to Protect Norm

Indictments and prosecutions serve a critical purpose in the battle to curb war crimes and limit the proliferation of atrocity crimes. But there are not enough courts, judges, prosecutors, and funds to cope with every conceivable atrocity amid civil war. Furthermore, courts act after the fact. There has long been a need to create an effective method of preventing unfolding genocides and ethnic cleansing operations in their early stages, or at least ending them before massive loss of life has occurred. A Canadian-sponsored international commission, which Hubert helped to staff, set in motion, in 2001, a broad international consideration of how best to keep civilian populations safe within individual nation-states, i.e., safe from their governments and safe within civil wars. Gareth Evans, former foreign minister of Australia; Lloyd Axworthy, the serving foreign minister of Canada; and several other members of the commission successfully proposed that world order and each nation-state had a "responsibility to protect" its citizens from grievous harm.[19] Their physical safety was a charge that overcame the doctrines of sovereignty. That responsibility was greater than and more appropriate given the circumstances of genocide and repeated massacres than an older, but little used and not generally accepted, right of "humanitarian intervention." The commission contemplated, indeed advocated, military intervention in aid of the "responsibility to protect," but only when and if mass killings were actual or imminent. Violence within a state that shocks "the conscience of mankind" could well trigger military intervention. (Kuwali calls this provision an "extremely high bar.") More precisely, the commission said that large-scale loss of life, whether or not with genocidal intent, or large-scale ethnic cleansing provided "just cause" for outside military action. How large "large-scale" had to be was not defined.[20]

The deliberations of the commission built, in part, on a fresh wave of rethinking about the sovereignty obstacle. Francis Deng and Sadako Ogata had already articulated that sovereignty carried responsibility not only to fend off potential outside interferers but also to have a positive responsibility for the welfare of all of a nation-state's citizens—not just for a clan, an ethnic entity, or some other particular group.[21] Then UN Secretary-General Kofi Annan had also addressed this problem, attempting in 1999 to redefine states as being entities responsible for serving their peoples "and not vice versa." He emphasized a "consciousness of human rights" that strengthened the rights of individuals within states. The aim of the UN Charter, he reminded UN members, was to protect individual human beings, "not to protect those who abuse them."[22]

From the point of view of the member states, particularly some of the key members of the Security Council, this attempt to reinterpret sovereignty seemed more pious than serious. Sovereignty—the inalienable, time-tested "right" of nation-states to control everything and everyone within national boundaries without outside "interference"—remained a bulwark against possibly well-meaning but conceivably sanctimonious busybodies concerned more with the rights of individuals (as Annan) than with the prerogatives of tyrannical, authoritarian, and quasi-democratic regimes. The power to govern well or badly within the confines of a state in practice has continued to trump the protection of individuals or groups at risk within the state.

This sadly is so despite the UN World Summit's acceptance in 2005 of the norm of "responsibility to protect" (R2P). This surprising embrace of the norm proposed by the commission in 2001 came more because of an avalanche of deaths in the Congo and Darfur than because of any norm cascade.[23] The R2P norm, as agreed upon in the 2005 World Summit Outcome Document, enshrines the obligation of world order and individual states to protect groups in harm's way within hitherto mostly sacrosanct national borders. That is, it impels world order first to do everything possible to prevent nation-states from targeting populations, not specifically religious, linguistic, racial, and ethnic communities, for attack; to deter such attacks; and to act decisively to rescue those who are attacked.[24] The norm, as ratified in 2005, imposes on "each state" the responsibility to protect its own populations specifically (and only) from genocide, war crimes, ethnic cleansing, and crimes against humanity (without defining those well-established principles of international law). This responsibility further entails the prevention of such crimes, "including their incitement." The heads of state and government, meeting in 2005, authorized the establishment of an early warning capability for preventing atrocities and committed themselves to helping states to build capacity to protect their populations from genocide, war crimes, ethnic cleansing, and crimes against humanity. In a penultimate phrase, they also promised to assist those under stress before crises and conflicts break out.[25]

Evans argues that the problems in the world that R2P was invented to solve are narrowly focused. In attempting to avert future Bosnias, Rwandas, and Cambodias, Evans suggests that R2P is not about general conflict or dampening human rights violations. Nor is it meant to address human security issues writ large. It is "not about solving all the world's problems." The special cases that merit R2P attention, he says, are no more than ten or fifteen in number at any one time. They appear in the countries where mass atrocity crimes are "clearly being committed, here and now; those where such crimes seem to be . . . about to be committed . . . and also . . . where there seems a serious risk that such crimes will be committed in the foreseeable future unless effective preventive action is taken. . . ."[26]

As Hubert points out, the UN's 2005 text was purposely vague. It did not give priority to the effective protection of civilian populations as opposed to the right of non-intervention. The precise obligations of the UN were undefined. The thresholds for action were left hanging, especially because ethnic cleansing had and still has no legal definition. "No guidelines are set out to govern the potential use of force" in situations that might meet the presumed thresholds.[27] Naturally, too, the text was silent on possible remedies if and when a permanent member vetoed a Security Council decision to intervene to protect human life. Hubert reminds us that intense lobbying was necessary even to obtain the limited language agreed upon in paragraphs 138 and 139 in 2005. Waxman contends, however, that although no new legal obligations flowed from the 2005 Outcome Document, it shaped "the normative terrain of intervention" by powerfully rejecting the argument that sovereignty shielded leaders and regimes from international concern. For the UN and world order, the two paragraphs in the Outcome Document emphasized "a responsibility to act" and a "momentum for action."[28]

In 2009, as three important chapters in this book delineate, UN Secretary-General Ban Ki-moon undertook to make operational the 2005 articulation of international responsibility to protect norms. That is, UN Secretary-General Ban Ki-moon committed his office, and a special preparatory task force led and staffed by one of this book's contributors, to help the Assembly and the UN Secretariat to fulfill the 2005 mandate. The hope of many proponents was that the member states would agree to set out under what circumstances and how the UN could take note of a pending crisis, seek to prevent and then to remediate it, and—if necessary—mobilize the UN under Chapters VI, VII, and VIII to intervene to protect peoples at risk. The three previously mentioned chapters in this book suggest exactly why the original desire to extend the principles of the norm into actions capable of being taken by the UN and member states individually and collectively came to naught. What transpired instead of modalities that could be acted upon in today's Congo and elsewhere was a coming together of different national actors wishing to make the norms work with those concerned at a potential diminution of sovereign rights. Sufficient consensus was achieved between those concerned to preserve sovereignty and those more concerned to protect persons to enable the norm to survive in a hortatory rather than in an operational state for a few years more.

Indeed, Edward C. Luck, the UN secretary-general's special adviser for R2P, suggests in his chapter in this book that R2P may never achieve the status of a "binding" legal norm.[29] But that deficiency may not prevent the emerging norm from being effective in curbing the behavior of states and armed groups. R2P's "relevance and power derive from its capacity to help to spur political will for implementing widely accepted and long codified international standards."[30] From Luck's optimistic perspective, R2P is or will shortly become the standard by which the behavior of states and non-state actors is judged. Thus, Luck believes, even if R2P never becomes a legal norm, it will condition the conduct of states, especially those nations that prey upon their own peoples. Implicitly, Luck argues that R2P is already a widely accepted informal norm, thus having achieved at least some of the goals of its creators. The Stanley Foundation's assessment of R2P progress in early 2010 was equally affirmative: "Support for the concept remains strong."[31] Claire Applegarth and Andrew Block, in their chapter in this volume, somewhat disagree, calling R2P "an unfulfilled promise."[32]

As his chapter hints, Luck and Secretary-General Ban Ki-Moon worked diligently and in a disciplined, constrained, and consistent manner throughout 2008 and 2009 to prevent the emerging norm and its implications from being stretched to cover a broad, rather than a narrow, range of global issues. A narrow application was better, and more productive in strengthening a political acceptance for the norm among members suspicious of its possible broad reach. Evans told the UN in 2009 that "if we are to be really serious about ending mass atrocity crimes once and for all" intervention must be an option. But such intervention need not imply the dispatch of a military force. It could mean diplomatic persuasion, high-level mediation, threats of international prosecution, arms embargoes, targeted sanctions, and the jamming of hate radio stations.[33] In that manner the norm was usefully employed by former Secretary-General Annan and others in Kenya, where thousands were killed in post-electoral combat; influential jaw-boning and intense mediation substituted in that case for outside military intervention.

But Evans and others were pleased that the R2P norm was not invoked in response to the nevertheless callous actions of the Burmese military junta in the wake of Cyclone Nargis' destruction of millions of homes and lives in 2008. Luck (and Evans) prefer a narrow construction of the norm for fear that a broader application would make the norm unusable and incoherent, and its application haphazard.

The use of military might to prevent nation-states from harming their own populations is widely opposed by some members of the General Assembly. Luck and the proponents of a robust R2P within the permanent five members (P5) of the Security Council, as Applegarth and Block's chapter explains, failed in the 2009 discussions at the UN to overcome the widespread worry that R2P contingencies would automatically occasion coercive measures from outside, strong states against weak states. To these skeptics, "humanitarian intervention" was anathema because it supposedly betokened renewed imperialism and major power infringement on the prerogatives of weak states.

Burma, Cuba, Nicaragua, North Korea, the Sudan, Venezuela, and Zimbabwe led the charge against R2P. Russia and China were largely supportive of the status quo, and were not stridently opposed to a more robust R2P initiative. India was a little more favorable than it had been in the 2005 debates, as were Vietnam and Egypt. A number of other Southeast Asian nation-states expressed themselves as hesitant, if less than supportive. Many of the strongest supporters of R2P in 2009, as opposed to in 2005, were African nations: Benin, Botswana, Cameroon, the Gambia, Ghana, Kenya, Lesotho, Mali, Nigeria, South Africa (a recent convert), Rwanda, Sierra Leone, Swaziland, and Tanzania. Most members of the Organization of American States, including Canada and, finally, the United States, were favorable. So were members of the European Union, Australia, New Zealand, Japan, Jordan, Morocco, and Qatar. Applegarth and Block reckon that ninety-four nations backed R2P positively in the 2009 General Assembly debate. There was a possible momentum; certainly those in favor were more numerous than those implacably opposed. Nevertheless, Applegarth and Block argue that it was less the antagonism to R2P from members of the Non-Aligned Movement and the G-77 that prevented the implementation of a R2P apparatus in 2009 than it was "the disinterest and disorganization of the norm's supporters."[34] Friends and backers of R2P could have done much more.

What is thus far missing, even among the champions of R2P, are national offices dedicated to advancing R2P. Too many country capitals regard R2P as primarily a UN issue in New York. There is little preparation within nations for the next atrocity-provoked crisis. There is little mainstreaming of R2P into home country institutions. Indeed, there is abundant lip service to the moral norm of R2P, but little advance planning or effective political will to ready even the norm's supporters for future crises and possible preventive actions. At the UN, a joint office for R2P and genocide prevention is being contemplated, but had not been created in early 2010. Secretary-General Ban Ki-moon has called for a system-wide UN effort with predictive and preventive abilities in mind, but the embrace of R2P, even in the Secretariat of the UN, remains tentative.

Evans, Luck, and other articulators of the R2P concept have always preferred that any of its remedies be pursued within the multilateral framework of the Security Council or regional organizations, and in accordance with the provisions of the UN Charter, in a timely and decisive manner "should peaceful means be inadequate and national authorities . . . manifestly [fail] to protect their populations from genocide, war crimes, ethnic cleansing and crimes against humanity."[35] In practice, R2P would mean (and means) a heightened awareness of injurious state actions that could lead to war crimes, ethnic cleansing, and so on; an attempt on the part of UN officials to call perpetrators to account; an investigation by or on behalf of the Security Council; a declaration of findings leading to mediation, high-level personal intervention, and the possibility of sanctions. Luck also points out that the sense of R2P could encompass peacekeeping deployments and Chapter VII enforcement missions to help nation-states being attacked by insurgents committing R2P crimes. If these multiple preventive and responsive options under R2P fail to halt a nation-state's attacks on its own populations, and other good faith initiatives are exhausted, then R2P could lead to interference by the forces of world order, as anticipated in the 2001 Commission report. But, to date, we have no illustrative examples of such actions and many political big power battles to win within the Security Council before there could be clear-sighted and robust responses to an unfolding tragedy somewhere within the confines of a distant nation-state.

The Military Option

Sarah Sewall, in her contribution to this volume, is less timid about sending troops to deter ongoing mass atrocity crimes. She argues that "the United States and the international community should proactively respond to the outbreak of widespread civilian massacres with military force as well as other tools of national and international power."[36] By focusing on non-militant or non-forceful methods of preventing mayhem, world order risks contributing to "operational paralysis." A tougher initial response may have more preventive heft than the modalities now presumed under R2P. Sewall indeed fears that "in an effort to make R2P sound benign" and acceptable to anxious members, "great powers are remaining silent about armed intervention."[37]

"Prevention *alone*," Sewall avers, "is an ineffective strategy."[38] She argues sensibly that only strong, early interference can effectively prevent the escalation of state-directed violence against disadvantaged citizens. Acting early is obviously better than acting after ethnic cleansing has been completed. The costs of acting too late, or of not acting at all, are always higher than the costs of acting—as the 2005 Outcome Document says—in a timely and decisive manner.

Sewall is also impatient with multilateralism. Under its natural umbrella, state sovereignty almost always vetoes the necessary humanitarian response. Thus, only a few nations have land and air capabilities sufficient to mount a rapid response to atrocities. Had the United States intervened robustly in Rwanda in 1994 (the UN was incapable of acting speedily), the lives of many hundreds of thousands would have been spared. An effective prevention strategy must therefore include a sound military option even though no nation, not even the United States, is presently ready institutionally (nor is the UN) rapidly to undertake on a large enough scale (thinking Rwanda or the Sudan) what a small force of British paratroopers did in Sierra Leone in 2000 or the larger ECOWAS forces accomplished in Liberia in 1990 and Sierra Leone in 1997. Sewall notes the lack of preparedness within the U.S. armed forces for the types of intervention that would be required to staunch on-going mass atrocities. The prevention of atrocities is not the same as counter-insurgency warfare.

Obtaining Early Warning Information

When and if the responsibility to protect norm becomes a robust instrument of world order, with the UN Security Council as the arbiter and wielder of the instrument, world order will require early warning capabilities. It will want an alert system to trigger first responders. It will also want a mechanism or a series of interlocking modalities capable of alarming the forces of world order about the dangers to citizens within a nation-state, and to the reality that those citizens are suddenly (or over a longer term) at risk, and in need of protection against war crimes, atrocities, ethnic cleansing, and genocide. Beyond raising the alarm, which is relatively easy, world order also needs to ensure a response. News of the Cambodian killings was not obscure for too long, the massacres in Darfur came to the attention of the world with relative speed, and the depredations in the eastern Congo are largely reported in real time. Before the Rwandan genocide erupted there was ample warning, but reasonably reliable premonitions and information went unheeded.[39] Three chapters in this book offer innovative approaches to the systematic gathering of intelligence about severe threats to the persons and groups needing protection within targeted countries.

Drawing on social network theory, Sarah E. Kreps suggests that new technological innovations can provide critical and timely information about impending human crises. The ubiquity of mobile phones, and the ease of text messaging, has already in very different contexts amplified and expanded protests against authoritarian actions. Text messaging can alert insiders and outsiders to harmful regime actions, as in Teheran, Manila, Beijing and many other tense cities. Even in beleaguered Somalia, text messaging provides warnings and mobilizes dissenters. In Kenya in 2008, it probably contributed to waves of destruction and killings, and, later, to calming messages of peace. Kreps recognizes as well that mobile telephone technology, including built-in cameras, allows citizen observers to become citizen journalists capable of reporting on violent incidents (rapes, riots, and forced displacements) and incipient war crimes. As Jennifer Leaning's chapter also elaborates, these decentralized and possibly uncoordinated outpourings can be organized usefully, graphed, and mapped to provide concrete information in real time that is more valuable and greater than the scattered contents themselves. The mobile phone has already demonstrated its vast capability as a vital early warning tool.[40]

Overhead surveillance has long provided another method of appreciating and interpreting unfolding events on the ground. As Leaning reminds us, old-fashioned aerial photography was helpful in accumulating intelligence about the location and extent of janjaweed depredations in Darfur. So was satellite imagery showing destroyed villages and population displacements. Now the availability in many circumstances of unmanned aerial vehicles, such as drones, permits more intensive observation and photography from the air; today's drones can hover for hours and can use infrared, as well as other forms of photographic technology, video, and radar, to provide almost instantaneous reporting of suspicious behavior and dangerous events. Fortunately, unmanned aircraft are less costly to build and operate than many larger fixed-wing aircraft. They can also be down-sized to maximize their utility and reduce their intrusiveness. Mechanical butterflies may soon sweep in and out of target zones to offer critical observations capable of alerting the UN and interested governments of unfolding threats to peace and order.

Satellites, high-orbit, low-orbit, and high- and low-resolution, have well-demonstrated their value—at least in clear weather and absent heavy tree cover on the ground—as key overhead surveillance tools. Various kinds of commercial satellites, Kreps reminds us, are already being used to document the scale and spread of human rights abuses. By comparing before and after images—especially the erasure of villages, for example, and the burning of crops—the possibility of ethnic cleansing can be noticed and preventive action taken. Satellites and infrared sensors can compare light signatures (signifying power usages) before and after to detect the onset of ethnic cleansing or other potential war crimes. A normalized vegetation index can be employed through overhead means to show dramatic deforestation and other potential indicators of harm to target populations. The mass dislocation of Tutsi during the Rwandan genocide would have been discernible by abrupt alterations in vegetation cover.

Employing these many different technologies conveys visual clues about events on the ground that might merit close attention, possibly even official preventive efforts. They assist, especially if statistical methods and other sophisticated aggregational approaches are utilized to obtain clues sufficient to anticipate the onset of mass atrocities and conceivably less catastrophic war crimes. But the knowledge that incipient killing fields and potential atrocity crime scenes are being watched from on high may also have even greater value by inhibiting assaults by despots and their associates. If they know that they are being watched and know that anything obtained by surveillance can be supplied to the ICC, tyrants may stay the worst of their mailed fists. Even closed junta-run societies such as Burma may not want to be embarrassed by satellite-collected data or other visual proof of atrocities. All of these technologies are to some extent intrusive and, implicitly, conceivable breaches of sovereignty. But they are too valuable in the battle against crimes against humanity to discard.

Information obtained in these and more traditional ways permits knowledgeable experts to discern patterns and to notice deviations from pre-existing patterns. As Leaning reminds us, John Snow ended a cholera epidemic in nineteenth century Britain when he mapped places of death in London and thus zeroed-in on the likely fount of contamination. In the 1990s, William Bratton and John Timoney employed similar techniques and more powerful probabilistic tools to curb crime in New York City.[41] Now we can use evidence of unusual population movements and the removal of villages, the proliferation of animal carcasses, or some other equally indicative repetitive pattern, to arouse appropriate concern and early warning. Realities on the ground only become important when they are noticed, and their out-of-the-ordinary patterning is revealed.

Anticipating where and when the next episode of ethnic cleansing will occur, and suggesting which countries might harbor the potential for, or which unfolding situations might lead to, genocide demands close attention to unfolding patterns, satellite images, and so on by dedicated teams at the UN and regional bodies, officials from the P5, and by well-respected and dedicated international NGOs such as the International Crisis Group, International Alert, Amnesty International, and Human Rights Watch. If and when a R2P mission is fully incorporated in the UN system, the collection and examination of much of this early warning information can be overseen there, and alarms issued. But, even when there is such a R2P office, much of the non- or at least low-tech indications of potential atrocity crimes will come from NGOs and civil society personnel on the ground in targeted countries, from regular journalists as well as citizen journalists, from foreign diplomats, and from a close examination of day-to-day occurrences on the ground.

Frank Chalk's chapter further argues that the monitoring of local mass media can positively "predict" the coming of mass atrocities. Arguing from classic studies of propaganda in Nazi Germany, Chalk reminds us that Joseph Goebbels consciously prepared Germans for policy departures through regular news releases and commentaries. If Europeans or Americans had paid attention to German domestic radio broadcasts, Hitler's intention to annihilate Jews would have been obvious. In the case of Rwanda, the messages of hate for Tutsi that Radio Television Libre des Mille Collines (RTLM) disseminated, especially in Kinyarwanda (and not necessarily in French), were tellingly indicative of the plans that the ruling Hutu and their allies had prepared. RTLM's messages "facilitated the genocide, contributed to the authoritativeness of the leaders' orders to kill, and gave important early clues as to the intentions and thinking within the paranoid world of the genocidaires."[42] Indeed, Canadian General Roméo Dallaire, head of a UN peacekeeping force in Kigali, begged to jam RTLM before the genocide began but was refused permission. At the time, Washington and London may have been less aware than necessary of the messages of hate spewing out of the Hutu-sponsored RTLM; they were inconsistently monitoring broadcasts in Kinyarwanda, and mostly listening to RTLM programs in French.

Most developing world citizens obtain their news and information from radio, and most developing world countries control their main radio outlets. Media monitoring of countries at risk, or tense countries, should be taken seriously. Chalk argues that attention should be paid particularly to obvious hate propaganda; omissions of key matters from news reports; intensifying governmental dictating of broadcast and news content; and reports about persons eliminated on the basis of ethnicity, race, religion, and political affiliation. Each of these factors foreshadowed the coming of atrocities in the Soviet Union, Nazi Germany, Sukarno's Indonesia, East Pakistan, Burundi, Cambodia, Rwanda, and Côte d'Ivoire. Unfortunately, as Chalk says, there is limited capacity today in the P5 and elsewhere for such a monitoring effort. Cost-cutting efforts have largely destroyed the once-vaunted broadcast monitoring capabilities of the United States and Britain, and newer techniques have not replaced them.

Conclusion

It should be evident from this and successive chapters in this book that the work of preventing mass atrocity crimes is very much in embryo. The norm of R2P, as much in the general atmosphere as it might be, has not yet achieved anything similar to a tipping point of acceptance or a cascade toward universal applicability. Too many nation-states still embrace sovereignty instead of protection for innocent civilians. Too many others are indifferent or hesitant. Hence, ethnic, religious, linguistic, and political groups remain as much at risk as they have been for decades. The force of international law against all manner of atrocity crimes applies, as the Rome Statute mandates, but the ICC has not yet extended its reach far enough or decisively enough to stay the hand of those despots or warlords in selected countries who continue to abuse their own peoples and perpetrate what clearly are war crimes—but are crimes difficult to indict or prosecute. Freshly sensitized to the recurrence of mass atrocities, and with ample early warning of such crimes against humanity available through older means or new technologies, the citizens of the world and the forces of world order will notice the next wave of ethnic cleansing, the next incipient genocide, and the commission of war crimes. But will world order be able to act in a timely and robust manner? That is the key question of our era. Easy answers are not forthcoming. The peoples of the globe remain very much at risk.

Notes

1. The writing of this chapter greatly benefited from the constructive comments of David M. Crane, Richard J. Goldstone, Dan Kuwali, Jennifer Leaning, and Edward C. Luck.

2. These numbers are derived from diverse standard sources and accord well with received wisdom except in the case of Sierra Leone, where the number comes from David M. Crane, in his chapter in this book. For the broader but critical question of what such numbers mean, and how they are amassed, see the important explanations and debate in Michael Spagat, Andrew Mack, Tara Cooper, and Joakim Kreutz, "Estimating War Deaths: An Arena of Contestation," *Journal of Conflict Resolution*, LIII (2009), 934–950; Ziad Obermeyer, Christopher J. L. Murray, and Emmanuela Gakidou, "Fifty Years of Violent War Deaths from Vietnam to Bosnia: Analysis of Data from the World Health Survey Programme," *British Medical Journal* (2008), available at www.bmj.com/cgi/content/full/bmj.a137 (accessed 25 February 2010); Bethany Lacina, Nils Petter Gleditsch, and Bruce Russett, "The Declining Risk of Death in Battle," *International Studies Quarterly*, I (2006), 673–680. The first article questions the number of estimated deaths in the Congo. See also E. Cameron, Michael Spagat, and Madelyn Hicks, "Tracking Civilian Casualties in Combat Zones using Civilian Battle Damage Assessment Ratios," *British Army Review*, CXLVII (2009), 87–93. For the number of civil war deaths in Sierra Leone and Liberia, Julia Mensah's thorough literature search produced a series of reputable estimates for Sierra Leone ranging from 120,000 to 500,000. For Liberia, she found much smaller numbers.

3. See www.preventgenocide.org/genocide/officialtext (accessed 15 February 2010).

4. Dan Kuwali, "Old Crimes, New Paradigms: Preventing Mass Atrocity Crimes," chapter 2 in this volume, 37.

5. See Gareth Evans, *The Responsibility to Protect: Ending Mass Atrocity Crimes Once and for All* (Washington, D.C., 2008), 13.

6. See Robert M. Hayden, "Schindler's Fate: Genocide, Ethnic Cleansing, and Population Transfers," *Slavic Review*, LV (1996), 731–734.

7. See M. Cherif Bassiouni, "Crimes against Humanity," Crimes of War Guide, available at www.crimesof war.org/ (accessed 15 February 2010).

8. See www.aegistrust.org/war-crimes (accessed 15 February 2010).

9. See www.aegistrust.org/War-crimes/what-are-war-crimes.html (accessed 15 February 2010).

10. See http://news.bbc.co.uk/2/hi/europe/1420133.stm (accessed 15 February 2010).

11. For Equatorial Guinea, see John R. Heilbrunn, "Equatorial Guinea and Togo: What Price Repression?" in Robert I. Rotberg (ed.), *Worst of the Worst: Dealing with Repressive and Rogue Nations* (Washington, D.C., 2007), 223–249.

12. Seretse Ian Khama, "State of the Nation Address," *Tautona Times* (13 November 2009), 27.

13. See Stephen D. Krasner, *Power, the State, and Sovereignty: Essays on International Relations* (New York, 2009), pp. 179–210; Hurst Hannum, *Autonomy, Sovereignty, and Self-Determination: The Accommodation of Conflicting Rights* (Philadelphia, 1990), 14–26; Edward C. Luck, "Sovereignty, Choice, and the Responsibility to Protect," *Global Responsibility to Protect*, I (2009), 10–21.

14. United Nations, *The Report of the Independent Inquiry into the Actions of the United Nations during the 1994 Genocide in Rwanda*, UN Doc. S/1999/1257 (New York, 1999), 50.

15. Richard J. Goldstone, "The Role of the International Criminal Court," chapter 3 in this volume, 60.

16. Ibid., 62.

17. Admittedly, innovative researchers could interview a succession of presumed perpetrators to discover whether their future actions would now be inhibited by the putative "long-arm" of the ICC.

18. David M. Crane, "Understanding Crimes against Humanity in West Africa: Giving the People What They Want," chapter 4 in this volume, 77.

19. For Evans's account of the commission and the development of the R2P concept, see his *Responsibility to Protect*, 38–48.

20. The Report of the International Commission on Intervention and State Sovereignty was published as *The Responsibility to Protect* (Ottawa, 2001), 31–32.

21. Deng, *Sovereignty as Responsibility: Conflict Management in Africa* (Washington, D.C., 1996). See also the commentary in Evans, *Resoponsibility to Protect*, 36.

22. Kofi Annan, "Two Concepts of Sovereignty," address to the 54th Session of the General Assembly, New York, New York, 18 September 1999.

23. For the cascade concept, see Martha Finnemore and Kathryn Sikkink, "International Norm Dynamics and Political Change," *International Organization*, LII (1998), 887–917.

24. For the history and evolution of the Responsibility to Protect norm, see the authoritative account of Evans, one of its inventors and first articulators: Evans, *Responsibility to Protect*, 38–54. See also the chapter by Edward C. Luck, "Building a Norm: The Responsibility to Protect Experience," chapter 6 in this volume, p. 112.

25. For the 2005 text, see Matthew C. Waxman, *Intervention to Stop Genocide and Mass Atrocities* (New York, 2009), 10.

26. Gareth Evans, "Implementing the Responsibility to Protect: The Need to Build on the 2005 Consensus," speech to the UN General Assembly, New York, New York, 23 July 2009, available at www.gevans.org/speeches (accessed 15 February 2010).

27. Don Hubert, The Responsibility to Protect: Preventing and Halting Crimes against Humanity," chapter 5 in this volume, 95–96.

28. Waxman, *Intervention*, 10.

29. Luck, "Building a Norm," 109.

30. Ibid.

31. Stanley Foundation Policy Memo, 21 January 2010.

32. Claire Applegarth and Andrew Block, "Acting against Atrocities: A Strategy for Supporters of R2P," chapter 7 in this volume, 128.

33. Evans, "Implementing the Responsibility to Protect."

34. Applegarth and Block, "Acting against Atrocities," 129.

35. UN General Assembly, Sixtieth Session, *2005 World Summit Outcome*, UN Doc. A/60/L.1, 2005, para. 139.

36. Sarah Sewall, "From Prevention to Response: Using Military Force to Oppose Mass Atrocities," chapter 8 in this volume, 160.

37. Ibid., 162.

38. Ibid.

39. See Alison L. Des Forges, "Making Noise Effectively: Lessons from the Rwandan Catastrophe," in Robert I. Rotberg (ed.), *Vigilance and Vengeance: NGOs Preventing Ethnic Conflict in Divided Societies* (Washington, D.C., 1996), 213–234. See also Rotberg, "Conclusions: NGOs, Early Warning, Early Action, and Preventive Diplomacy," in his *Vigilance and Vengeance*, 263–268.

40. See also Anand Giridharadas, "Africa's Gift to Silicon Valley: How to Track a Crisis," *New York Times* (12 March 2010).

41. See William Bratton, "Crime by the Numbers," *New York Times* (17 February 2010).

42. Frank Chalk, "Monitoring African Governments' Domestic Media to Predict and Prevent Mass Atrocities: Opportunities and Obstacles," chapter 11 in this volume.

DAN KUWALI

2

Old Crimes, New Paradigms: Preventing Mass Atrocity Crimes

The thresholds for intervention under the responsibility to protect (R2P) norm, as endorsed in the 2005 World Summit Outcome Document, are serious human rights violations in the form of genocide, war crimes, crimes against humanity, and ethnic cleansing. The same thresholds apply for intervention under Article 4(h) of the Constitutive Act of the African Union (AU Act). However, acts that shock the conscience and elicit a basic humanitarian impulse remain politically elusive. As these thresholds have no precise contours, it is not clear what mechanisms are to be used to determine the preconditions for intervention. For example, the mass atrocity crimes in Darfur test the efficacy of the political commitment of international actors under R2P and the AU's right to intervene under Article 4(h) of the AU Act. To determine intervention based on the prior occurrence of such amorphous international crimes overlooks the preventive function of R2P and Article 4(h).[1] This discussion seeks to address two key questions: 1) When does the situation cease to be essentially a domestic matter and become one that calls for international intervention? and 2) How is it determined that the national government is manifestly unable or unwilling to protect its citizens?

Human Rights Violations as a "Threat to" or "Breach of" International Peace and Security

The United Nations (UN) Security Council is responsible for the maintenance or restoration of "international peace and security." The Security Council may authorize the use of force in response to "any threat to the peace, breach of the peace or act of aggression."[2] By giving the Security Council jurisdiction to use force for any "threat to the peace," rather than for any threat to international peace, Article 39 does not permit the Security

Council to authorize interventions to end human rights violations that have trans-boundary effects.[3] The practice of the Security Council shows that it does not necessarily consider an international crime as a threat to peace.[4] For this reason, the Security Council does not act in response to widespread breaches of basic human rights obligations, but rather threats or breaches of international peace.[5] This position is substantiated by reference to the "essentially political function of the maintenance of the peace."[6] However, the Security Council is a political organ, and not a court of law. As such, it decides only what is politically possible and desirable. The determination of a situation as a threat to peace entails a political and factual judgment rather than a legal one. Hence, a determination in any one case cannot be treated as a binding precedent.[7] The Security Council is not bound to use uniform criteria and consequently may treat similar crimes differently.

The Security Council has shown that human rights violations may, under certain circumstances, be regarded as threats to peace and that rampant and egregious violations of essential human rights may constitute "breaches" of the peace.[8] The UN's interventions in Northern Iraq (1991), Somalia (1992), Rwanda (1994), and Haiti (1994) attest to the practice of the Security Council to authorize the use of military force under Chapter VII of the UN Charter to end massive human rights abuses.[9] The Security Council has declared that the absence of armed conflicts among states does not in itself ensure international peace and security as non-military sources of instability ranging from economic, social, humanitarian, and ecological realms have equally been threats to peace and security.[10]

Expanding the permissible range of threats to peace to include human rights violations that threaten international peace allows greater consistency than a trans-boundary effects test.[11] Given that such a test is not explicitly required by the UN Charter, it should be avoided as it may provide absurd results. Under trans-boundary effects tests, loss of life, on the same scale in different countries, may or may not lead to a Chapter VII mandate merely on the basis of whether this loss produces refugee flows across borders, spill-over effects, or is likely to provoke intervention by particular states. Instead, an interpretive approach, focused on preserving human life and safeguarding other fundamental human rights, would avoid such inconsistencies.[12] Under what circumstances is the international community justified in overriding sovereignty to protect victims of human rights violations? To justify such action under the UN Charter, there must be a threat to international peace and security. However, there is a growing consensus that massive human rights violations in a country constitute such a threat.[13]

Thus, the notion that human rights, and peace and security, are two sides of the same coin is rendered more concrete now that the Security Council has taken an expansive view of what constitutes international peace and security. The interventions in Iraq, Somalia, Rwanda, Liberia and Haiti confirm that a "threat to the peace" is necessary for Security Council action. The essence of the "threat" for these interventions did not lie in the trans-boundary effects of the human rights violations but, rather, in the violations themselves.[14]

Protection of human rights is certainly relevant to the maintenance of international peace and security. Today the Security Council includes human rights in existing peace and security instruments such as UN peace-keeping and peace enforcement operations.[15] The Security Council established both the International Criminal Tribunal for the former Yugoslavia (ICTY) and the International Criminal Tribunal for Rwanda (ICTR) as measures for the restoration of peace and security under Chapter VII of the UN Charter.[16] The Security Council has recognized that "massive and systematic breaches of human rights law and international humanitarian law constitute threats to international peace and security and therefore demand its attention and action."[17]

The notion of R2P ascertains that the Security Council can, and should, respond to mass atrocity crimes even in the absence of wider threats to international peace and security.[18] The reference to Chapter VII in paragraph 139 of the World Summit Outcome Document suggests the fact that states remain reluctant to acknowledge that human rights violations by a government against its own people are sufficient justification for intervention by the international community. The Security Council ought to determine that such actions are a threat to international peace and security.[19] By specifying in the World Summit Outcome Document that R2P intervention must be taken through the Security Council, UN member states placed a heavy responsibility on the Security Council and on its individual members. However, the political commitment of R2P and the AU's Article 4(h) are new paradigms that may reduce the Security Council's margin of discretion to authorize intervention in the face of mass atrocity crimes: war crimes, genocide, and crimes against humanity.

Mass Atrocity Crimes: Serious Human Rights Abuses as International Crimes

The concept of international crime should not be confused with "crime under international law." The latter relates to the responsibility of the individual, rather than to the state.[20] The obligation to punish individuals in a personal capacity for wrongs that entail an international crime is not part of a state's international responsibility nor does it necessarily exhaust the state's responsibility.[21] There is no necessary nexus between international crimes and individual responsibility.[22] Bassiouni views, and correctly so, international crimes more broadly as "those international criminal law normative proscriptions whose violation is likely to affect the peace and security of humankind or is contrary to fundamental humanitarian values, or which is the product of state action or a state-favoring policy."[23] The R2P and Article 4(h) crimes, namely, war crimes, genocide, and crimes against humanity, are recognized as the most classic international law crimes.[24]

An international crime cannot be committed through negligent behavior. These crimes are characterized by the fact that they can only be committed with willful intent or premeditation. Any state committing genocide or engaging in war crimes and crimes against humanity displays its *animus* to do what it is doing. If it had no such *animus*, one would expect it to act to suppress the conduct of its organs. In fact, none of the crimes in Article 4(h) can be committed without the active cooperation of high-placed state organs, such as top government officials and high-up police and military officers.[25] Genocide "means any of the following acts committed with intent to destroy, in whole or in part, a national, ethnical, racial or religious group."[26] Further, the existence of a "widespread" and "systematic" practice would suffice to establish the willful intent or premeditation on the part of the state.[27] The same is true for the commission of grave breaches of international humanitarian law (IHL) under the 1949 Geneva Conventions. The fact that war crimes, genocide, and crimes against humanity constitute serious human rights violations is obvious. A shorthand term—mass atrocity crimes—is used in this discussion to describe these serious crimes under international law.[28]

When Does a Situation Cease to Be "Essentially a Domestic Matter"?

Although the inchoate notion of R2P is now gaining international legal salience, it remains a controversial concept. Similarly, Article 4(h) intervention presents questions regarding a member state's sovereignty. The crucial question is how to determine the deterioration or tolerance threshold after which a situation ceases to be a matter essentially within the domestic jurisdiction of a state.[29] For example, despite the humanitarian rationale, the Economic Community of West African States (ECOWAS)'s intervention in Liberia in 1990 was beset by acrimony and controversy as some ECOWAS' states, notably Côte d'Ivoire and Burkina Faso, contested the political and legal basis of the intervention, arguing that the Liberian crisis was an internal problem that did not require regional military intervention.[30] What are grave circumstances (i.e., genocide, crimes against humanity, and war crimes), given that the international community has been reluctant to intervene despite evidence of a government's widespread violation of its own citizens? Subjectivity in assessing grave circumstances undermines the implementation of R2P.[31]

The point is that every life counts and should, therefore, be protected. In terms of the obligations under the UN Charter, every sovereign state is responsible for saving succeeding generations from the scourges of war (and certainly from serious human rights violations). Therefore, to suggest that the international community should not intervene until conscience-shocking situations occur is a misstatement of gargantuan proportions. This is particularly so with respect to the high threshold for crimes against humanity, which require "widespread and systematic attacks" and that of war crimes, which require "a plan or policy as part of a large-scale commission" of crimes. The same applies to genocide, which requires a specific intent (*dolus*). Understandably, the rationale behind limiting the thresholds for serious violations is not to dilute an attempt to protect civilians against massive savagery, but to reduce the possibility that the right to launch Article 4(h) interventions will be abused. This fact underscores the need for definitive thresholds for deciding upon and implementing Article 4(h) interventions.

The international community cannot wait for an all-out, large-scale war with its accompanying devastation before it condemns and punishes the perpetrators of mass atrocity crimes. Although the rule against intervention in internal affairs encourages states to solve their own problems and prevents them from becoming a threat to international peace, the "just cause" theory provides a benchmark for determining when rules protecting sovereignty yield to intervention to protect the rights of individuals at risk of mass atrocity crimes. A common yardstick for R2P and Article 4(h) interventions is to save humanity from such crimes. International human rights and humanitarian law instruments clearly provide the definitions of war crimes, genocide, and crimes against humanity, yet there is lack of consensus on when a national government is unable or unwilling to protect its citizens. The same questions apply to what constitutes "grave circumstances" under Article 4(h).

The 1994 Rwandan genocide and the continuing Darfur crisis clearly show that valuable time may be wasted debating labels for ominous events. Imprecise terms such as "grave circumstances" or "supreme humanitarian emergency," as well as "severe violations of international human rights and humanitarian law" may be prone to subjective definitions. The government of the Sudan has manifestly been unable or unwilling to stop the atrocities against civilians in Darfur, but now it is the AU and, arguably, the international community, that are unable or unwilling to draw the line. There is a need for intervening states to make a convincing case to the effect that the violations of human rights within the target state have reached such a magnitude that they "shock the conscience of humanity." How many people must die before R2P or Article 4(h) intervention can be justified? Certainly, it is not the exact number that is killed or tortured that matters. There cannot be a precise threshold.

The standard set by the UN Economic and Social Council (ECOSOC) with respect to "consistent patterns" of "gross violations" of human rights and fundamental freedoms represents a minimum threshold for intervention.[32] A supreme humanitarian emergency exists when the only hope of saving lives depends on an outsider coming to the rescue.[33] Where a state disregards the fundamental rights of its own citizens, other states "are authorized by international law to intervene on the ground of humanity."[34] Extreme harm to citizens is evidence that sovereignty is no longer an absolute shield against international intervention.[35] The provision of R2P in paragraph 138 of the outcome document does not spell out a clear-cut threshold that would warrant international intervention. The key disagreement in the Security Council over Kosovo, for example, was whether the humanitarian crisis met the threshold for UN military intervention; determining whether a particular situation reaches the requisite threshold for international intervention is the fundamental problem for the international community when deciding whether to implement R2P and Article 4(h). Below is an examination of the various thresholds that should trigger R2P and Article 4(h).

The Thresholds for Intervention under R2P and Article 4(h) of the AU Act

When, if ever, are outsiders entitled to use force to protect people from their governments?[36] The ICISS Report sets an extremely high bar for the use of military force for human protection, calling for intervention in cases of "serious and irreparable harm occurring to human beings," characterized by large-scale loss of life or large-scale ethnic cleansing.[37] Similarly, the AU Act calls for intervention without the consent of the concerned state only in the case of "grave circumstances, namely war crimes, genocide, and crimes against humanity." The terms "war crimes," "genocide," and "crimes against humanity" are defined in relevant international conventions and instruments, suggesting that the 1949 Geneva Conventions, the Genocide Convention, and the Rome Statute of the International Criminal Court (ICC) provide the key references.[38]

War Crimes: The Challenges of Victor's Justice

While war crimes can trigger R2P and Article 4(h), accountability for war crimes is limited to persons in armed conflicts. The 1949 Geneva Conventions and 1977 Additional Protocols provide protection for non-combatants during armed conflicts.[39] Additional Protocol I defines war crimes as grave breaches of the Geneva Conventions and the Protocols. The Rome Statute of the ICC has filled the protection gap in internal armed conflicts by placing individual criminal responsibility on the perpetrators of grave breaches contained in common Article 3 and Protocol II.[40] According to Article 8(2) of the Rome Statute, war crimes may be perpetrated in the course of either international or internal armed conflicts.[41] War crimes are serious violations of customary or, when applicable, treaty rules concerning IHL.[42] While the ICC provides a comprehensive list of war crimes, according to Article 8(1) of the Rome Statute, the ICC only has jurisdiction over these crimes where they are "part of a plan or policy or as part of a large-scale commission of such crimes."

War crimes could be perpetrated by military personnel against enemy servicemen or civilians or by civilians against members of the enemy armed forces. Conversely, crimes committed against friendly forces do not constitute war crimes. Criminal offences, if they are to amount to war crimes, must also have a link with an international or domestic armed conflict.[43] Statutory limitation does not apply to war crimes. Yet the lack of any "exact, objective criterion" defining "armed conflict" poses challenges to determining when a conflict began. It is generally agreed that a conflict involves the use of armed forces, as opposed to police, and involves the actual firing of weapons.[44] It is important to recognize that a high threshold of violence is necessary to constitute a genuine armed conflict, distinct from lower-level disturbances such as riots, isolated and sporadic acts of fighting, or unilateral abuses committed by a government in the absence of a widespread armed resistance by the target population.[45] Moreover, to qualify as an international armed conflict, the situation must constitute an armed conflict involving two or more states or a partial or total occupation of the territory of one state by another.[46]

The grave breaches provision (Protocol I) serves to criminalize a core set of violations of the 1949 Geneva Conventions by mandating that states enact penal legislation and then extradite or prosecute offenders.[47] In practice, however, the picture that emerges of a common attitude toward war crimes in history is that in a just war, there can be no war crimes; one side's heroes are the other side's war criminals. The point is rendered valid by an African adage that "as long as lions will not have their own historians, hunting stories will continue to glorify the hunters." Looking at the spectrum of justice of warfare, this proverb proves to be absolutely correct.[48] For example, Foday Sankoh, in Sierra Leone, continued to wage war on civilians despite being given his state's vice presidency.

States have proved reluctant to prosecute their own soldiers for war crimes unless such crimes are especially heinous and publicized; "they have thus justified impunity, or a small administrative punishment, on the exigencies of warfare."[49] States often hesitate to prosecute their opponent's soldiers if the opponent is still holding some of their prisoners, for fear of reprisal.[50] In an internal armed conflict it is usually the government that has functioning courts. Hence, the rebels may not prosecute their war criminals, but the government may prosecute those rebels that it is holding, rather than prosecute its own military personnel. If an international criminal tribunal is established, it may also depend on the parties' cooperation to hand over perpetrators, who may justify their acts on grounds of military necessity.[51] Though prohibited, war crimes continue to be committed with impunity. Contrary to the aims and aspirations of the UN, the scourge of war continues to plague civilians while most of the abusers go unpunished.

Experience shows that perpetrators of atrocities are often rewarded with access to political power. In the Democratic Republic of the Congo (DRC), for instance, former warlords were safely contained in the transitional government. Therefore, until the responsibility for ensuring civilian protection is respected by state and non-state actors, the norm of protection will remain rhetorical.

Nevertheless, the establishment of the ICC is a quantum leap toward the protection of human rights, given that it can deter future war criminals and bring closer the day when no perpetrator anywhere can commit mass atrocity crimes with impunity. The same holds true for the *ad hoc* ICTY and the ICTR, as well as the Special Court for Sierra Leone (SCSL). Thus, as of 2009, the international community does not tolerate unpunished war crimes. The Geneva Conventions and Additional Protocols provide for certain formal mechanisms to monitor compliance with the law during hostilities. It is clear from the wording of Article 4(h) that the insertion of the right to intervene into the AU Act was a means of repentance for the crimes committed against civilians in armed conflicts on the African continent. Nevertheless, intervention to prevent war crimes will be problematic to implement if the loopholes to such crimes are not addressed. According to Greenwood, the most important means of ensuring compliance with IHL is "scrutiny by, and pressure from, third parties."[52] In the absence of a protective power system, the International Committee of the Red Cross (ICRC) has attempted to fill the protection gap. However, there is a need to complement the ICRC in such a monumental humanitarian function.[53] In this case, the AU should have a mechanism to detect violations and put pressure on the recalcitrant parties to comply with IHL.

There are several options for tying up the loose ends in the protection of civilians in armed conflicts: 1) states should make a declaration pursuant to Article 90 of the 1977 Additional Protocol I to the Geneva Conventions recognizing the competence of the International Fact-finding Commission; 2) states should ensure that countries at risk declare a state of emergency pursuant to Article 4 of the International Covenant on Civil and Political Rights (ICCPR). Otherwise there can be no derogations of fundamental human rights; and 3) states should ensure that perpetrators of war crimes are brought to justice (whether they are from the government's side or the insurgent's). There is also a need for a proactive disarmament regime for small arms and light weapons since they are readily accessible and easy to use even by untrained belligerents. The paucity of regulation has exacerbated the commission of war crimes.

Genocide: Numerical Issues and Evidentiary Problems of Intent

While genocide is a condition for intervention pursuant to R2P and Article 4(h), problems remain regarding the *actus reus* (unlawful act) and *mens rea* (intent to commit a crime) of genocide, the nature of protected groups, and the quantitative dimensions of the crime.[54] However, much debate about genocide revolves around the proper definition of "genocide." While the Genocide Convention allows preventive action against potential perpetrators, the question whether genocide is actually occurring or about to occur is both epistemologically and legally complex. For, if there is action to prevent genocide and this action is successful, there is no genocide and then it cannot be proven that genocide has been prevented. If there is a legal finding that genocide has occurred, then it is too late for prevention.[55]

The concern about the inability to prevent or to halt the Rwandan genocide led to the establishment of an International Panel of Eminent Personalities to Investigate the 1994 Genocide in Rwanda and Surrounding Events

(IPEP). This panel blamed the neighboring countries, but also the predecessor of the AU, the erstwhile Organization of African Unity (OAU), the UN, and the international community at large, for failing to call the killings in Rwanda genocide and for failing to stop the violence.[56] According to Article 6 of the Rome Statute, "genocide" refers to the intentional killing, destruction, or extermination of groups or members of a group.[57]

Genocide acquired autonomous significance as a core crime upon the adoption of the 1948 Convention on the Prevention and Punishment of the Crime of Genocide by the General Assembly, a day before the proclamation of the Universal Declaration.[58] Article I of the Genocide Convention contains an obligation to prevent acts of genocide and to punish persons guilty of genocide, within a state's own jurisdiction.

The ICJ has recognized that the prohibition of genocide is a customary legal norm, *erga omnes* (obligations toward all other member states of the international community), and also has the status of *jus cogens*—peremptory norms that may not be derogated from by either international agreement or *a fortiori* by national legislation.[59] The ICTY and the ICTR, as Schabas has noted, consider genocide to be a "crime of crimes."[60] In the same vein, in its Advisory Opinion on Reservations to the Convention on Genocide, the ICJ held that the principles underlying the Genocide Convention are recognized by civilized nations as binding on states, even without any conventional obligation.[61] Apart from being endorsed by the Security Council in Resolution 808 (1993), this position has been echoed in the ICTR case, *Akayesu*, and the ICTY case, *Krstić*.[62] At the level of state responsibility, it is now apparently accepted that customary rules of genocide impose *erga omnes* obligations and at the same time confer on any state the right to require that acts of genocide be discontinued. Further, those rules are *jus cogens*.[63]

Genocide constitutes any of the following acts committed with intent to destroy, in whole or in part, a national, ethnical, racial or religious group: 1) killing members of the group; 2) causing serious bodily or mental harm to members of the group; 3) deliberately inflicting on the group conditions of life calculated to bring about its physical destruction in whole or in part; 4) imposing measures intended to prevent births within the group; and 5) forcibly transferring children of the group to another group.[64] Genocide is, thus, comprised of three main elements: first, the commission of at least one of the acts enumerated in the definition; second, the act is to be directed at a specified group(s); and third and important, the intent to destroy the group wholly or partially.

The Genocide Convention's scope is confined to the physical destruction of groups to which persons normally belong involuntarily and, usually, by birth. The intention must be to destroy a group and not merely one or more individuals who are coincidentally members of a particular group. The group itself is the ultimate intended victim of this type of massive criminal conduct.[65] At the heart of the definition is the fact that the perpetrator identified the group for destruction. The test is subjective, not objective.[66]

The language of the Genocide Convention indicates that there is a quantitative threshold "where mass murder turns into genocide."[67] The quantitative test is more than a numbers game. The language refers to the genocidal intent and not to the physical act. Given that genocide is a crime of intent, "the real question is what is the purpose of the offender, not what is the result."[68] It is not necessary to have the intention of achieving the complete annihilation of a group; although the crime of genocide by its nature requires the intention to destroy at least a substantial part of the group. Nevertheless, the actual quantitative result is relevant in order to draw conclusions about the offender's intent based on its behavior. The greater the number of actual victims, the more plausible the deduction is that perpetrators intended to destroy the group, in whole or in part. It is not the particular number of persons killed or the killing which is essential to the crime of genocide. The most distinguishing feature of genocide is the presence of an intent to destroy the group as such.[69]

The number of victims may vary depending on the constituent nature of the victims and the proportion of the total population that the group represents.[70] The protected group may be defined qualitatively as well as quantitatively or, put differently, a "significant" rather than a "substantial" part of the group must be targeted. The totality, *per se*, may be a strong indication of genocide, regardless of the actual number killed.[71] Using the significant group approach, the test is whether the destruction of the social strata threatens the group's survival as a whole.

For genocide to occur the involvement of a government is not required and genocide may be committed without an organized plan or policy of a state or similar entity. However, according to *Prosecutor v. Kayishema*, a plan or policy may facilitate strong evidence of a specific intent for the crime.[72] This is evident in Article IV of the Genocide Convention, which states that persons committing genocide or any of the other acts outlined in Article III shall be punished, whether they are constitutionally responsible rulers, public officials, or private individuals.

Prosecutor v. Akayesu confirmed that the enumeration of genocidal acts in Article II is exhaustive and that the term clearly includes bodily or mental torture, inhuman treatment, and persecution.[73] In this case, the ICTR found the accused guilty of genocide for acts of rape and mutilation. This landmark case defined rape as an act of genocide when committed with the intent to destroy a particular ethnic group. In determining whether an act is genocidal, the key is the Genocide Convention's primary focus on preventing the physical destruction of groups. The perpetrators must possess specific intent to be guilty of genocide; if the perpetrator merely knew his or her actions would further the destruction of a group but did not have the specific intent to do so, the perpetrator can only be found guilty of complicity in genocide.[74] The intent to destroy needs be directed at a protected group for the perpetrator to be convicted of genocide.[75]

Still, determining what constitutes genocide and which acts are merely criminal or inhuman behavior are not clear-cut matters. An accusation of genocide is certainly not taken lightly and will almost always be controversial and disputed.[76] However, genocide has a clear, precise, and narrow legal definition spelled out in the 1948 Genocide Conventions and repeated in the Rome Statute.[77] The hesitation to use the word "genocide" is governed by political considerations, although in a legal context.[78] Admitting that genocide occurred leads to invoking the commitment and responsibilities under Article VII of the Genocide Convention. Although the Genocide Convention does not impose any right or duty to intervene, it obligates state parties to "call upon the competent organs of the UN to take action to suppress acts of genocide." This is why many states deliberately played down the scale of the killings in Rwanda; they were fearful that an acknowledgment that genocide was occurring would create a legal obligation to intervene to stop it.[79] Such dithering on the part of the international community, exacerbated by the lack of a common mechanism to establish the existence of genocide, reinforces the need rapidly and effectively to arrest any genocidal intent in crisis situations.[80] For example in Darfur, how many more people had to have been killed before the international community acknowledged the commission of genocide?[81]

The situation in Darfur is further complicated by the ambiguous report of the UN International Commission of Inquiry on Darfur (ICID). For instance, the ICID concluded that while the government of the Sudan did not have a policy of genocide, it was implicated in numerous war crimes and crimes against humanity. Moreover, the ICID found that "[i]n some instances individuals, including government officials, may commit acts with genocidal intent."[82] The ICID observed that only a competent court would be able to determine whether specific crimes were genocidal. In this sense, the report may fall short of expectation and unintentionally risk deflecting international attention from the real issues on the ground—justice for the innocent victims.

Paradoxically, the U.S. Congress observed that "the atrocities in Darfur, Sudan, are genocide," and called on the members of the UN "to undertake measures to prevent the genocide."[83] This determination shows that the tougher issue is not whether to intervene but when and how. The international community has grappled with the latter two questions in the face of mass atrocity crimes. The enforcement mechanisms envisaged by the Genocide Convention are ineffective since the convention contemplates trials before the courts of the state in whose territory the genocide has occurred or before an international penal tribunal pursuant to Article VI has been established. Yet history demonstrates that the hand of the state, or those who wield state-like power, is behind contemporary genocide and national prosecutors will, therefore, be reluctant to act.

In Darfur, religious sects overlap with political groups. The definition in the Genocide Convention does not include cultural genocide; for instance, the destruction of the language and culture of a group or the extermination of a group on political grounds is not included.[84] The limitations of the definition of genocide, particularly the restricted list of protected groups and intent requirement, pose significant hurdles to making a case for genocide in instances where it is difficult to determine whether victims constitute a cohesive group that the Genocide Convention protects. There is no justification for including groups based on religion, nationality, and ethnicity, while excluding those based on political views, or social or economic status.[85]

Although the ICTR expressed judicial activism in expanding the interpretation of the definition in the *Akayesu* case, judicial interpretation is challenging and is coupled with political hurdles to amend the Genocide Convention. The most promising route for the evolution of the international law on genocide is through the expansion of customary law. It is, therefore, suggested that states expand the definition of genocide under their domestic law and press for recognition of a more expansive interpretation of the crime in international fora.[86] In order to address fully the most heinous international offences, states need to encompass in their definition of genocide the mass destruction of any human collective based on any core element of human identity.

From the perspective of R2P, states can use the provisions of Article VIII and—subject to jurisdictional requirements—Article IX of the Genocide

Convention as whistleblowers. Article IX of the Genocide Convention enables a signatory state to take a case to the ICJ relating to the interpretation, application, or fulfillment of the convention, including those relating to the responsibility of a state for genocide or for any other acts enumerated in Article III. The idea is to prevent or suppress genocide and not necessarily to react after the fact, as has been the case. In the former approach, the question is, however, which UN organ would be the most competent to act? Article VIII of the Genocide Convention permits the Security Council to authorize military intervention to stop genocide from occurring. As the Security Council is generally the UN organ with the primary responsibility for peace and security, its approval would be needed before any concerted international effort might be launched on this basis. The UN Charter, with its rules on the use of force, remains the law to which Article VIII of the Genocide Convention is subject.

Further, the General Assembly can request that the ICJ, in accordance with Article 96 of the UN Charter, give its opinion on the legal question relating to the commission of genocide by a member state. Although the opinions of the ICJ do not bind the organs that request them or the members of the UN, unless there is a prior express agreement to that effect, they serve to enlighten the requesting organ "on the course of action it should take." It is true that in advisory proceedings a state's consent is not necessary and, therefore, no state, whether a member of the UN or not, can prevent the preparation of an Advisory Opinion. Referring a matter to the ICJ does not preclude it from being discussed by the Security Council.[87]

Time is of the essence to prevent genocide and there is an issue of time under the ICJ Statute and Rules of Procedure to decide in a given case whether or not a proposed intervention is justified. These matters are of the highest urgency, and a decision to intervene to prevent or to stop genocide cannot possibly await the decision of the ICJ. Harhoff has suggested that a way out of this dilemma is to institute a "quick procedure" under Chapter IV of the ICJ Statute. Upon the secretary-general's request, a specially designated chamber of the ICJ would be asked to render an Advisory Opinion on the matter within a certain (short) time frame.[88] However, given the uncertainty of the secretary-general's authority to request Advisory Opinions from the ICJ and the possible reluctance of the Security Council to see its inherent authority to prescribe the use of force, this option might not gain immediate support. Another important option, specific for AU member states, would be to bring the question of genocide before the African Court of Justice and Human Rights pursuant to Article 28 of the Statute of the African Court of Justice and Human Rights (the ACtJHR Statute). The ACtJHR Statute extends the jurisdiction of the African Court to all cases and disputes submitted to it concerning the interpretation and application of the African (Banjul) Charter on Human and Peoples' Rights, the Protocol that established the African Court, and any other relevant human rights instruments ratified by the states.[89]

It is clear that the Genocide Convention is concerned with both prevention and punishment. However, it is the punishment mandate that has received the most attention.[90] What the Genocide Convention means by preventing genocide remains ambiguous. According to the framers of the convention and of the mission of the UN Special Advisor for the Prevention of Genocide, states should focus on prevention and response to a potential genocidal action and generate political support where needed. To achieve this goal, there is a need to build human security architecture with early warnings and corresponding early responses to eradicate the root causes of genocide and punish the perpetrators. In this context, regional human rights institutions should work closely with both the UN bodies and the international community to suppress genocidal intent.

Crimes against Humanity: Can Intervention Save Humanity?

The term "crimes against humanity" has come to mean anything atrocious committed on a large scale, although this is neither the original meaning nor the technical formulation. Crimes against humanity seem to be the most diffusely defined of the three thresholds in Article 4(h), as contrasted with genocide's narrow focus on attempted exterminations of defined groups, or the relatively limited focus of war crimes on the most egregious behaviors associated with armed combat.[91] Crimes against humanity are defined in Article 6(c) of the 1945 Charter of the International Military Tribunal (IMT), also known as the London Charter, which conceived them as: "murder, extermination, enslavement, deportation, and other inhumane acts committed against civilian populations, before or during a war; or persecutions on political, racial or religious grounds in execution of, or in connection with, any crime within the jurisdiction of the Tribunal, whether or not in violation of the domestic law of the country where perpetrated." The World Summit Outcome Document, like Article 4(h) of the AU Act, refers to crimes against humanity as a condition for intervention. The definition of such crimes in the ICC Statute, as well as in customary international law, includes widespread or systematic murder, torture, persecution, and the like. It also covers other inhumane acts of a similar character that intentionally cause great suffering, or serious injury to body or to mental or physical health. In the *Erdemovic* case, the ICTY decided that crimes against humanity are serious acts of violence that harm human beings by striking what is most essential to them: their life, liberty, physical welfare, health, and dignity. The Trial Chamber said that these crimes "are inhumane acts that by their extent and gravity go beyond the limits tolerable to the international community, which must perforce demand their punishment."[93] The Trial Chamber said that these crimes also transcend the individual because when the individual is assaulted, humanity comes under attack and is negated. It is the concept of humanity as a victim that essentially characterizes crimes against humanity.[94] The ICTY's Statute, for example, acknowledges this critical point in its Article 5, and enumerates eight categories of specific acts as crimes against humanity: murder; extermination; enslavement; deportation; imprisonment; torture; rape; and persecution on political, racial, and religious grounds. A ninth category, "other inhumane acts," was included to make the list potentially all-inclusive.[95] The definition of crimes against humanity, then, contains four general criteria, namely: the acts must be inhumane in character; widespread or systematic; directed against a civilian population; and committed on national, political, ethnic, racial, or religious grounds.[96]

Considering the novelty of the international legal concept of crimes against humanity in the immediate post–WWII era—and insofar as these crimes transcend the ambit of ordinary war crimes—Dinstein argues that Article 6(c) of the London Charter did not follow customary international law at the time of its adoption. This view is supported by Cassese, who suggests that Article 6(c) constituted a new law as explained by both the limitations to which the notion was subjected and the extreme caution and reticence of the IMT.[97] Further, there is still no specialized international convention on crimes against humanity. Nonetheless, crimes against humanity have been included in the Statutes of the ICTY in Article 5 and ICTR in Article 3, as well as in the ICC Statute in Article 7.

The central dimension of crimes against humanity is that they are directed against the civilian population, rather than against individual civilians in isolation. The term "civilian" need not raise questions insofar as it is generally regarded as the antonym of "combatants" as articulated in Article 48 of the 1977 Additional Protocol I to the Geneva Convention. In the *Tadić* case, a wide definition of civilian population is intended, given that the emphasis is not on the individual victims but rather on the collective. The individual is victimized not because of his or her individual attributes but because of his or her membership in a targeted civilian population.[98] In this sense, the presence of some non-civilians in the midst of a targeted population does not change the overall civilian character of the population.

A crime against humanity does not arise only out of mass action involving a large number of victims, as "an attack on a single individual may constitute a crime against humanity, provided that it has a specific character which shocks the human conscience."[99] Crimes against humanity are not isolated or sporadic events, but are part of either a governmental policy or a widespread or systematic practice of atrocities that are tolerated, condoned, or acquiesced to by a government or a *de facto* authority. There are two general conditions for acts to qualify as crimes against humanity: First, it requires the inhumane acts to be committed in a systematic manner as a preconceived plan or policy; and second, they should be committed on a large scale.

Each individual offence will either be a particular crime that is frequently repeated; be part of a string of such crimes (widespread practice); or be a particular manifestation of a policy or a plan drawn up or inspired by state authorities, an entity holding *de facto* authority over a territory, or an organized political group (systematic practice). Jurisprudence of the international criminal tribunals points to the fact that the requirement that the crimes be widespread or systematic is disjunctive.[100]

In the cases of *Tadić* and *Jelesic* the ICTY acknowledged that a single act might qualify as a crime against humanity if it were part of a large scale plan or policy to commit such offences.[101] In this sense, the occurrence of a couple of reprehensible acts would not suffice to establish a systematic—even if not widespread—course of conduct; rather, a clear pattern of behavior must emerge. The cruel and terrible actions, which are essential elements of the offence, must be undertaken in pursuance of a policy of discrimination or persecution of an identifiable group or race.[102]

Many concepts underlying this category of crimes derive from, or overlap with, those of human rights law. There are at least eleven international instruments defining crimes against humanity, but they all differ slightly in their definition of these crimes and their legal elements.[103] However, what all of these definitions have in common is that they refer to specific acts of violence against persons irrespective of whether the person is a national or non-national and irrespective of whether these acts are committed in time of war or peace.

Crimes against humanity constitute customary international law and are subject to universal jurisdiction, meaning that all states can exercise their jurisdiction in prosecuting a perpetrator irrespective of where the crime was committed.[104] All states have the duty to prosecute or extradite, no person charged with that crime can claim the "political offense exception" to extradition, and states have the duty to assist each other in securing evidence needed to prosecute. No perpetrator can claim the "defense of obedience to superior orders" and no statute of limitation contained in the laws of any state can apply. No one is immune from prosecution for such crimes. Immunities or special procedural rules that may attach to the official capacity of a person, whether under national or international law, shall not bar the court from exercising its jurisdiction over such a person.[105]

The list of the specific crimes contained within the meaning of crimes against humanity has been expanded since Article 6(c) of the London Charter to include, in the ICTY and the ICTR, rape and torture in Articles 5 and 3 of the respective statutes. The Rome Statute also expands the list of specific acts. In particular, the Rome Statute adds the crimes of enforced disappearance of persons, and of apartheid. Further, the Rome Statute contains clarifying language with respect to the specific crimes of extermination, enslavement, deportation or forcible transfer of a population, torture, and forced pregnancy. Although crimes against humanity overlap with genocide and war crimes to some extent, crimes against humanity are distinguishable from genocide in that they do not require intent to destroy in whole or in part an identified racial, ethnic, or religious group. Similarly, though, crimes against humanity are widespread or systematic violations that target victims from a given group with illicit forms of violence, including violent acts referred to as "grave breaches" of the laws of war.[106] Crimes against humanity are also distinguishable from war crimes in that they do not apply only in the context of war but rather both in war and peace.[107] Crimes against humanity are strictly confined to acts hostile to the civilian population as opposed to war crimes, which are usually directed against combatants. Further, crimes against humanity, unlike war crimes, postulate widespread or systematic criminal action.

The daunting task for the international community in terms of R2P and equally for the AU in terms of Article 4(h) intervention is how to ensure that all perpetrators of crimes against humanity, be they states or non-state actors, do not slip away with impunity. In the case of crimes against humanity, more often than not, there are difficulties with bringing perpetrators to justice.[108] Thus, unless interventions are progressively shifted from emergency reactive activities to proactive initiatives, such as deterring potential perpetrators from crimes against humanity, the international community will continue to witness impunity for those who commit atrocities.

Therefore, the international community should develop a concerted approach for intervention to prevent crimes against humanity, where conflicts are simmering, through conflict resolution measures with targeted strategies. There is also a need to deter potential perpetrators while gathering evidence for the possible prosecution of violators. If humanity is to be protected from crimes against humanity, then perpetrators of human rights violations must be brought to justice at all costs. This may seem to be an unrealistic demand, but it is not. It is mainly a matter of political will, and political will is influenced by outside pressure. Peer pressure is also imperative where systematic patterns of human rights violations are revealed. Since such mass atrocity crimes are subject to universal jurisdiction, states should cooperate in judicial proceedings to overcome the legal problems connected to the principle of non-extradition of a state's nationals. Further, there must be early warning mechanisms in human rights monitoring and reporting and in the collection of evidence.

When to Intervene: The Culpability of the Government

While the thresholds for Article 4(h) intervention directly mirror the just cause thresholds of R2P, there are conundrums as to the gravity that a situation has to reach to be included in the particular thresholds. For example, some AU member states not only disputed the view of the United States that the government of the Sudan was complicit in the genocide in Darfur, but they also disputed the UN's high level missions' findings that senior government officials were implicated in widespread and systematic war crimes and crimes against humanity.[109]

Notably, the general thresholds for R2P, as well as for an Article 4(h) intervention, are "grave circumstances." The question, therefore, arises: Is the phrase ". . . war crimes, genocide, and crimes against humanity" merely illustrative and does it include other *jus cogens* crimes? Given the disparity between the institutionalization of the AU's right to intervene and R2P, it would be advisable to build congruence between these norms for ease of implementation. The lacuna in a common definition of genocide or the threshold of seriousness involving war crimes and crimes against humanity may cause paralysis in deciding on R2P and Article 4(h) intervention. Defining when abuses are grave or when there is a humanitarian emergency is highly subjective and the nature of the decision, whether it is made by the UN Security Council or other institutions, is inevitably highly politicized.

The AU is confined to assessing the existence of legally defined situations, rather than making a political finding, as the UN Security Council would do when it establishes a threat to international peace and security.[110] However, there is no provision in the AU Act as to how the existence of these crimes is to be determined, as well as to when this legal assessment should be made. The World Summit Outcome Document is also silent on both these issues. Given the high speed with which mass atrocity crimes occur, it would be wise to say that the international community should prioritize intervention over legal ascertainment of Article 4(h) conditions.[111] However, noting that Article 4(h) intervention and R2P are contingent on the existence of these mass atrocity crimes, any intervention carried out prior to the requisite assessment will be legally deficient. Although the conceptual contours of war crimes, genocide, and crimes against humanity are not entirely clear, they are increasingly well understood and are the subjects of considerable jurisprudential exploration.[112] For example, in Resolution 1820 (2008), the UN Security Council noted that "rape and other forms of sexual violence can constitute a war crime, a crime against humanity, or a constitutive act with respect to genocide."[113] Moreover, these thresholds have been clarified and crystallized by the judgments of the *ad hoc* tribunals and their codification in the Rome Statute.

War crimes that trigger Article 4(h) and R2P imply the complicity of the state or of its organs, yet it is usually the vanquished, not the victors, who are prosecuted. Certain groups are not included in the Genocide Convention's protective scheme, and the convention's requirement of a specific intent is a high threshold and is frequently difficult to prove. Further, there is an overlap between genocide and crimes against humanity, as well as an overlap between these two crimes and war crimes. These overlaps need to be clarified.[114]

Uncertainty abounds regarding the precise conceptual contours of these thresholds, which leaves room for political discretion to determine when violations warrant international intervention. If intervention under Article 4(h) and R2P aims at prevention of mass atrocity crimes, it seems contradictory to require grave circumstances before lives are saved. Preventive intervention is particularly pertinent in cases of impending mass atrocity crimes. Hence, this scenario militates against the option to wait for legal ascertainment of the thresholds. In order to overcome this conundrum, it is suggested that, for R2P and Article 4(h) intervention to prevent these atrocities, there should be a broader definition for the thresholds while the strict definition under international criminal law should be retained.[115] This broader threshold will define violations of human rights that do not reach the level of grave circumstances as legitimate causes for intervention.[116] The subjectivity in assessing grave circumstances or the inability or unwillingness of a government to act undermines the implementation of Article 4(h) and R2P.

Indeed, labeling atrocities as genocide may prove to be a recipe for inaction since the concept is contentious. This problem is evident in the Extraordinary Chambers of Cambodia, where prosecutors have not yet filed a charge of genocide for the deaths of one-third of the Cambodian population that resulted from the murderous policies of the Khmer Rouge.[117] To overcome such a legal quagmire, there is a need to broaden the thresholds to view crimes against humanity as mass atrocity crimes for purposes of intervention. The generic term "mass atrocity crimes" should be used for policy discussion purposes and the prosecutors can couch the legally appropriate term for a particular case.[118]

The downside of expanding the thresholds is that this expansion would add a new meaning to the provisions that the signatory states had not intended. A general formulation referring to gross violations of human rights may also open a door too widely for outsiders to act.[119] However, it should be noted that both R2P and Article 4(h) do not entail military intervention. International human rights law regulates how states behave toward their citizens and elevates the protection of human rights as a concern for the international community as a whole.[120] Even the *ad hoc* tribunals' interpretations of the thresholds have become less restrictive.[121] If based on the extent of crimes actually committed or the number of casualties, these thresholds fail to take into account the preventive function of R2P and Article 4(h). The objective of R2P and Article 4(h) is, and should be, to prevent mass atrocity crimes.

As such, the rationale for intervention must depend crucially on the culpability of the national government in either causing or allowing such harm. Under the "theory of relational sovereignty," extreme harm to citizens is evidence that sovereignty is no longer an absolute shield against international intervention.[122] As such, intervention could be invoked if two conditions are met: 1) "should peaceful means be inadequate" and 2) "national authorities are manifestly failing to protect their populations" from mass atrocity crimes.[123] In determining the thresholds for Article 4(h) intervention, it may be necessary to engage the apolitical opinion of relevant institutions such as the African Court of Justice and Human Rights or the ICJ.

In the face of impending or on-going mass atrocity crimes, AU member states should invoke Article 34 of the UN Charter, which calls for the Security Council to investigate a looming crisis and engage in prevention in a timely manner. Regional arrangements should consider imposing the appropriate enforcement action within the terms of Article 53 of the UN Charter. In order to reinforce political support for such efforts and enhance confidence in their legitimacy, the international community should consider the following factors: 1) the scope of the breaches of human rights and IHL, including the number of people affected and the nature of the violations; 2) the inability of local authorities to uphold legal order or identification of a pattern of complicity by local authorities; 3) the exhaustion of peaceful or consent-based efforts to address the situation; 4) the ability of the UN Security Council and the international community to monitor responses; and 5) the limited and proportionate use of force to prevent or to stop mass atrocity crimes and to protect civilians with attention to repercussions upon civilian populations.[124]

Conclusion: The Challenges to Broadening the Thresholds

The jurisdiction of the Security Council under Chapter VII of the UN Charter is only triggered by the determination of a threat to the peace, a breach of the peace, or an act of aggression. However, since the end of the Cold War, the Security Council has increasingly interpreted the phrase "threats to the peace" broadly to include mass atrocity crimes as either a symptom, or a cause, of threats to peace and security.[125] This position seems to indicate that respect for human rights might be a prerequisite for peace.[126] The Security Council is a political, not a judicial or humanitarian, body.[127] It will inevitably rely on political considerations, which, if overlapping with humanitarian concerns, may lead to enforcement action to protect human rights under Chapter VII.

As to the question of when a situation justifies R2P and Article 4(h) interventions, the answer is that intervention must not depend on actual crimes or hard numbers, but rather on the culpability of the national government in either causing or tolerating atrocities.[128] Where non-state actors commit atrocities, the state, as the primary protector of its citizens' rights, should act to stop such crimes.

There is a need to adopt a broader term of mass atrocity crimes for purposes of R2P and Article 4(h) interventions, while limiting the legal definition for purposes of prosecution. It is not necessary to prove beyond doubt that war crimes, genocide, or crimes against humanity have been committed before action is taken, as that task belongs to the criminal courts. Legal nomenclature characterizing the crimes matters to the victims. Of course semantics may matter to garner media and international attention.[129]

Nevertheless, the use of a generic term, "mass atrocity crimes," gives a new formulation to the thresholds stipulated in paragraph 138 of the World Summit Outcome Document and Article 4(h) of the AU Act. However, Article 4(h) and R2P are not, and should not be viewed as, synonymous with military intervention. Article 4(h), like R2P, is about prevention. Yet, R2P and Article 4(h) in their present formulations seem to suggest that intervention will occur upon the commission of war crimes, genocide, and crimes against humanity. This reactive theory is not in line with the preventive agenda in the protection of human rights. The challenge is to formulate a paradigm that is preventive as opposed to the prevailing reactive model. For this reason, R2P and Article 4(h) should not be confined to military intervention but should include a panoply of preventive and early warning tools to avert mass atrocity crimes. These remedies should be linked to other extant early warning and monitoring mechanisms, such as the Fact Finding Commission under Article 90 of the 1977 Additional Protocol I and UN Resolution 1235, as well as the 1503 special procedure.

Article 28 of the ACtJHR Statute for preventing Article 4(h) crimes is important for Africa, given that it accords with the African Court of Justice and Human Rights' wide jurisdictional latitude concerning the interpretation and application of human rights treaties. States should engage in persuasive prevention of mass atrocity crimes, for example, by adopting universal jurisdiction. The prospect that one may be prosecuted anywhere in the world for mass atrocity crimes may act as a serious deterrent to potential perpetrators. Needless to say, persuasive prevention to ensure the observance of the law in prospect, as opposed to intervention and penalization after the fact, is important in ending atrocities.

Notes

1. Ademola Abass, "Consent Precluding State Responsibility: A Critical Analysis," *International and Comparative Law Quarterly*, LIII (2004), 211–225.

2. *Charter of the United Nations* (San Francisco, 1945). The charter entered into force on 24 October 1945.

3. J.L. Holzgrefe, "Humanitarian Intervention Debate," in J.L. Holzgrefe and Robert O. Keohane (eds.), *Humanitarian Intervention: Ethical, Legal and Political Dilemmas* (New York, 2003), 15–52, 41.

4. André de Hoogh, *Obligations Erga Omnes and International Crimes—A Theoretical Inquiry into the Implementation and Enforcement of the International Responsibility of States* (The Hague, 1996), 406.

5. Cited in ibid.

6. Ibid., 3, 16.

7. Mattias Falk, *The Legality of Humanitarian Intervention—A Review in Light of Recent UN Practice* (Stockholm, 1996), 62.

8. See Brian D. Lepard, *Rethinking Humanitarian Intervention: A Fresh Legal Approach Based on Fundamental Ethical Principles in International Law and World Religions* (University Park, 2002), 177.

9. Holzgrefe, "Humanitarian Intervention Debate," 41; Richard Caplan, "Humanitarian Intervention: Which Way Forward?" *Ethics and International Affairs*, XVII (2000), 23–38.

10. UN Security Council, 3046th Meeting, *Statement Concerning the Council's Responsibility in the Maintenance of International Peace and Security*, UN Doc. S23500, 1992, 143.

11. Lepard, *Rethinking Humanitarian Intervention*, 171.

12. Ibid., 175.

13. Francis Deng, "Foreword," in John Akokpari and Daniel S. Zimbler (eds.), *Africa's Human Rights Architecture* (Cape Town, 2008), xii.

14. Sean D. Murphy, *Humanitarian Intervention: The United Nations in an Evolving World Order* (Philadelphia, 1996), 284. Although trans-boundary effects were a relevant element for the intervention, they were not the central focus of the Security Council's deliberations.

15. See Lepard, *Rethinking Humanitarian Intervention*, 257; Peter Malcontent, "Human Rights and Peace: Two Sides of the Same Coin," in Ramesh Thakur and Peter Malcontent (eds.), *From Sovereign Impunity to International Accountability: The Search for Justice in a World of States* (New York, 2004), 1–12.

16. See UN Security Council, 3217th Meeting, Resolution 827, UN Doc. S/RES/827, 1993; UN Security Council, Forty-eighth Session, UN Doc. S/INF/49, 1993; UN Security Council, 3453rd Meeting, Resolution 955, UN Doc. S/RES/955, 1994; UN Security Council, Forty-ninth Session, UN Doc. S/INF/50, 1994.

17. UN Security Council, Resolution 688 (1991) on Iraq; Resolution 941 (1994) on Bosnia and Herzegovina; Resolution 955 (1994) on Rwanda; Resolution 1203 (1998) on Kosovo; Resolution 1244 (1999) on Kosovo; *Report of the Secretary-General to the UN Security Council on the Protection of Civilians in Armed Conflict*, UN Doc. S/1999/957 (New York, 1999), paras. 30–31.

18. Don Hubert, "The Responsibility to Protect: Preventing and Halting Crimes against Humanity," chapter 5 in this volume.

19. Jennifer M. Welsh, "The Responsibility to Protect: Securing the Individual in International Society," in Oliver Jütersonke and Keith Krause (eds.), *From Rights to Responsibilities: Rethinking Interventions for Humanitarian Purposes* (Geneva, 2006), 23–44.

20. Lyal S. Sunga, *International Responsibility in International Law for Serious Human Rights Violations* (Dordrecht, 1992), 132.

21. *Case Concerning the Application of the Convention on the Prevention and Punishment of the Crime of Genocide (Bosnia and Herzegovina v. Serbia and Montenegro* Case*)*, ICJ Judgment, General List No. 9 (2007), para. 82. Hereinafter: *Bosnia v. Serbia* Case.

22. Sunga, *International Responsibility*, 32.

23. M. Cherif Bassiouni, *Introduction to International Criminal Law* (Boston, 2003), 24, 118–122.

24. Jan Wouters, "The Obligation to Prosecute International Law Crimes," (2005), 3, available at www.law.kuleuven.be/iir/nl/opnies/obligatiointoprosecute.pdf (accessed 1 May 2008).

25. Ibid., 59–60.

26. UN High Commissioner for Human Rights, "Convention on the Prevention and Punishment of the Crime of Genocide," 78 U.N.T.S. 277, Article 2, 1951. Hereinafter the "Genocide Convention."

27. Ibid., 61.

28. Gareth Evans, *The Responsibility to Protect: Ending Mass Atrocity Crimes Once and For All* (Washington, D.C., 2008), 11–13.

29. See for example UN Security Council, 4988th Meeting, UN Doc. S/PV.4988, 2004; see also UN Security Council, 4988th Meeting, Resolution 1547, UN Doc. S/RES/1547, 2004; Alex J. Bellamy and Paul D. Williams, "The UN Security Council and the Question of Humanitarian Intervention in Darfur," *Journal of Military Ethics*, V (2006), 144–160.

30. See Festus B. Aboagye and Alhaji M.S. Bah, "Introduction," in Festus B. Aboagye and Alhaji M.S. Bah (eds.), *A Tortuous Road to Peace: The Dynamics of Regional, UN and International Humanitarian Intervention in Liberia* (Pretoria, 2005), 1–20.

31. Thelma Ekiyor, "Implementing the Responsibility to Protect Doctrine in Africa," FES Briefing Paper 1 (Berlin, 2007), 2–4.

32. UN Economic and Social Council, Forty-second Session, Resolution 1235, Supplement 1, UN Doc. E/4393, 1967; UN, Economic and Social Council, Forty-eighth Session, Resolution 1503, Supplement 1A, UN Doc. E/4832/Add.1, 1970; Murphy, *Humanitarian Intervention*, 325.

33. Kithure Kindiki, "Humanitarian Intervention in Africa: The Role of International Organizations," PhD diss., University of Pretoria, 2005, 285; see Nicholas J. Wheeler, *Saving Strangers: Humanitarian Intervention in International Society* (New York, 2000), 34.

34. Edwin M. Borchard, *The Diplomatic Protection of Citizens Abroad* (New York, 1914), cited in Manor K. Sinha, *Humanitarian Intervention by the United Nations* (New Delhi, 2002), 41.

35. Helen Stacy, "Humanitarian Intervention and Relational Sovereignty," *Stanford Journal of International Relations*, VII (2006), 6.

36. Bellamy and Williams, "The UN Security Council," 144.

37. International Commission on Intervention and State Sovereignty (ICISS), *The Responsibility to Protect* (Ottawa, 2001), 34–36. Herein after "ICISS Report."

38. Greg Puley, "The Responsibility to Protect: East, West, and Southern African Perspectives on Preventing and Responding to Humanitarian Crises," Working Paper, Project Ploughshares 05–5 (2005), 12–13.

39. *Geneva Conventions*, 1949; *Additional Protocols*, 1977, para. 7, available at www.icrc.org/eng/party_gc#7 (accessed 1 May 2009); UN, *Report of the Secretary-General in pursuance of UN Security Council Resolution 808*, UN Doc. S/25704, (New York, 1993).

40. *The Rome Statute of the International Criminal Court*, 2187 U.N.T.S. 90, 2002, Article 8(2)(c). Hereinafter *Rome Statute*; Steven R. Ratner and Jason S. Abrams, *Accountability for Human Rights Atrocities in International Law—Beyond the Nuremberg Legacy* (New York, 2001) 82, 98–99.

41. *Prosecutor v. Dusko Tadić*, Decisions on the Defence Motion for Interlocutory Appeal on Jurisdiction, Appeals Chamber (1995), para. 94; see also *Rome Statute*, Article 8.

42. *Charter of the International Military Tribunal* (Nuremberg, 1945).

43. Antonio Cassese, "International Criminal Law," in Malcolm D. Evans (ed.), *International Law* (New York, 2003), 720–754.

44. See Ratner and Abrams, *Accountability for Human Rights Atrocities*, 84.

45. "Additional Protocol to the Geneva Conventions of 12 August 1949 and Relating to the Protection of Victims of Non-International Armed Conflicts (Protocol II)," Art. 1(2), 1977. Protocol II "shall not apply to situations of internal disturbances and tensions, such as riots [and] isolated and sporadic acts of violence. . . ."

46. *Geneva Conventions I, II, III and IV*, Common Article 2.

47. *Geneva Convention I*, Article 49; *Geneva Convention II*, Article 50; *Geneva Conventions III*, Article 129; *Geneva Conventions IV*, Article 146; Ratner and Abrams, *Accountability for Human Rights Atrocities*, 86.

48. See also Carla Del Ponte, "Civilian Peace Building and Human Rights in South-East Europe," keynote speech, Annual Conference of Political Affairs Division IV, New York, New York, 1 September 2005, available at www.un.org/icty/pressreal/2005/p1001-e.htm9 (accessed 10 September 2005); see generally the International Criminal Court Fact Sheet, available at www.un.org/News/facts/iccfact.htm (accessed 25 May 2007).

49. Ratner and Abrams, *Accountability for Human Rights Atrocities*, 106.

50. Ibid., 106–107.

51. Ibid., 107; Scott Worden, 'The Justice Dilemma in Uganda," U.S. Institute of Peace Briefing (Washington, D.C., 2008), 1.

52. Christopher Greenwood, "The Law of War (International Humanitarian Law)," in Evans (ed.), *International Law*, 798–823.

53. Ibid., 820–821.

54. *Prosecutor v. Jelesic*, IT–95–10–T, 1999.

55. Tod Lindberg, "The Only Way to Prevent Genocide," *Wall Street Journal* (2 April 2009), available at http://online.wsj.com/article/SB123870435894683767.html (accessed 14 May 2009).

56. Organization of African Unity/African Union, *Rwanda: The Preventable Genocide* (Addis Ababa, 2000); W.A. Schabas, "Was Genocide Committed in Bosnia and Herzegovina? First Judgments of the International Criminal Tribunal for the Former Yugoslavia," *Fordham International Law Journal*, XXV (2001), 23–53, citing the gravity of the sentences in *Prosecutor v. Krstić*, IT–98–33–T, 2001, and *Prosecutor v. Kambanda*, ICTR–97–23S, 1998, para. 16.

57. Raphael Lemkin, *Axis Rule in Occupied Europe: Laws of Occupation—Analysis of Government—Proposals for Redress* (Washington, D.C., 1944), 79.

58. *Bosnia v. Serbia*, para. 161.

59. See, for example, International Court of Justice, *Reports of Judgments, Advisory Opinions and Orders: Case Concerning Barcelona Traction, Light and Power Company, Limited (Belgium v. Spain), (Second Phase)* (The Hague, 1970), paras. 33–34; see also William A. Schabas, *Genocide in International Law* (New York, 2000), 3–4; Ratner and Abrams, *Accountability for Human Rights Atrocities*, 41.

60. Schabas, *Genocide in International Law*, 30.

61. International Court of Justice, *Reservations to the Convention on the Prevention and Punishment of the Crime of Genocide, Advisory Opinion* (New York, 1951), 15, 23–24.

62. *Prosecutor v. Jean-Paul Akayesu*, ICTR–96–4–T, 1998, para. 516, 495; *Krstić*, para. 541.

63. Cassese, "International Criminal Law," 744.

64. See Article 2 of the "Genocide Convention"; Sunga, *International Responsibility*, 67; Ratner and Abrams, *Accountability for Human Rights Atrocities*, 33–36.

65. See UN, *Draft Code of Crimes Against the Peace and Security of Mankind 1996* (New York, 2005); UN General Assembly, Fifty-first Session, Official Records, Article 17, Commentary 6, UN Doc. A/51/101996.

66. William Schabas, "The Genocide Convention at Fifty," Special Report No. 41 (Washington, D.C., 1999), 3.

67. See Schabas, *Genocide in International Law.*

68. Schabas, "The Genocide Convention at Fifty," 3.

69. Sunga, *International Responsibility*, 68.

70. See Schabas, "The Genocide Convention at Fifty," 3; Schabas, *Genocide in International Law*, 40.

71. M. Cherif Bassiouni, "The Commission of Experts Established Pursuant to Security Council Resolution 780: Investigating Violations of International Humanitarian Law in the Former Yugoslavia," *Criminal Law Forum*, V (1994), 279, 323; Schabas, *Genocide in International Law*, 4–45.

72. *Prosecutor v. Kayishema and Ruzindana*, ICTR–95–1–T, 1999, para. 94; Schabas, *Genocide in International Law*, 30; *Akayesu*, para. 516.

73. *Akayesu*, paras. 497–499, 502–504, 705–707; Ratner and Abrams, *Accountability for Human Rights*, 29–30.

74. Article III of the Genocide Convention; *Akayesu*, paras. 485, 538–548; Ratner and Abrams, *Accountability for Human Rights*, 32–37.

75. Ratner and Abrams, *Accountability for Human Rights*, 38.

76. Alhaji M. S. Bah, "The Intervention Dilemma," in Aboagye and Bah (eds.), *A Tortuous Road to Peace*, 21–49.

77. Evans, *Responsibility to Protect*, 12.

78. Olof Beckman, *Armed Intervention: Pursuing Legitimacy and the Pragmatic Use of Legal Argument* (Lund, 2005), 135.

79. Schabas, "The Genocide Convention at Fifty," 6; David Mepham and Stephen Ramsbotham, *Safeguarding Civilians—Delivering on the Responsibility to Protect in Africa* (London, 2007), 2.

80. Ibid.

81. Refugees International, "Military Intervention and Peacekeeping in Darfur," (Washington, D.C., 2005).

82. UN Human Rights Commission, *Report of the International Commission of Inquiry on Darfur to the United Nations Secretary-General* (Geneva, 2005), 4, available at www.relief web.int/library/documents/2005/ici-sud-25feb.pdf (accessed 2 May 2008).

83. Quoted in Bah, *A Tortuous Road to Peace*, 32–42.

84. Cassese, "International Criminal Law," 743.

85. Ratner and Abrams, *Accountability for Human Rights*, 44–45.

86. Ibid., 45.

87. *Armed Activities on the Territory of the Democratic Republic of the Congo* (*Democratic Republic of the Congo* v. *Uganda)* (Request from the Indication of Provisional Measures), available at www.icj-cij.org/decisions/summaries/iCO_summary_20000704.html (accessed 1 May 2005); D. D. Ntanda Nsereko, "Aggression Under the Rome Statute of the International Criminal Court," *Nordic Journal of International Law*, LXXI (2002), 497–521.

88. Frederik Harhoff, "Unauthorised Humanitarian Interventions—Armed Violence in the Name of Humanity?" *Nordic Journal of International Law*, LXX (2001), 65–119.

89. See *Statute of the African Court of Justice and Human Rights*, Article 28, available at www.africa-union.org/root/au/Documents/Treaties/treaties.htm (accessed 12 December 2008).

90. Schabas, "The Genocide Convention at Fifty," 2.

91. Stanley Foundation, *Actualizing the Responsibility to Protect: 43rd Conference on the United Nations of the Next Decade* (Muscatine, 2008), 12.

92. Gareth Evans, "Facing Up to Our Responsibilities," *The Guardian* (17 May 2008).

93. *Prosecutor v. Erdemović*, 1996, IT–96–22–T paras. 27–28.

94. Ibid.

95. Christopher C. Joyner, "Arresting Impunity: The Case for Universal Jurisdiction in Bringing War Criminals to Accountability," *Accountability for International Crimes and Serious Violations of Fundamental Human Rights*, LIX (1996), 153–172; see, generally, *Statute of the ICTY*, Article 5.

96. Michael Scharf, "The Letter of the Law: The Scope of the International Legal Obligation to Prosecute Human Rights Crimes," *Law and Contemporary Problems*, LIX (1996), 41–61.

97. Yoram Dinstein, "Crimes against Humanity after *Tadić*," *Leiden Journal of International Law*, XIII (2000), 373–393.

98. *Prosecutor v. Dusko Tadić*, 1997.

99. International Law Commission, *Yearbook of the International Law Commission: Fourth Report on the Draft Code of Offences against the Peace and Security of Mankind*, Part I (New York, 1986), 56.

100. *Tadić*, paras. 644–646; *Akayesu*, para. 579; *Kayishema and Ruzindana*, para. 123.

101. *Tadić*, paras. 645–649.

102. *Finta*, 1994, 814; *Tadić*, ibid.; see *Jelesic*, para. 53; Dinstein, "Crimes against Humanity after Tadić," 388–390; UN General Assembly, Fifty-first Session, *Report of the International Law Commission on the Work of Its Forty-Eighth session*, Official Records, Supplement 10, UN Doc. A/51/10, 1996; Ratner and Abrams, *Accountability for Human Rights*, 61.

103. *Rome Statute*, Article 7; *ICTY Statute*, Article 5; *ICTR Statute*, Article 3; Official Gazette Control Council for Germany, *Control Council Law No. 10, Punishment of Persons Guilty of War Crimes, Crimes against Peace and against Humanity*, 1945, Article II(c), (Berlin, 1946).

104. Ibid.

105. *The Convention on the Non-Applicability of Statutory Limitations to War Crimes and Crimes against Humanity*, Article 1; *Rome Statute*, Article 27.

106. The Stanley Foundation, *Actualizing the Responsibility to Protect*, 12.

107. According to the *Tadić* case, "Customary international law may not require a connection between crimes against humanity and any conflict at all"; *Tadić*, paras. 140–141, 627; Dinstein, "Crimes against Humanity after Tadić," 393.

108. MONUC, *MONUC and the Bukavu Crisis 2004*, report by the Best Practices Officer in MONUC to the Under Secretary-General for Peacekeeping Operations, 6–8.

109. Alex J. Bellamy, "Whither the Responsibility to Protect? Humanitarian Intervention and the 2005 World Summit," *Ethics and International Affairs*, XX (2006), 143–169.

110. See African Union "Protocol relating to the Establishment of the Peace and Security Council of the African Union," Article 7(1)(e), (Durban, 2002).

111. Ademola Abass, "The Darfur Crisis: The Role of the African Union in Darfur," *Utrecht Journal of International and European Law*, XXIV (2007), 47–57.

112. *Rome Statute*, Article 9; Cassese, "International Criminal Law," 739.

113. UN Security Council, 5916th Meeting, Resolution 1820, UN Doc. S/RES/1820, 2008.

114. M. Cherif Bassiouni, "Searching for Peace and Achieving Justice: The Need for Accountability," *Law and Contemporary Problems*, LIX (1996), 10–28.

115. Schabas, "The Genocide Convention at Fifty," 3.

116. Centre for Conflict Resolution, *Preventing Genocide and the Responsibility to Protect: Challenges for the UN, Africa, and the International Community: Policy Advisory Group Seminar Report* (Stellenbosch, 2007), 12.

117. Diane Orentlicher, "From Nuremberg to Darfur: Accountability for Crimes against Humanity," testimony to the United States Senate Judiciary Subcommittee on Human Rights and the Law, 24 June 2008, 5. It should be noted that prosecutors have charged some members of the Khmer Rouge with crimes against humanity.

118. Scheffer, "Genocide and Atrocity Crimes"; William A. Schabas, "Preventing the 'Odious Scourge': The United Nations and the Prevention of Genocide," *International Journal on Minority and Group Rights*, XIV (2007), 379–397; Evans, *The Responsibility to Protect.*

119. Welsh, "The Responsibility to Protect," 42.

120. Falk, *The Legality of Humanitarian Intervention*, 17–18.

121. *Akayesu*; see also *Krstić*.

122. Stacy, "Humanitarian Intervention and Relational Sovereignty," 6.

123. UN General Assembly, Sixtieth Session, *2005 World Summit Outcome*, UN Doc. A/60/L.1, 2005, para. 139; *Report of the Secretary-General to the UN General Assembly on Implementing the Responsibility to Protect*, UN Doc. A/63/667 (New York, 2009), 22.

124. *Report of the Secretary-General to the Security Council on the Protection of Civilians in Armed Conflict*, 22.

125. Anne Orford, *Reading Humanitarian Intervention: Human Rights and the Use of Force in International Law* (New York, 2003), 3.

126. See Penelope C. Simons, "Humanitarian Intervention: A Review of Literature," *Ploughshares Monitor*, XXI (2000), 12.

127. International Court of Justice, *Case Concerning Military and Paramilitary Activities in and against Nicaragua (Nicaragua v. United States of America)* (The Hague, 1986).

128. Boutros Boutros-Ghali, "Address by the Secretary-General of the United Nations at the Opening of the World Conference on Human Rights," Vienna, Austria, 1993, available at www.unhchr.ch/huricane/huricane.nsf/view01/F4F9573477975320C12570210077FC48?opendocument (accessed 15 May 2009).

129. Jennifer Trahan, "Why the Killing in Darfur Is Genocide," *Fordham International Law Journal*, XXXI (2008), 990–1057, available at www.genocidewatch.org/images/Sudan_08_05_12_Why_the_Killing_in_Darfur_is_Genocide.pdf (accessed 15 May 2009).

RICHARD J. GOLDSTONE

3 *The Role of the International Criminal Court*

Other chapters in this collection consider the nature, identification, and prevention of the commission of crimes against humanity. This chapter considers the prosecution of persons alleged to have committed crimes against humanity. Thus, it deals with events that, by their nature, come after such egregious crimes have been committed.

As in the case of all prosecutions, for what are increasingly being called "atrocity crimes," there are substantial benefits. I discuss six of them, namely:

—Bringing an end to impunity for war criminals;
—Providing justice to the victims;
—Ending fabricated denials;
—Deterring potential criminals;
—Advancing international humanitarian law; and
—Increasing the capacity of states.

Ending Impunity

Before the Nuremberg Trials, international law did not recognize criminal liability for the perpetrators of war crimes. Indeed, international law only regulated the responsibility of states.[1] The only international court, the Permanent Court of Justice, like its successor, the International Court of Justice, had jurisdiction in cases between states and, by definition, could exercise no criminal jurisdiction.

Until the Nuremberg Trials, there was impunity for war criminals. They were hardly ever prosecuted by their own domestic authorities and war criminals were too frequently hailed by their own people as war heroes. There was no international court in existence and courts of countries other than those of the victims seldom had domestic jurisdiction over the perpetrators. Piracy was the only crime that attracted universal jurisdiction.

This position changed with the prosecution of Nazi leaders at Nuremberg under the terms of the London Agreement between the four victorious nations in World War II: France, the Soviet Union, Britain, and the United States. It was there agreed that German leaders would be indicted for international crimes and would be given a fair trial before judges appointed by the allied nations.[2] One of the crimes recognized in the London Agreement was crimes against humanity.[3] It must be recognized that the Nuremberg Tribunals and the Tokyo Tribunals that followed were at most multi-national courts established by the victors.[4] They were not international courts. That in no way should detract from the manner in which those war crimes courts recognized individual criminal liability for the commission of war crimes.

The Nuremberg Trials were sufficiently successful to create an expectation, certainly in the minds of many international lawyers, that there might be a permanent international criminal court in the then near future. There was, of course, the Permanent International Court of Justice. However, like its successor, the International Court of Justice, they could determine disputes only between nations and possessed no criminal jurisdiction at all. One sees that expectation reflected in Article 6 of the 1948 Genocide Convention, which provides that "[p]ersons charged with genocide or any of the other acts enumerated in article III shall be tried by a competent tribunal of the State in the territory of which the act was committed, or by such international penal tribunal as may have jurisdiction with respect to those Contracting Parties which have accepted its jurisdiction."[5] This provision was repeated in the 1973 Apartheid Convention.[6] However, partly as a result of the Cold War, there was no political will by the leading member states of the United Nations (UN) and the endeavor was effectively put on hold for almost half a century.

It was only in 1993 that the UN Security Council established the first truly international war crimes tribunal, the International Criminal Tribunal for the former Yugoslavia (ICTY).[7] In order to do this, the Security Council used its peremptory powers under Chapter VII of the Charter of the UN and established the ICTY as a tool designed to assist in the restoration of international peace and security.[8] It, thus, made a direct connection between peace and justice. Indeed, had it not done so, it would have lacked jurisdiction to take such actions.

Here, then, was the first international criminal tribunal with authority to prosecute individuals suspected of having committed war crimes in the former Yugoslavia. Similar use of its Chapter VII powers led the Security Council, in 1994, to establish the International Criminal Tribunal for Rwanda (ICTR).[9] Since then, we have witnessed the establishment of other international criminal courts. The so-called "mixed tribunals" for East Timor, Sierra Leone, Cambodia, and Lebanon were established by agreement between the respective national governments and the UN (rather than the Security Council under its Chapter VII powers) in 2001, 2002, 2003, and 2009, respectively. On July 1, 2002, the permanent International Criminal Court (the ICC) came into operation, pursuant to the 1998 Rome Statute.[10] The Rome Statute established the ICC by way of an international treaty. At the time of writing, 108 nations had ratified the statute and they make up the Assembly of States Parties that control the ICC and elect its judges and prosecutor.

The war crimes tribunals to which I have made reference have jurisdiction only over atrocity crimes, of which crimes against humanity is an important component. Since 1993, we have, thus, witnessed a rapid development of international criminal justice, and accountability of individuals before those courts for the commission of war crimes. In this way, impunity for war criminals has been halted.

Only a few years ago there would have been disbelief that well over half of the members of the UN would have ratified the Rome Statute by the first decade of the twenty-first century, thereby making their nationals amenable to the jurisdiction of an international criminal court.

Nevertheless, there are a significant number of leaders around the world who feel less secure than they would have a few years ago. Some are no longer able to travel freely. I refer in this context to President Omar al-Bashir of the Sudan. The ICC issued a warrant for his arrest for crimes against humanity that he allegedly committed in the Darfur region of his country. He was unable to attend the inauguration of Jacob Zuma as president of South Africa in May 2009 because, under the Rome Treaty, the South African authorities were obliged to arrest him and send him to The Hague. Similarly, there are a host of countries that have informed President Robert Mugabe of Zimbabwe that he would not be allowed entry for analogous reasons.

Justice for the Victims

Without justice, without courts with jurisdiction, the victims of atrocity crimes have no way of receiving acknowledgement of what they suffered. Most atrocity crimes are surrounded by what Winston Churchill, in a different context, called "a bodyguard of lies." Thus, in the former Yugoslavia, for example, all three of the main parties, Bosniaks, Croatians, and Serbs, denied that they were perpetrators of serious war crimes and claimed to be the victims of such crimes committed against them by one or both of the other groups.

Concurrent with international criminal institutions, states have established alternative justice mechanisms, which are mandated to find truth, reconcile communities, and recompense victims.[11] The most notable of these is the South African Truth and Reconciliation Commission, which granted amnesty to perpetrators of human rights violations in exchange for truth.[12] These institutions acknowledge that justice for victims often means more than retribution. At times they have acted concurrently with domestic or international prosecutions (e.g., Sierra Leone's Special Court and Truth and Reconciliation Commission), but they have a broader mandate than punitive institutions because they are less constrained in subject matter, and temporal and personal jurisdiction. Nevertheless, there are limits to the extent to which they can ascertain truth, particularly where they do not offer the carrot of amnesty. The trial of Drazan Erdemovic is a case in point.

The Case of Drazan Erdemovic

In the case of the genocide committed in July 1995 by Bosnian Serb forces in Srebrenica, the Bosnian Serb leaders initially denied the massacre of more than 8,000 civilian men and boys. Frequently, Western nations and, in particular, the United States, referred to these acts as anti-Serb propaganda. Those denials had a double-edged consequence for many of the families of those who had been slaughtered. Many knew what had occurred and were enraged by the denials and failure by the Bosnian Serbs to take responsibility for what had befallen them. Some used the denials to nurture the hope that their loved ones were still alive and possibly being held in a Serb prison camp.

It was one of the members of the Bosnian Serb Army, Drazan Erdemovic, who effectively put an end to those denials. For personal reasons, he decided to publicize the part he played in the massacre and his participation in a firing squad ordered to murder the Bosniaks. He gave an interview in Serbia to a journalist from a U.S. television company. The film was confiscated by the Serb security police. However, after a highly publicized order from a judge of the ICTY, the government of Prime Minister Slobodan Milosevic agreed to send him to The Hague. The information that Erdemovic provided to my office enabled us to locate and identify the mass grave in which many of those who had been slaughtered were buried.[13] The United States government was able to furnish to us, in confidence, satellite photographs that corroborated the evidence from Erdemovic. Some months later, those photographs were given to the media by Madeleine Albright, then the U.S. ambassador to the UN.

The immediate reaction from the Bosnian Serb Army was to deny that such a grave contained the dead from any recent battle. If it existed at all, they claimed, it contained the bodies of people killed many years before. With the assistance of Physicians for Human Rights, the mass grave was exhumed and the bodies recovered. The dead were all men and boys who had died with their hands tied behind their backs and from a single bullet wound to the back of the head.[14] This is hardly the manner in which people die in battle. That evidence, when it became public, effectively put an end to the denials.

It is not difficult to understand the importance of Erdemovic's evidence to the victims and to their families. For many, it brought closure to their vain hope that their loved ones were somehow still alive. For all of the victims, and, indeed for the people of Bosnia and Herzegovina, it provided public and official acknowledgement of what had happened.

Truth and Reconciliation

There has been an outpouring of evidence from the hundreds of witnesses who have testified at war crimes trials, whether in The Hague, in the case of the ICTY; in Arusha, Tanzania, in the case of the ICTR; or in Freetown, in the case of the Special Court for Sierra Leone. That evidence has brought justice and acknowledgement to a substantial number of victims. As with truth and reconciliation commissions, these courts have also helped to establish a historical record of the wars that resulted in the deaths, rapes, and injuries of so many. It is that history that can assist reconciliation between people who have been at each other's throats for centuries. Acknowledgment of the truth can help to avoid people nursing grievances that are exacerbated by false denials and that so often lead to hatred and calls for revenge. Truth commissions alone cannot find truth. In the case of massive atrocity crimes, such as crimes against humanity, the number of victims who stand to benefit from prosecutions is large.

There is no single approach to or mechanism for exposing and establishing the truth that might best apply to all situations of transitional justice. The South African Truth and Reconciliation Commission worked well in the post-apartheid era. However, the world has changed since then and, with the ICC now functioning, it might well not be open to a nation similar to South Africa to escape with a truth and reconciliation commission. The prosecution of those most responsible for the commission of what was clearly a crime against humanity might well now be unavoidable. This is especially the position with regard to those countries that have ratified the Rome Statute.

Whether prosecution or a truth and reconciliation commission is the most appropriate solution for a particular transitional justice situation will depend on many factors: political, military, and economic. The common factor or the common aim is to ensure that the truth be exposed for the benefit of the victims and to provide a basis for peace in the future.

Ending Fabricated Denials

My description of how the testimony of Erdemovic helped to bring an end to the false denials that were broadcast by the Bosnian Serb Army illustrates a general trend in the Balkans. The testimony of many hundreds of witnesses before the ICTY effectively put an end to the widespread denials of war crimes committed during the wars that were waged between 1991 and 1994. The complaints have since changed. They are now that the ICTY was not even-handed. Serb nationalists, in particular, point to the far greater number of Serbs indicted by the Tribunal in comparison with the number of Croats and Bosniaks indicted. The reason that a greater number of Serbs were indicted, however, is that a greater number of war crimes were committed by the Serbs and Bosnian Serbs than by the other two parties.[15] What is significant is that the complaint carries with it an admission that war crimes were committed by the Serb and Bosnian Serb armies.

In the case of Rwanda, the ICTR has established in fine detail the extraordinarily efficient genocide and crimes against humanity that led to the murder of some 800,000 children, women, and men in fewer than 100 days. Those most responsible, including Prime Minister Jean Kambada, and political leaders such as Theoneste Bagasora (former minister of cabinet and defense), Aloys Simba (former Member of Parliament), Jean de Dieu Kamuhanda (former minister for higher education), and Eliezer Niyitegeka (former minister of information), were brought before the tribunal and are now serving lengthy prison sentences. Before the work of the ICTR began, there were denials from some that genocide and crimes against humanity had been committed in Rwanda. The deaths were ascribed to tribal enmity that resulted in some kind of "spontaneous" uprising, leading to another cycle of violence in that part of Africa. The ICTR proceedings have been central to combating these denials.

Deterring Potential Criminals

It is obviously difficult to prove the deterrent effect of justice. It usually would require some kind of counter history—a description of what would have happened if it were not for prosecutions. Given the relative youth of international criminal justice, we are yet to see the kind of empirical studies that would provide evidence of such deterrent effects.[16] That notwithstanding, there is some anecdotal history that tends to establish that prosecutions can deter the commission of war crimes, including crimes against humanity.

"Operation Storm" was the name given to the massive offensive launched by the Croatian Army in 1995 to take repossession of those enclaves of Croatia that had been occupied by the Serb Army. The Croatian leaders were concerned about being accused of committing war crimes by the ICTY. President Franjo Tudjman and his army leaders made well-publicized statements calling upon their army to take care not to imperil the lives of civilians unless that was unavoidable for military purposes. Those entreaties notwithstanding, as subsequent trials established, the Croatian Army did commit serious war crimes. I would suggest, however, that in the absence of the ICTY, more civilian lives would have been lost and many more would have been injured.

A more graphic illustration can be found in the manner in which NATO forces fought the humanitarian war against Serbia in 1998 in order to protect the lives of the Albanian population of Kosovo. The bombing was the heaviest since World War II and lasted for seventy-eight days. There was a remarkably low civilian casualty rate—fewer than 2,000 civilians were killed or injured. The reason given to me by leaders of both the U.S. and German armies was that, first, the precision bombing capability had been developed and used, and second, the ICTY was able to investigate any war crimes that might have been committed by the NATO forces. This combination resulted in the NATO generals seeking and following advice from military lawyers, identifying appropriate military targets, and so sparing the lives, to the extent possible, of civilians. Such coordination can lead to greater dialogue and transparency in the military actions of states, and greater reluctance to violate humanitarian and human rights obligations in times of armed conflict or humanitarian intervention.

The distinction made by the NATO forces between combatants and noncombatants is a far cry from the previous wars of the twentieth century. In World War II, all sides intentionally targeted civilians. One need only recall the blitz bombings of London and Coventry, the fire bombings of Berlin and

Dresden, and the dropping of atom bombs on Hiroshima and Nagasaki. In the Vietnam War, the civilian casualty rate compared with that of members of armies was approximately 90 percent, and in almost all civil wars in the second half of the twentieth century, innocent civilians were targeted as a matter of military policy. The presence of war crimes tribunals and the publicity given to International Humanitarian Law (IHL) as a consequence has since exercised the minds of political and military leaders.

In any country, an efficient criminal justice system does not deter all potential criminals.[17] However, there can be no doubt that it reduces the crime rate. The same applies in the case of international crimes. If leaders are aware that they no longer benefit from impunity for atrocity crimes, some must be deterred from committing such crimes, if not now, then in the future. The language of war leaders has changed since the establishment of international criminal courts. Wars are now preceded, even if disingenuously in some cases, by claims that civilians will be protected. Those claims, even if not genuine, provide some indication that the presence of courts having jurisdiction to investigate them has had an effect.

Advancing International Humanitarian Law

When law is not used, it stagnates and does not develop. That was the case with IHL. For more than a century, the International Committee of the Red Cross (ICRC) was the custodian, guardian, and interpreter of the Geneva Conventions. Indeed, the four Geneva Conventions of 1949 were the result of an international diplomatic conference called by the ICRC. However, until the ICTY began to operate, those conventions were seldom, if ever, applied by courts of law. Domestic courts in some countries had jurisdiction to prosecute war crimes, but their own war criminals were all too frequently regarded at home as war heroes. IHL was not taught outside army colleges in some of the democratic nations. It was not taught at regular law schools.

That changed with the establishment of international war crimes courts. From the very first trial before the ICTY, that of Dusko Tadić, IHL began to be developed. I mention only three areas of that development.[18] The first was the narrowing of the traditional distinction between international and non-international armed conflict. Prior to the Tadić trial, civilians were substantially less protected in non-international armed conflict than in international armed conflict. However, the decisions of the Appeals Chamber in that case narrowed the difference.[19] In particular, the judges held that customary law crimes applied not only to international war but also to civil war situations.

This facilitated prosecutions of complex situations, such as those in the former Yugoslavia, where at times it was difficult to establish whether a particular war crime was committed in an international or non-international armed conflict.

The second area of development relates to gender crimes. Gender crimes, such as rape, sexual assault, sexual slavery, and forced prostitution have always been perpetrated during war, yet the laws of war have been slow to acknowledge such crimes and to bring their perpetrators to justice. The Security Council condemned rape in war for the first time in 1992; the council was "appalled by reports of the massive, organized and systematic detention and rape of women, in particular Muslim women, in Bosnia and Herzegovina."[20] The UN Tribunals for the former Yugoslavia and Rwanda then developed the law by fashioning more progressive definitions of rape, including enumerating rape as a crime in the definition of crimes against humanity, as a war crime, and as a violation of common Article 3 of the Geneva Conventions.[21] For the first time, they also imaginatively and successfully prosecuted gender related crimes as genocide, crimes against humanity, grave breaches of the Geneva Conventions, and other war crimes.[22] The statutes also contained procedural safeguards to protect victims of and witnesses to sexual assaults and facilitate the prosecution of gender crimes.[23] This was in "stark contrast" to the approach taken by the Nuremberg Tribunal, which was essentially one of avoidance.[24] It is an important development that recognizes the mental and physical harm that arises as a result of sexual violence, and counters the previously dismissive legal attitude toward women.

The Rome Statute has further developed the law by providing that rape, sexual slavery, forced pregnancy, enforced sterilization, persecution on gender grounds, and other forms of sexual violence are each instances of crimes against humanity that do not need to be subsumed under personal outrages against dignity, and are instances of war crimes in both international and non-international armed conflicts.[25] The statute, for the first time, acknowledged the crime of forced pregnancy.[26] The prosecutor also has an obligation to appoint legal advisors with expertise on specific issues including sexual and gender violence.[27] While there are still issues to be resolved, such as the definition of gender, these developments are a significant step toward dealing with gender and sexual violence.

The third area of development to which I refer relates to the definition of crimes against humanity.[28] We have already looked at the definition fashioned for the Nuremberg Trials. With few changes, it was one of the crimes recognized in the Security Council's statutes for the ICTY and

ICTR. However, the drafters of the Rome Statute significantly changed and extended the concept of crimes against humanity. They departed from the approach in the ICTY Statute by not requiring any nexus to "armed conflict." They also adopted the ICTR requirement that the crime be committed as part of a "widespread or systematic attack." Article 7 of the Rome Statute also requires that the crime be committed with "knowledge of the attack," i.e., that it be directed at a civilian population. Perhaps the most significant innovation introduced by the Rome Statute is the inclusion of new crimes in the list of criminal acts that might constitute crimes against humanity. They include "imprisonment or severe deprivation of physical liberty in violation of fundamental rules of international law," "rape, sexual slavery, enforced prostitution, forced pregnancy, enforced sterilization, or any other form of sexual violence of comparable gravity," and the "crime of apartheid."[29]

These innovations and developments would have been unthinkable prior to the jurisprudence of the ICTY and ICTR.

Increasing the Capacity of States

The failure of states to investigate and prosecute international crimes, despite treaty-based obligations to do so, was a compelling reason for the establishment of international criminal courts and tribunals.[30] The *ad hoc* and mixed tribunals, and in particular, the ICC, were established to combat widespread impunity. All institutions, except for the ICC, were established on the basis of universal jurisdiction, such that they had jurisdiction over conduct irrespective of whether the state was investigating or intending to prosecute.[31] Universal jurisdiction was rejected in favor of complementarity by negotiating states at the Rome Conference.[32] The ICC can now exercise jurisdiction where a state is unwilling or unable to do so, or where domestic investigations or prosecutions purposefully shielded the perpetrator, or were inconsistent with an intent to bring a person to justice.[33]

Complementary jurisdiction then aims to motivate states to conduct prosecutions at home. This objective is supported by the preamble, which provides that member states "recall that it is the duty of every state to exercise its criminal jurisdiction over those responsible for international crimes . . . [and to] emphasize that the International Criminal Court established under this Statute shall be complementary to national criminal jurisdictions."

While it is too early to tell whether complementary jurisdiction will result in genuine, independent, and impartial investigations within domestic jurisdictions, it is beginning to have an effect in situations that the ICC is investigating. Following indictments and arrest warrants issued for leaders of the Ugandan rebel group, the Lord's Resistance Army (LRA), the government of Uganda started investigating ways in which it might establish institutions to conduct prosecutions at home.[34] While these shifts might be largely the result of pressure by the LRA to exchange peace for a withdrawal of arrest warrants, it remains to be seen whether domestic mechanisms will be put in place.[35] It does indicate that the Rome Statute has the potential to have a positive effect in combating impunity on the domestic level.

The Expectations for International Criminal Justice Are Too High

Too much is often expected from criminal justice. It is but one of a number of important tools available to the international community for dealing with the commission of atrocity crimes. Others include domestic prosecutions and truth and reconciliation commissions. They all have in common the official, and usually efficient, gathering and recording of the truth about the perpetration of these heinous crimes. Victims of serious violations of their human rights usually seek public acknowledgement of what they suffered. That is crucial for them to begin the healing process and helps to assuage demands for revenge. Institutions of transitional justice undoubtedly assist in peace-making. They are, however, no substitute for serious endeavors to prevent the commission of such egregious atrocity crimes.

Notes

1. Following World War I, there were unsuccessful attempts to establish international criminal institutions to prosecute individuals for international crimes. See Antonio Cassese, "From Nuremberg to Rome: International Military Tribunals to the International Criminal Court," in Antonio Cassese, Paola Gaeta, and John R.W.D. Jones (eds.), *The Rome Statute of the International Criminal Court: Commentary, Volume 1* (New York, 2002), 4–5.

2. It must be acknowledged that the Nuremberg Trials represented "victors' justice." However, by the standards of the mid-twentieth century, the trials were substantially fair. It must also be recognized that Winston Churchill's wish was summarily to execute the Nazi leaders. See Cassese, Gaeta, and Jones, *The Rome Statute*, 6.

3. Crimes against humanity were defined by Article 6 of the Charter of the International Military Tribunal (Nuremberg) and Principle VI of the Principles of the Nuremberg Tribunal 1950 as "murder, extermination, enslavement, deportation, and other inhuman acts done against any civilian population, or persecutions on political, racial, or religious grounds, when such acts are done or such persecutions

are carried on in execution of or in connection with any crime against peace or any war crime."

4. The Tokyo Tribunals are officially known as the International Military Tribunals for the Far East. The tribunals were established between 1946 and 1948 to try alleged Japanese war criminals for crimes committed by Japanese leaders.

5. United Nations (UN) General Assembly, *Convention on the Suppression and Punishment of the Crime of Genocide*, Resolution 260A (III), UN Doc. A/RES/260A, 1948. It entered into force on 12 January 1951.

6. UN General Assembly, *Convention on the Suppression and Punishment of the Crime of Apartheid*, Resolution 3068 (XXVIII), UN Doc. A/RES/3068, Article 5, 1973. It entered into force on 18 July 1976.

7. UN Security Council, 3175th Meeting, Resolution 808, UN Doc. S/RES/808, 1993.

8. Acting under Articles 24 (authority with respect to international peace and security), 39 (power to issue binding resolutions), and 41 (measures not involving the use of force) of the UN Charter. Article 39 provides that the "Security Council shall determine the existence of any threat to the peace, breach of the peace, or act of aggression and shall make recommendations, or decide what measures shall be taken in accordance with Articles 41 and 42, to maintain or restore international peace and security."

9. UN Security Council, 3637th Meeting, Resolution 955, UN Doc. S/RES/955, 1994.

10. *Rome Statute of the International Criminal Court*, A/CONF.183/9, 1998. It entered into force on 1 July 2002.

11. Martha Minow, "Making History or Making Peace: When Prosecutions Should Give Way to Truth Commissions and Peace Negotiations," *Journal of Human Rights*, VII (2008), 180.

12. This is provided a range of other criteria were met, including that the perpetrator must have acted pursuant to a political, rather than personal, objective.

13. At the time I was the Chief Prosecutor for the ICTY.

14. Physicians for Human Rights is a Boston-based, not-for-profit organization.

15. The prosecutor, in exercising his or her discretion, must assess the gravity of crimes, which might include the number of victims, the seriousness of the crime, and the perpetrator's role. Where the crimes of one party to a conflict were of greater gravity when compared with the other, it is inappropriate for a prosecutor to prosecute an equal number from each side for political purposes.

16. There are also concerns that the threat of international criminal prosecution for political leaders might lead to greater crimes in order to maintain power. For example, President al-Bashir now has an interest in maintaining power so that he can avoid arrest. One of the ways in which he has done so is through "divide and rule" tactics; ongoing conflicts serve to support his goal. See Sarah Maria Heiltjen Nouwen, "Sudan's Divided Peace Agreements," *Hague Yearbook for International Law*, XIX (2006), 130.

17. The ability of any system to deter, whether national or international, is restricted by the extent to which perpetrators might be rational or non-rational actors.

18. Another development is the extension of liability through joint criminal enterprise and aiding and abetting. Should the decision of the ICTR in *Prosecutor v. Rutaganira* (Judgment and Sentence, Case No. ICTR–95–1C–T, 2005) be adopted by other courts, liability could also extend to civilian leaders for omissions.

19. *The Prosecutor v. Dusko Tadić*, IT–94–1–A, 1999.

20. UN Security Council, 3150th Meeting, Resolution 798, UN Doc. S/RES/798, 1992.

21. Article 5(g) of the *ICTY Statute*; Articles 3 and 4 of the *ICTR Statute*, respectively.

22. *The Prosecutor v. Jean-Paul Akayesu*, ICTR–96–4–T, 1998, paras. 685–695, 706. For torture, see *Prosecutor v. Anto Furundzija*, IT–95–17/1–A, 2000; *Prosecutor v. Delalic and others (Celebici case)*, ICTY IT–96–21–A, 2001.

23. Richard J. Goldstone and Estelle A. Dehon, "Engendering Accountability: Gender Crimes under International Law," *New England Journal of Public Policy*, XIX (2003), 122. For example, Rule 96(i) of the ICTY Rules of Procedure and Evidence states that the testimony of a victim of sexual violence does not need to be corroborated to be admissible, and Rule 96(iv) prevents admission of evidence regarding prior sexual conduct.

24. Ibid.

25. Articles 7, 8(2)(b)(xxii) and 8(2)(c)(6) of the *ICC Statute*, respectively.

26. Goldstone and Dehon, "Engendering Accountability," 135.

27. Article 42(9) of the *Rome Statute*. Also see Article 54(1)(b), which requires the prosecutor to take into account issues associated with sexual and gender violence when investigating and prosecuting cases. The ICC Rules of Procedure and Evidence also mirror those of the tribunals, including rules on corroboration and protective measures.

28. See generally Leila Sadat, *The International Criminal Court and the Transformation of International Law: Justice for the New Millennium* (Boston, 2002), 146–160.

29. Articles 7(1)(e); 7(1)(g); and 7(1)(j) of the *Rome Statute*.

30. UN General Assembly, *Convention on the Prevention and Punishment of Genocide*, Resolution 260 (III), UN Doc. A/RES/260 (III), Article 4, 1948. The article entered into force on 12 January 1951 and provides that persons committing genocide shall be "punished." UN General Assembly, *Convention against Torture, and Other Cruel, Inhuman or Degrading Treatment or Punishment*, Resolution 39/46, UN Doc. A/RES/39/46, Article 7, 1984. The article entered into force 26 June 1987 and provides that states must extradite or prosecute perpetrators of torture. Article 4 provides that states must make offences punishable by appropriate penalties taking into account their grave nature; The Geneva Conventions: *Convention on the Amelioration of the Condition of the Wounded and Sick in Armed Forces in the Field*, Article 49, 7 UNTS 31, 1949; *Convention for the Amelioration of the Wounded, Sick and Shipwrecked Members of the Armed Forces at Sea*, Article 50, 17 UNTS 85, 1949;

Convention Relative to the Treatment of Prisoners of War, Article 129, 75 UNTS 135, 1949; *Convention Relative to the Protection of Civilian Persons in Time of War*, Article 146, 75 UNTS 287, 1949. The duty to extradite or prosecute is confirmed by Article 85 of Additional Protocol to the Geneva Conventions of 12 August 1949, and relating to the Protection of Victims of International Armed Conflicts (Protocol I), 1977 (entered into force 7 December 1979), which requires states to prosecute grave breaches; *Convention on the Suppression and Punishment of the Crime of Apartheid*, Article 4, 1973. It entered into force 18 July 1976 and requires states to prosecute and punish perpetrators of apartheid.

31. A court or tribunal may, nevertheless, be subject to the principle of *ne bis in idem*, such that it could not prosecute for conduct that has already been subject to an effective prosecution elsewhere.

32. *Report of the Preparatory Committee on the Establishment of an International Criminal Court*, UN Doc. A/CONF.183/2/Add.1, 1998, 41, available at www.un.org/law/n9810105.pdf (accessed 21 April 2009).

33. *Rome Statute*, Articles 17 and 20.

34. William W. Burke-White and Scott Kaplan, "Shaping the Contours of Domestic Justice: The International Criminal Court and an Admissibility Challenge in the Uganda Situation," in Carsten Stahn and Göran Sluiter, *The Emerging Practice of the International Criminal Court* (Boston, 2009), 82–84.

35. Ibid.

DAVID M. CRANE

4 Understanding Crimes against Humanity in West Africa: Giving the People What They Want

The Land of the "Blood Diamond"

In March 1991, the tragedy of the civil war in Sierra Leone began with an invasion from Liberia into the eastern diamond fields of the country. The invading forces consisted of various units and criminal elements from across West Africa, including the Revolutionary United Front (RUF), led by Foday Sankoh; Guineans; Burkinabe; Liberians; and Special Forces from Libya.

For more than ten years, a joint criminal enterprise, led by then President Charles Taylor on behalf of Muammar Qaddafi, murdered, raped, maimed, and mutilated close to 1.2 million human beings to further its own criminal purposes, trading diamonds for guns and cash. The guns and cash were used in the overall geopolitical plan to turn all of West Africa into a Libyan fiefdom. Many of the players in this horror were graduates of the terrorist training camps in Libya. In this internal armed conflict, the combatants committed atrocities beyond description. Sierra Leone became a killing field, truly a hell on earth.

The Conflict

Due to a disastrous combination of bad governance and socio-economic changes, Sierra Leone has been politically unstable since gaining its independence from Britain in 1961.[1] The unchecked corruption of the ruling

Portions of this chapter are taken from various speeches, notes, and articles by the author over the past few years. See also M. Cherif Bassiouni, "The Special Court for Sierra Leone," in his *International Criminal Law* (Boston, 2008, 3rd ed.), 195; David M. Crane, "Prosecuting West Africa's Warlords," in William A. Schabas, Ramesh Thakur, and Edel Hughes (eds.), *Atrocities and International Accountability: Beyond Transitional Justice* (Tokyo, 2007). The author wishes to acknowledge his research assistants, Ben Flam and Sarah Marquez.

elite has further provoked the situation.[2] Although rich in natural resources, including diamonds and minerals, Sierra Leone remains among the poorest countries in the world since the 1980s.[3] Since independence, corruption and mismanagement have dominated politics in Sierra Leone. In 1985, military commander Joseph Momoh became president when dictator Siaka Stevens, in his late eighties and facing a student uprising, resigned.[4] Initially, Momoh was quite popular, but problems with student activists and dissidents, such as Foday Sankoh, whom Libya trained and funded, persisted.[5]

Early on in the conflict, the RUF carried out attacks principally in the countryside, killing countless civilians. After several months, soldiers on the front line, unhappy about not being paid, went to Freetown to protest. On April 29, 1992, these soldiers overthrew President Momoh, establishing the National Provisional Ruling Council (NPRC) under Army captain and paymaster Valentine Strasser. Sierra Leone's army sought the help of the Economic Community of West African States Military Observer Group (ECOMOG) of the Economic Community of West African States (ECOWAS), but was unable to prevent the overthrow of its government and the establishment of the NPRC. The NPRC entered into peace talks with the RUF, which proved to be unsuccessful, and the civil war continued. Strasser remained in power for four years, despite the civil war, until he was overthrown in 1996.

In March 1996, Sierra Leone held its first multi-party elections, with Ahmed Tejan Kabbah elected president.[6] Kabbah's new government, with the support of Executive Outcomes, a private security group, and its newly organized "kamajor" (traditional tribal hunter) fighters, pushed the RUF to the brink of defeat. Under the leadership of Kabbah's deputy defense minister, Chief Sam Hinga Norman, the kamajors were transformed from an unorganized "home guard" into a Civilian Defense Force (CDF), a military organization capable of trailing the rebels into the bush.

Despite the regime change, the RUF continued fighting.[7] In November 1996, the RUF signed the Abidjan Peace Accord, thereby entering into a cease-fire agreement with the new government, which granted amnesty to members of the RUF in exchange for the demobilization of RUF forces.[8] However, peace did not result from the accord. Hostilities ensued, mainly due to the lack of organization concerning the implementation of key provisions in the accord, such as demobilization of forces and registering the RUF as a political party.[9] With the hostilities continuing, the Armed Forces Revolutionary Council (AFRC), a rebel group of military officers, staged a successful coup and seized control of Freetown, inviting the RUF to join them.[10]

President Kabbah fled to Guinea, where he struggled to attract international attention and generate support for the situation in Sierra Leone. With the help of ECOMOG, the beleaguered president was able to regain control of the government in March 1998.[11] Although Kabbah regained power, the hostilities raged on, with the RUF in control of more than half of the country.[12] In 1999, the RUF forces invaded Freetown, effecting another series of atrocities.[13] In response to the international community's encouragement, Kabbah decided to negotiate with the rebels. The negotiations resulted in a cease-fire agreement, and led to the signing of the Lomé Peace Accord in July 1999.[14] In June 2000, the government of Sierra Leone officially asked for help from the international community. Kabbah sought the assistance of the United Nations (UN) to establish a special court that could try those who were responsible for the atrocities committed during the decade-long conflict. The ultimate purpose of the court was, according to President Kabbah, to bring and maintain peace in Sierra Leone, and the region, through accountability.[15]

The Response

The UN was compelled to act, despite a great deal of initial reluctance on the part of the Security Council. At the time, the world was frustrated with the cost of international criminal justice. The International Criminal Court (ICC) did not exist and the two *ad hoc* tribunals in Yugoslavia and Rwanda were moving slowly forward with no end in sight, as neither had a prosecution plan nor an exit strategy. The cost was enormous, coming in at more than $250 million per year to sustain the efforts in The Hague and Arusha. The total cost for the two tribunals in 2000 was more than $1.2 billion. The Security Council was not going to sanction another *ad hoc* effort. The question at the time was: Could international criminal justice be effectively and efficiently applied within a politically acceptable time frame?

In August 2000, the Security Council passed Resolution 1315 calling upon the secretary-general to study the problem and recommend an alternative accounting mechanism to deal with what took place in Sierra Leone. The result was the development of the world's first hybrid international war crimes tribunal: the Special Court for Sierra Leone. In January 2002, the UN, on behalf of the international community, signed a treaty with Sierra Leone creating this bold new experiment in international accountability.

Resolution 1315 recommended that the Special Court should have jurisdiction over crimes under international law and selected crimes under Sierra

Leonean law. [16] To this effect, Resolution 1315 endorsed President Kabbah's appeal to create an accountability mechanism in Sierra Leone. In accordance with the Statute of the Special Court (the Statute), the crimes to be charged under international law were those recognized in customary international law at the time that the alleged crimes were committed.[17] The Statute did not create the crimes to which it refers; rather, it simply granted the Special Court jurisdiction over existing crimes.[18]

As a result of negotiations with the government of Sierra Leone, then UN Secretary-General Kofi Annan submitted his report to the Security Council, presenting recommendations for the structure of the new tribunal.[19] When the Security Council chose to support Kabbah's request to create the special court, it unequivocally refused to establish another UN international criminal tribunal that necessitated a direct, prolonged UN role in its functioning.[20] Therefore, the Special Court for Sierra Leone would differ from the International Criminal Tribunal of Yugoslavia (ICTY) and the International Criminal Tribunal of Rwanda (ICTR). To this effect, the court would exist as an independent institution, having its legal basis in an agreement, rather than having the UN administer and finance the subsidiary entity.

The UN and the government of Sierra Leone oversaw jointly the Special Court; it was to be comprised of both international and domestic judges, prosecutors, and staff.[21] The Special Court's temporal jurisdiction started in November 1996, and would continue to a date yet to be decided.[22] Also, the amnesty provisions featured in the Lomé Peace Accord did not constrict the Special Court's jurisdiction, because the amnesty agreements did not apply to violations of international law, such as crimes against humanity.[23]

The Mandate

In April 2002, this author was appointed Chief Prosecutor. I arrived in Sierra Leone in August 2002 with a ten-phase prosecution plan. We were already in phase three when I arrived with my special assistant and political advisor, along with my chief of investigations.

Our mandate was to prosecute those who bore the greatest responsibility for war crimes and crimes against humanity stemming from the ten-year civil war in Sierra Leone. International tribunals are creatures of political events and their conception is one of political compromise. The compromise for this international tribunal was "greatest responsibility." This mandate allowed me to accomplish my goals within a politically acceptable time frame.

The Crimes against Humanity—Believe the Unbelievable

Article 2 of the Statute for the Special Court presents two categories of elements for crimes against humanity—contextual elements and the elements of the acts enumerated.[24] There are four contextual elements: 1) an attack against a civilian population; 2) the attack is widespread or systematic; 3) the act in question was committed as part of that attack; and 4) the accused knew of the broader context in which their acts were committed.[25] Once these four elements have been satisfied, one or more of the nine types of acts enumerated must be established.[26]

Although the concept of crimes against humanity originated with the 1907 Hague Convention Concerning the Laws and Customs of War on Land, the term was not defined until 1945, when it was included in the Nuremberg Charter for the purpose of prosecuting crimes committed in Europe during World War II.[27] There, the term included "murder, extermination, enslavement, deportation, and other inhumane acts committed against any civilian population, before or during the war, or persecutions on political, racial or religious grounds."[28] Although the charter included the words "before or during the war," in practice, the tribunal only prosecuted acts occurring after the declaration of war, drastically limiting the charter's definition.[29]

Following the Nuremberg prosecutions, the international community continued toward a working definition of "crimes against humanity." The UN led the effort, which created the International Law Commission (ILC) in 1947 with the goal of developing and codifying international law.[30] The ILC adopted a definition similar to that enumerated in the Nuremberg Charter, although it omitted the words "before or during war."[31] However, since its inception, the ILC has developed several different formulations for crimes against humanity in a document known as the "Draft Code of Crimes against the Peace and Security of Mankind," which was modified in 1954, 1991, and 1996.[32] In general, the Draft Codes were viewed as the international community's attempt to enumerate international crimes, thus reducing the Nuremberg Charter to a document that defines the legal jurisdiction of the International Military Tribunal.[33]

The ILC's most recent effort, in 1996, contains two requirements that must be met in order for an act to be considered a crime against humanity.[34] First, an act must be systematic, meaning that it was committed "pursuant to a preconceived plan or policy."[35] Second, a government or an organization or group must instigate or direct the acts, although the entity does not necessarily need to be one that is officially recognized.[36] Although this definition is a valuable addition to international law, it has still faced criticism from numerous sources and it is likely that the ILC will make additional modifications in the future.[37]

Tribunals have also contributed to the development of a definition of crimes against humanity. Both the ICTY and the ICTR have been recognized for shaping these acts as international crimes, rather than merely philosophical and historical concepts.[38] The UN Security Council created these tribunals in 1993 and 1994, respectively, in response to atrocities in those countries, and adopted similar, two-part definitions of crimes against humanity.[39]

The first requirement that the ICTY and ICTR adopted, in Article 5 and Article 2 of their statutes, respectively, sets forth the general conditions that must exist in order for acts to constitute crimes against humanity under international customary law.[40] The following elements must be present: a widespread and systematic attack against any civilian population, a link between the acts of the accused and the attack, and the appropriate *mens rea* on the part of the perpetrator.[41] The second part of the definition requires that the act be one of the following: murder, extermination, enslavement, deportation, imprisonment, torture, rape, prosecutions on political, racial, and religious grounds, or other inhumane acts.[42]

The ICTY's and ICTR's definitions and the decisions made interpreting this law are important sources of international law.[43] In 1998, the Rome Conference was held pursuant to UN General Assembly Resolution 52/160.[44] The goal of the Rome Conference was to establish the ICC, and to discuss the jurisdiction of the court, as well as definitions of crimes.[45] After several rounds of negotiations and decision-making, the conference released the following definition of crimes against humanity: "any of the following acts when committed as part of a widespread or systematic attack against any civilian population and with knowledge of the attack." The underlying acts that are prohibited include murder, extermination, enslavement, deportation or forcible transfer of population, imprisonment, torture, rape, persecution, forced disappearance of persons, apartheid, and other inhumane acts.[46]

The definition of crimes against humanity has taken many different forms. However, despite its evolution, the term has gained coherence, given its relatively brief history. From its earliest enumeration, requiring that the acts take place after a formal declaration of war, to the Rome Statute's precondition of a widespread and systematic attack, the definition has been revised and adapted to fit the needs of the international community.[47]

Reaching Out to the People

Public recognition of the importance of the rule of law and good governance is essential to the success of any international tribunal. This was no truer than in Sierra Leone where the law and government were perceived to be the problem, not the solution. Early on, we factored a "town hall" concept into our overall strategic plan for the Office of the Prosecutor. In order to understand the crimes that the warring factions perpetrated, we let the people of Sierra Leone tell us what had happened. Eventually we turned this forum and the outreach strategy over to the registry, which had a robust program that was headed by a Sierra Leonean and a dedicated staff.[48] During the first four months our goal was to visit every district and every major town within those districts.[49] We accomplished this task in late December 2002.[50] The town hall concept continues even to this day in Sierra Leone. Court personnel ask citizens regularly to report to them on how the court is doing.

Though planned and developed well in advance, a typical outreach event was a two-day-long affair. An outreach team arrived a day prior to the events to talk to various chiefs and elders and to brief them on the next day's events. The team was usually present during the town hall meeting and ran the program. On the day of the event, the outreach team would talk to the assembled locals about the Special Court. We, the prosecution team, would arrive, and after brief remarks, open up the floor for comments and questions.[51] It was in these settings that the citizens got to meet their prosecutor and, in turn, allowed their prosecutor to understand in some small way the horrors of the past conflict. Our focus was never on the indictees but on the court and its process. The central themes of our outreach program were that the rule of law was more powerful than the rule of the gun, no one was above the law, and that the law was fair.

Our legacy program existed from the beginning of the Special Court. As stated above, the Special Court was for and about the people of Sierra Leone: the victims of the ten-year civil war. We needed to leave them with not just the newly built complex, where the Special Court was located, just off Jomo Kenyatta Road in Freetown, but a cadre of trained and dedicated court personnel to carry on the hard work after we departed. The court worked closely with the Sierra Leonean Bar Association, NGOs, and other civil society organizations to develop creative projects that local and international organizations could sponsor to help to rebuild a devastated judiciary.[52] In many ways, the legacy program means that the court will never leave Sierra Leone.

Not only does a town hall program allow a prosecution team to understand fully and appreciate the crimes against humanity perpetrated in the region, but it allows the victims, their families, the town, and its citizens to relate their stories to the investigative team. The sessions started a long-term relationship between the court and the people of Sierra Leone in the hope that the citizens would develop an understanding of the tribunal's mandate, the prosecution plan, and where they fit into the plan to develop a justice mechanism with which they could feel comfortable as they moved on with their shattered lives.[53]

Reflecting back over those three amazing years that I was the prosecutor, I realized the enormity of the atrocities that took place, particularly crimes against humanity, among the other crimes our mandate allowed us to investigate and charge. The key to a crime against humanity is the "widespread and systematic" nature of the act. Though the legal definition of such crimes hints at the massive extent of the plan to commit inhumane acts, one has to walk the countryside, talking and listening to the people, to fully understand what "massive" means.

From the hills of northeastern Sierra Leone to the moon-like landscape of the diamond fields of Kailihun, from the steamy southern Mende region, to the jungles of the western part of the country, the conflict consumed the entire region and its peoples. The RUF's or the AFRC's military operations were named "No Living Thing" and "Pay Yourself," respectively, with the intent of consuming whole parts of Sierra Leone "down to the ants."[54] Everything was killed, including humans, livestock, wildlife, and all of the crops that the rebels did not need. It was complete and utter devastation.

The way that the people died was truly "beyond description," as was noted in one of my opening statements against the leadership of one of the combatant groups.[55] Rape, maiming, and mutilations usually accompanied an eventual murder. A horrific example of such an event is the massacre at Penduma where several dozen people were killed, separated by gender and age. Some were forced into a hut, which was torched, while others were gutted or had their throats cut. Some were allowed to live to give testimony as to the result of not supporting the rebels. Those who lived all had limbs or other body parts amputated. Their appendages were collected in a blood-soaked burlap sack, which was carried around by child soldiers as a trophy. Severed heads were a popular hood ornament on the various vehicles that the rebels used.

A Penduma-type massacre was typical for the combatants and was a tactic used throughout the country to gain control of all or part of the country and certainly to intimidate the populace into submission; such attacks were widespread in Sierra Leone.[56] Those who bore the greatest responsibility for the atrocities in Sierra Leone perpetrated crimes against humanity such as rape, maiming, mutilation, burning, looting, and murder.

Prosecuting the Crimes

How did a prosecutor and his team understand the magnitude of the atrocity, the scope of the crime, the horror of the victims, and the anguish of the survivors? The answer lies in going out and walking the countryside; standing in front of the survivors, listening to their testimonials; being taken to the sites of the massacres and the burnings; touching, feeling, smelling, and tasting it all. Only when this happens does one fully understand what a crime against humanity entails. When drafting the indictments I only had to close my eyes to relive the perpetration of the crimes because of my physical presence at the scene of the crimes with the survivors and the bones of the victims all around me.[57]

Figure 4-1 illustrates the complexity of prosecuting crimes against humanity. Prosecution teams are trained in the law, as well as in procedure and evidence. Rarely, if at all, are the other aspects of prosecuting crimes against humanity considered, yet the other aspects of seeking justice for victims of crimes against humanity are crucial. Each of these dynamics—political, diplomatic, practical, cultural, as well as legal—needs to be considered and appreciated when one develops an appropriate prosecution plan for these horrific crimes.

The political dimension is crucial and is ultimately the key to a successful prosecution plan. At the end of the day, politics is the bright red thread that runs through international crimes. The UN Security Council, a regional organization, and a nation-state make a political decision to set up a tribunal. The tribunal's mandate is normally a political compromise to ensure its support and eventual success. As alluded to in the introduction, the mandate for the Special Court for Sierra Leone was just such a compromise. Prosecuting those with the "greatest responsibility" allowed for the creation of the tribunal. Without this compromise there would not have been a justice mechanism for the victims of crimes against humanity in West Africa. The decision as to who should be indicted also was a political decision on the part of the chief prosecutor. My decision to indict President Charles Taylor of Liberia, and not two other heads of state, Blasé Compare of Burkina Faso and Muammar Qaddafi of Libya, was purely political, as I felt that the political blow-back for indicting three sitting African leaders would have overwhelmed the tribunal.

Figure 4-1. *Multidimensional Aspects of Seeking Justice for Crimes against Humanity*

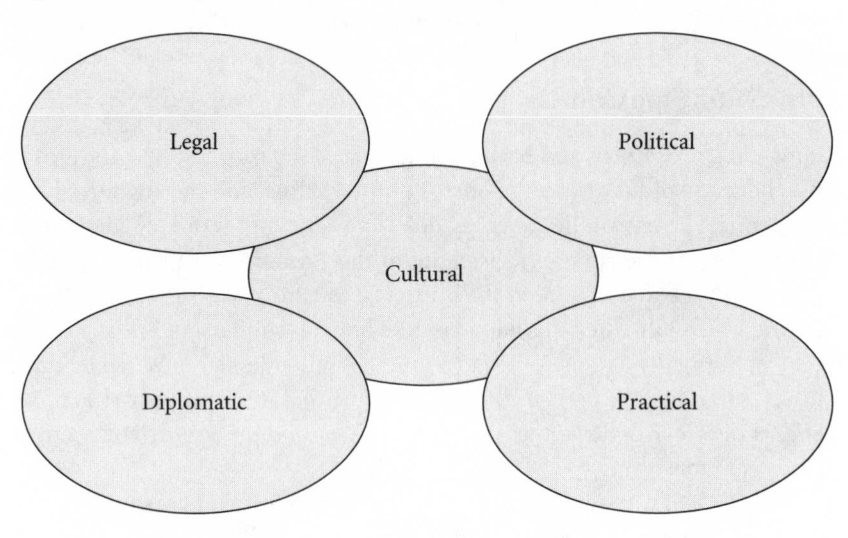

A chief prosecutor has to have a deft understanding of diplomacy and how a tribunal fits into the circumstances of geopolitics and the world stage. Prosecuting purely in the name of the law is laudable and appropriate, but doing so without considering the diplomatic ramifications of that prosecution can lead to unrest in a region or country and even threaten the mandate of the tribunal. It is the diplomats who provide the political support for the judicial effort. Meeting with key diplomats within the country, the region, and discussing the process internationally, seeking diplomats' perspectives, and those of others leads to a crucial understanding of why the prosecution strategy has been shaped the way that it has been. While I was chief prosecutor, it was crucial that permanent members of the UN Security Council, various foreign offices, as well as regional and domestic legislators be consulted for their views and support. It took two years of discussion, visits, and meetings before the diplomatic (and political) decisions were made to hand over former President Taylor to the tribunal for prosecution. The political and diplomatic aspects of prosecuting crimes against humanity in West Africa occupied most of my time once the prosecution plan was put into place.

A naïve chief prosecutor develops a plan for prosecution of crimes against humanity, and other international crimes, without considering the practical aspects of that plan. Leadership and management skills are essential to guiding an international team of trial counsel, investigators, paralegals, and support staff. Caring for these talented and dedicated professionals who are away from home, living in extreme conditions where the threat of catastrophic disease is a daily concern, and ensuring their safety should be a chief prosecutor's number one concern. It certainly was mine. In places such as West Africa, called "the white man's grave," small things make a big difference. We had an extensive personal support system ensuring that no one in the Office of the Prosecutor ever was alone.

Finally, considering the cultural perspectives of justice is crucial. Though I explore this further in my concluding thoughts, the prosecution of individuals who commit crimes against humanity must ensure that the victims feel that they, their families, and the country at large have received justice. As discussed above, an effective outreach program greatly assists in cultural considerations of justice. It is critical to understand that international justice is not the only answer when seeking prosecution for international crimes. There are other valid justice mechanisms, such as truth telling, confessional ceremonies, and reconciliation commissions, among others. Justice has to be produced. If it is not, time is being wasted.

Conclusion: Is the Justice That We Seek the Justice That Victims Want?

As mankind stumbles forward into the twenty-first century, it is armed with a judicial framework and mechanisms to deal with international crimes at the domestic, regional, and international levels. How it chooses to do so will largely be a political decision.

Regardless of the decision, the type of justice that is sought is important. The purpose of international justice is multi-faceted to be sure, but the core reason for these varied justice mechanisms is to bring a sense of justice to the victims. If victims feel the various methods of that justice are unfair, unclear, or nonexistent, then they will turn away from the law and pick up a gun.

An important question to ask ourselves as we consider how best to seek justice for crimes against humanity and other international crimes should be: Is the justice that we seek the justice that they want? If we do not carefully consider that answer, we may find that what we do as an international community will be a form of "white man's justice" and not a culturally refined justice that factors in not only the legal, diplomatic, political, and practical results of the decision to seek justice for the victims of an atrocity, but also the cultural ramifications of that decision.

A vignette here is instructive. I recall my arrival for the first town hall meeting in Kenema in the Kalihun district of Sierra Leone, the location of the now infamous blood diamond fields. The white UN helicopter landed in a field just outside of the town. Blue-helmeted Pakistani peacekeepers ringed the field. Sierra Leonean citizens watched with great trepidation as the ramp went down and off stepped a tall white man from the United States. One recalls thinking about the 1950s movie, "The Day the Earth Stood Still," where an alien landed on the Mall in Washington, D.C. It was the same type of moment. I was as alien to my clients, the people of Sierra Leone, as that fictional alien was in that classic movie.

The point here is that the type of justice that I represented was potentially no more helpful to Sierra Leonean citizens' sense of justice than was an alien justice system. It is a fatal move for a chief prosecutor to step over this all-important local sense of justice without considering the ramification of one's mandate on the victims' sense of the expected outcome, or failing to factor in that local sense of justice, where practical.

At a minimum, creating a communications mechanism that allows for a dialogue between the people living in a destroyed region of the world and the international tribunal that is set up to seek justice in and for that region would help an Office of the Prosecutor plan a more realistic investigative and trial strategy. It has been my experience at the domestic and the international levels that if a victim of a crime has a sense of control, of being a participant in the investigation, and of being listened to appropriately, he or she will develop more respect and confidence in the legal process and the rule of law.

Our town hall program, which eventually evolved into the Special Court Outreach Program, was an essential part of building that confidence and respect for the international justice being brought to bear on the atrocities in West Africa.

When dealing with crimes against humanity, we must appreciate that these acts are crimes against all of us. A wrong on humanity is an injury to our moral fiber. Yet, these horrific crimes are locally perpetrated against a people who may not be able to comprehend the international ramifications. Yet, they want justice, a justice that they can appreciate, understand, and respect.

Notes

1. Jeana Webster, "Sierra Leone—Responding to the Crisis, Planning for the Future: The Role of International Justice in the Quest for National and Global

Security," *Indiana International and Comparative Law Review,* XI (2001), 731, 733–734, citing Bankole Thompson, *The Constitutional History and Law of Sierra Leone (1961–1995)* (Lanham, MD, 1996) 194–195.

2. See Karsten Nowrot and Emily W. Schabacker, "The Use of Force to Restore Democracy: International Legal Implications of the ECOWAS Intervention in Sierra Leone," *American University Law Review,* XIV (1998), 321.

3. Webster, "Sierra Leone—Responding to the Crisis, Planning for the Future," 731, 735, citing Eliphas G. Mukonoweshuro, *Colonialism, Class Formation and Underdevelopment in Sierra Leone* (Lanham, MD, 1993), 201–240.

4. For an overview of the conflict, see David Pratt, "Sierra Leone: The Forgotten Crisis," (1999), available at www.globalsecurity.org/military/library/report/1999/crisis-e.htm (accessed 24 January 2010). For a more detailed history of the ten-year civil war, see Babafemi Akinrinade, "International Humanitarian Law and the Conflict in Sierra Leone," *Notre Dame Journal of Law, Ethics and Public Policy*, XV (2001), 391.

5. Pratt, "Sierra Leone: The Forgotten Crisis."

6. Matthew Griffin, "Accrediting Democracies: Does the Credentials Committee of the United Nations Promote Democracy through Its Accreditation Process, and Should It?" *New York University Journal of International Law and Politics*, XXXII (2000), 725, 747, citing Jeremy Levitt, "Humanitarian Intervention by Regional Actors in Internal Conflicts and the Cases of ECOWAS in Liberia and Sierra Leone," *Temple International and Comparative Law Journal*, XII (1998), 333, 364–365.

7. The RUF seemed willing to discuss peace terms. The fighters from Executive Outcomes were successfully reclaiming control of RUF-held diamond mines. The diamond mines provided essential funding for the war, and without access to them, the RUF would have been unable to support their troops. See Ian Smillie, Lansane Gberie, and Ralph Hazelton, "The Heart of the Matter: Sierra Leone, Diamonds, and Human Security," (2000), available at www.reliefweb.int/library/documents/2001/pac-sie-jan00.pdf (accessed 24 January 2010). The peace that the Abidjan Agreement fostered lasted approximately nine months. Under the agreement, Executive Outcomes was forced to leave Sierra Leone and was replaced by Nigerian peacekeepers. The RUF also achieved increased political legitimacy, and it appeared it would be recognized as a political party. However, since the RUF never adopted any political platform, the widespread sentiment was that they were fighting for control of the diamonds, not political change. See "Footpaths to Democracy," (1995), available at www.fas.org/irp/world/para/docs/footpaths.htm (accessed 24 January 2010). In 1997, Johnny Paul Koroma of the Armed Forces Revolutionary Council (AFRC), which soon after 1997 joined with the RUF to form the AFRC/RUF, overthrew President Kabbah. The AFRC/RUF proved to be an especially brutal regime. Determined to protect innocent civilians, the Economic Community of West African States (ECOWAS), with the support of the UN Security Council, increased the number of Nigerian troops stationed in Sierra Leone. See UN Security Council, 3889th Meeting,

Resolution 1171, UN Doc. S/RES1171, 1998. The AFRC/RUF signed an agreement with Kabbah's deposed government, and, with ECOWAS support, President Kabbah was returned to Freetown. The RUF continued to commit war crimes in the east, replenishing its war chest through diamond sales to President Taylor of Liberia. During this time, Foday Sankoh was captured in Nigeria and returned to Freetown, where he was tried and sentenced to death for his role in the civil war. In January 1999, the RUF once again attacked Freetown, this time defeating the peacekeepers in "Operation No Living Thing." Thousands of children were forcibly conscripted into the RUF army, drugged, killed, burned alive, or raped before the rebels were driven away. See "Getting Away with Murder," available at www.hrw.org/reports/1999/sierra/SIERLE99.htm (accessed 24 January 2010). In early 1999, there was essentially a stalemate. Economic Community of West African States Monitoring Group (ECOMOG) peacekeepers protected the capital (although they also stood accused of summary executions, rapes, and murders), but seemed unable to defeat the RUF and its allies. The RUF seemed content holding only the diamond-mining districts.

8. See "Peace Agreement between the Government of Sierra Leone and the Revolutionary United Front of Sierra Leone," 30 November 1996, Article 1, available at www.sierra-leone.org/abidjanaccord.html (accessed 24 January 2010); Diane Marie Amann, "Message as a Medium in Sierra Leone," *International Law Students Association Journal of International and Comparative Law*, VII (2001), 239.

9. See Webster, "Sierra Leone—Responding to the Crisis, Planning for the Future," 738–739; Jeremy Levitt, "Humanitarian Intervention by Regional Actors in Internal Conflicts, 333, 343.

10. Abdul Tejan-Cole, "Notes from the Field, The Complementary and Conflicting Relationship between the Special Court for Sierra Leone and the Truth and Reconciliation Commission," *Yale Human Rights and Development Law Journal*, VI (2003), 139, 141.

11. See Webster, "Sierra Leone—Responding to the Crisis, Planning for the Future," 739; Matthew S. Barton, "ECOWAS and West African Security: The New Regionalism," *DePaul International Law Journal*, IV (2000), 79, 80.

12. See Tejan-Cole, "Notes from the Field," 141.

13. The rebel forces committed the most atrocious human rights violations of Sierra Leone's civil war during their invasion of the capital. See, for example, Jon M. Van Dyke, "The Fundamental Human Right to Prosecution and Compensation," *Denver Journal of International Law and Policy*, XXIX (2001), 77. ECOMOG forces were eventually able to regain control over Freetown. However, the fighting was fierce, resulting in the deaths of approximately 7,000 people and two-thirds of Freetown being destroyed. See UN, *Fifth Report of the Secretary-General on the United Nations Observer Mission in Sierra Leone,* UN Doc. S/1999/237 (New York, 1999), para. 1 (describing the RUF attack on Freetown and the resultant effects). As a result of the anarchy, about 600,000 of Sierra Leone's estimated 4 million people sought sanctuary in neighboring nations, and two-thirds of those who remained in Sierra

Leone were internally displaced. See UN, *Sixth Report of the Secretary-General on the United Nations Observer Mission in Sierra Leone,* UN Doc. S/1999/645 (New York, 1999), para. 9 (describing the then-current status of the Sierra Leonean refugees and internally displaced persons).

14. See Webster, "Sierra Leone—Responding to the Crisis, Planning for the Future," 739; "Peace Agreement between the Government of Sierra Leone and the Revolutionary United Front of Sierra Leone," 7 July 1999 [hereinafter Lomé Peace Agreement], available at www.sierra-leone.org/lomeaccord.html (accessed 24 January 2010). Most controversially, the Lomé Peace Agreement granted complete amnesty to all combatants. Article IX reads in part: "(2) After the signing of the present Agreement, the Government of Sierra Leone shall also grant absolute and free pardon and reprieve to all combatants and collaborators in respect of anything done by them in pursuit of their objectives, up to the time of the signing of the present Agreement. (3) To consolidate the peace and promote the cause of national reconciliation, the Government of Sierra Leone shall ensure that no official or judicial action is taken against any member of the RUF/SL, ex-AFRC, ex-SLA or CDF in respect of anything done by them in pursuit of their objectives as members of those organizations, since March 1991, up to the time of the signing of the present Agreement. In addition, legislative and other measures necessary to guarantee immunity to former combatants, exiles and other persons, currently outside the country for reasons related to the armed conflict shall be adopted ensuring the full exercise of their civil and political rights, with a view to their reintegration within a framework of full legality." The Lomé Peace Agreement also established a Truth and Reconciliation Commission (TRC), created as an instrument for addressing the abhorrent violence to promote and facilitate reconciliation for a deeply fragmented people (Lomé Peace Agreement, Part Two art. VI and XXVI). Disregarding the terms of the Agreement, the RUF resumed its practice of committing violent acts against the people of Sierra Leone. See Daniel J. Macaluso, "Absolute and Free Pardon: The Effect of the Amnesty Provision in the Lomé Peace Agreement on the Jurisdiction of the Special Court for Sierra Leone," *Brooklyn Journal of International Law,* XXVII (2001), 347, 350. Seeking to take power from the AFRC, the RUF did not fully comply with the Lomé Peace Agreement. In May 2000, rebel forces took 500 UN peacekeepers hostage, attracting the international community's attention. Thereafter, Foday Sankoh, leader of the RUF, was captured and arrested, initiating a dialogue calling for the creation of an international criminal court for Sierra Leone to try those responsible for the grave crimes committed in violation of international law.

15. Not only did the national courts of Sierra Leone lack the expertise and resources to prosecute the crimes committed during the conflict, but the existence of an amnesty and gaps in Sierra Leonean criminal law posed problems. President Kabbah suggested that the Special Court should have as its applicable law a combination of international and domestic law. Kabbah requested, "[o]n behalf of the Government and people of the Republic of Sierra Leone," that a court be set up in order

"to try and bring to credible justice those members of the Revolutionary United Front (RUF) and their accomplices responsible for committing crimes against the people of Sierra Leone and for the taking of United Nations peacekeepers as hostages." In August 2000, the UN Security Council adopted Resolution 1315, which requested that the secretary-general consult with the government of Sierra Leone on the creation of an independent international court that would have jurisdiction over those most responsible for the notorious human rights violations committed during the conflict, such as crimes against humanity and war crimes. See Avril McDonald, "Sierra Leone's Shoestring Special Court," *International Review of the Red Cross*, LXXXIV (2002), 124; see also *Letter from the President of Sierra Leone to the UN Secretary-General*, UN Doc. S/2000/786, Annex, available at www.sc-sl.org (accessed 24 January 2010).

16. In 2000, UN Security Council Resolution 1315 created a framework for the establishment of an independent special court in Sierra Leone to address "crimes against humanity, war crimes and other serious violations of international humanitarian law, as well as crimes under relevant Sierra Leonean law committed within the territory of Sierra Leone." See UN Security Council, 4186th Meeting, Resolution 1315, UN Doc. S/RES/1315, 2000.

17. See UN, *Report of the Secretary-General to the Security Council on the Establishment of a Special Court for Sierra Leone*, UN Doc. S/2000/915 (New York, 2000), para. 12. Examples include: crimes against humanity, violations of common Article 3 of the Geneva Conventions and Additional Protocol II, and other serious violations of international law, such as crimes committed against peacekeepers and the use of child soldiers.

18. "Rome Statute of the International Criminal Court," (1999), Article 28, available at http://untreaty.un.org/cod/icc/statute/romefra.htm (accessed 24 January 2010). The language "persons who bear the greatest responsibility" from Article 1 of the Special Court's Statute came from the Rome Statute. Distinct from the ICTR and the ICTY Statutes, but succinct with the Special Court's Statute, sexual crimes are defined as crimes against humanity by the Rome Statute. See, SCSL Statute, Article 2(g); see also ICC Statute, art. 7(1)(g). Article 4(b) of the Special Court's Statute mirrors Article 8(2)(b)(iii) of the ICC Statute. Both operate to protect humanitarian assistance and peacekeeping missions. See Statute, Article 4(b); see also ICC Statute, Article 8(2)(b)(iii). These incorporations of the Rome Statute into the Special Court's Statute indicate gradual development in international criminal law.

19. UN, *Report of the Secretary-General on the Establishment of a Special Court for Sierra Leone*, UN Doc. S/2000/915 (New York, 2000), 1.

20. Operative paragraph 1 of Resolution 1315 "[r]equests the Secretary-General to negotiate an agreement with the Government of Sierra Leone to create an independent special court."

21. UN, *Report of the Secretary-General on the Establishment of a Special Court for Sierra Leone*. This includes the abuse of girls in violation of the Prevention of Cruelty

to Children Act (1926), for the rape of countless girls under fourteen years of age and the abduction of girls under sixteen subjected to forced marriage. This also includes the wanton destruction of property carried out in violation of the Malicious Damage Act (1861), such as burning people in their homes, burning down homes with people locked inside, and burning public buildings.

22. UN Security Council, *Statute of the Special Court for Sierra Leone* (New York, 2002), Article XII(1)(a), available at www.unhrc.org/refworld.docid/3dda29f94.html (accessed 18 March 2010) [hereinafter Statute].

23. Statute, Article X. The subject matter jurisdiction of the SCSL is similar to the Statutes of the ICTR and the ICTY. Article 2 of the Statute of the SCSL lists the crimes against humanity that the SCSL will have the power to prosecute. These include crimes such as murder, extermination, enslavement, imprisonment, torture, rape, or other inhumane acts, if they were committed as "part of a widespread or systematic attack against any civilian population." Article 3 covers Violations of Article 3 Common to the Geneva Conventions and of Additional Protocol II. The crimes in Article 3 are defined exactly the same as those in Article 4 of the Additional Protocol for Non-International Armed Conflict. These crimes include mutilation, torture, collective punishments, hostage-taking, terrorism, pillage, summary executions, and outrages on personal dignity. Article 4 enumerates Other Serious Violations of International Humanitarian Law, including intentional attacks on civilian targets, intentional attacks on humanitarian and peacekeeping personnel, and abduction and recruitment of children under the age of fifteen into armed groups. Not included on this list of crimes is genocide, since the attacks on civilians in Sierra Leone do not appear to have had an ethnic element. In addition to the crimes against humanity, war crimes, and other serious violations of international humanitarian law, Article 5 of the Statute provides jurisdiction for Crimes under Sierra Leonean law. The ICTR and ICTY did not provide jurisdiction for Rwandan and Yugoslavian crimes.

24. Article 2 of the Statute confers "the power to prosecute persons who committed the following crimes as part of a widespread or systematic attack against any civilian population: (a) Murder; (b) Extermination; (c) Enslavement; (d) Deportation; (e) Imprisonment; (f) Torture; (g) Rape, sexual slavery, enforced prostitution, forced pregnancy and any other form of sexual violence; (h) Persecution on political, racial, ethnic or religious grounds; (i) Other inhumane acts." Statute, Article II.

25. An "attack against a civilian population" refers to conduct that involves repeated commission of one or more of the acts enumerated in Article 2. The "attack" need not be physical, as alternate forms of inhumane mistreatment of a civilian population qualify. Further, customary international law does not necessitate discriminatory intent surrounding the "attack." (Although the ICTR Statute, Art. 3, limits ICTR jurisdiction in crimes against humanity cases to attacks made on discriminatory grounds, the Statute of the Special Court does not.) A civilian population is one that is predominantly civilian in nature, meaning that the people do not directly take part in the hostilities, or have ceased to take part in the hostilities (including

those who are injured or incapacitated.) See, for example, common article 3 to the Geneva Conventions and the Additional Protocols. A population will not lose its civilian character simply because non-civilians are found within it. See *Prosecutor v. Tadić,* IT–94–I, 1997. To establish a crime against humanity, showing that a civilian population was the primary target of an attack is sufficient (there is no requirement that the whole population be victimized by the attack). See *Prosecutor v. Bailishema,* ICTR–95–1, 2001. To establish the contextual elements for a crime against humanity, an attack must be either widespread or systematic. To be widespread, the attack must have taken place on a large scale directed against a large number of victims. To be systematic, the attack must have been carried out according to an organized plan. See Rome Statute, Article 7. To establish that the act was committed as a "part of" the attack against a civilian population, it must be shown that the act was related to the attack. This effectively excludes random or isolated acts from qualifying under the definition of crimes against humanity. However, a single act could constitute a crime against humanity if it is shown that it was perpetrated as a part of a larger, deliberate attack. See ICTY Trial Chamber Rule 61; *Prosecutor v. Tadić,* IT–94–I, 1997. This requirement represents the mental facet that must be proven to establish crimes against humanity. It must be shown that the accused had knowledge of the extensive nature of their actions, and that they had knowledge that their acts contributed to the broad attack on the civilian population.

26. Whereas the ICTY and ICTR did not consider all of the acts, the Special Court had the power to do so. See Statute, Article 2, para. (a)-(i).

27. Phyllis Hwang, "Defining Crimes against Humanity in the Rome Statute of the International Criminal Court," *Fordham International Law Journal,* XXII (1998), 457, 459.

28. Ibid., 459–460.

29. Beth Van Schaack, "The Definition of Crimes against Humanity: Resolving the Incoherence," *Columbia Journal of Transnational Law,* XXXVII (1989), 787, 803.

30. Mohamed Elewa Badar, "From the Nuremberg Charter to the Rome Statute: Defining the Elements of Crimes against Humanity," *San Diego International Law Journal,* V (2004), 73, 83.

31. Ibid., 84.

32. Ibid.

33. Matthew Lippman, "International Law and Human Rights Edition: Crimes against Humanity," *Boston College Third World Law Journal,* XVII (1997), 141, 231.

34. Badar, "From the Nuremberg Charter to the Rome Statute," 84.

35. Ibid.

36. Ibid.

37. Ibid.

38. Guaneal Mettrax, "Crimes against Humanity in the Jurisprudence of the International Criminal Tribunals for the Former Yugoslavia and for Rwanda," *Harvard International Law Journal,* XLIII (2002), 237, 238.

39. Ibid., 239–240.

40. Ibid., 244.

41. Ibid. The ICTR and ICTY do differ in an important respect. The ICTY required that the crime be "committed in armed conflict," while the ICTR required that the offense be committed on "national, political, ethnic, racial, or religious grounds."

42. Ibid.

43. Hwang, "Defining Crimes against Humanity," 488.

44. Ibid., 494.

45. Ibid., 500.

46. Ibid.

47. Van Schaack, "The Definition of Crimes against Humanity," 850.

48. The Outreach Section of the Registry was headed by Binta Mansarey, a citizen of Sierra Leone, who is now the Registrar of the Court. The section, headed by an outreach officer, again Sierra Leonean, would expand its operational capability into the various districts within the country. These dedicated officers became the backbone of the program, setting up the town hall meetings, distributing information on the court, and showing videos of the court proceedings.

49. Our first town hall meeting was on September 24, 2002, six weeks after my arrival. The town of Kalihun was chosen, as it is the center of the diamond district and a place that was the heart of the civil war for the full ten years.

50. The last town was Port Locko on the Guinean/Sierra Leonean border.

51. After being introduced by the appropriate official, usually the local paramount chief, I would step off the high table and move right into the audience. Instead of launching into a lecture about why I was there, I would thank them for the privilege of being among them and then tell them about my wife, my children, even my pets. I would then state that since I had left my family in the United States for up to three years, I asked them for permission to be a part of their families. Any tension in the room evaporated and I would be welcomed with open arms. After they had welcomed me, then I would say: "Since you have given me this honor to be in your family, let's talk about what happened to you here." The session usually went on for three or four hours.

52. The legacy program has expanded since I left Sierra Leone in 2005. The senior leadership, many now from Sierra Leone, are members of the law faculty at the University of Sierra Leone.

53. A few days prior to my departure from Sierra Leone in July 2005, I was made an honorary paramount chief by the Civil Societies of Sierra Leone. I would like to think this honor was given to me by a citizenry who knew me personally and who had seen me many times "in the bush" talking to them for three years.

54. This phrase is taken from a statement that one of the victims gave to one of my investigators.

55. I told the tribunal in my opening statement in the joint criminal trial against the Civil Defense Force that they would have to "believe the unbelievable." I took this

phrase from a comment by a Jewish partisan who fought in the Warsaw ghetto during World War II, and wrote to the World Jewish Council in New York City saying, "They are killing us all, believe the unbelievable!"

56. I used this horrific episode in my opening statement in July 2004 in the joint criminal trial against the leadership of the RUF.

57. I signed nine of the indictments on March 3, 2003. In all, there were thirteen indictments.

DON HUBERT

5 The Responsibility to Protect: Preventing and Halting Crimes against Humanity

At the September 2005 United Nations (UN) World Summit in New York, the world's leaders formally accepted an international responsibility to protect civilian populations from genocide, war crimes, ethnic cleansing, and crimes against humanity. Widely hailed as one of the few successes of the World Summit, the commitment was, in many ways, a restatement of "never again," the phrase frequently invoked in the wake of genocide. The "responsibility to protect" is rapidly becoming part of the international lexicon, but what was actually agreed upon at the summit and will it ever have an impact?

In this chapter, I trace the intellectual antecedents of the responsibility to protect throughout the long-standing legal debate over humanitarian intervention and illustrate how this debate was reframed by the collective experiences of a series of interventions in humanitarian crises during the 1990s. After setting out the central contributions of the International Commission on Intervention and State Sovereignty, I account for the ascendancy of these ideas from obscurity in 2001 to their inclusion in the World Summit Outcome Document in 2005 and assess the agreed-upon text against the broader doctrine. Finally, I challenge the prevailing view that Darfur demonstrates the futility of the concept of the responsibility to protect and highlight key factors that will determine the effectiveness of the doctrine's implementation.

Humanitarian Intervention

Under what circumstances, if at all, can outside powers intervene with military force to stop a government from committing atrocities against its own population? A controversial question since the end of the Cold War, the debate is long-standing. Since the late nineteenth century, following a series of interventions by European powers on behalf of Christian minorities within the Ottoman Empire, states have, at various times, asserted a right to intervene in another country on humanitarian grounds.[1] Early debates about the potential emergence of such an international legal norm were put to rest, however, with the signing of the UN Charter in 1945.[2] The prohibition on the use of force, save only in cases of self defense, clearly made such interventions illegal in the absence of explicit Security Council authorization.

International debate reappeared during the 1970s in the context of three prominent cases: the 1971 Indian invasion of East Pakistan (modern-day Bangladesh), following a brutal response to a secessionist movement that resulted in hundreds of thousands killed and ten million refugees; the 1978 Vietnamese invasion of Cambodia to overthrow the genocidal Khmer Rouge; and the 1979 Tanzanian invasion to remove Idi Amin from power in Uganda. Although humanitarian rationales were not invoked in any of these cases, the humanitarian benefits of these interventions were self-evident.[3] Yet the combination of Cold War politics and the unfinished process of decolonization stifled any attempt to articulate new legal grounds for external military intervention.[4]

The end of the Cold War spawned an intense period of international action in response to humanitarian crises. With more failures than successes, UN-mandated missions were deployed to a series of crises from northern Iraq, the former Yugoslavia, Somalia, and Rwanda to Haiti, Sierra Leone, Liberia, Kosovo, and East Timor. A compelling case can be made that over this period, significant advances were made in the capacity of the UN and member states to oversee, implement, and even enforce peace agreements.[5] But the same cannot be said for their ability to provide protection to the civilian populations who were at grave risk. Epitomized by the Rwandan genocide and the crimes at Srebrenica, this shortcoming was a persistent feature of most UN missions throughout the decade.[6]

If the events had profound implications for this controversial debate, so too did their subsequent assessments. Two reports, published in late 1999 and early 2000, were particularly influential. The first, the *Report of the Secretary-General on the Fall of Srebrenica*, concluded that "the cardinal lesson of Srebrenica is that a deliberate and systematic attempt to terrorize, expel or murder an entire people must be met decisively with all necessary means, and with the political will to carry the policy through to its logical conclusion." It further highlighted the "pervasive ambivalence within the [UN] regarding the role of force in the pursuit of peace" and "an institutional ideology of impartiality even when confronted with attempted genocide."[7] The second document, the *Report of the Independent Inquiry into the Actions of the United Nations during the 1994 Genocide in Rwanda*, took the UN Assistance Mission for Rwanda and the UN secretariat to task for focusing on the breakdown of the cease-fire as opposed to the on-going genocide. It concluded that "the [UN] had an obligation to act which transcended traditional principles of peacekeeping. In effect, there can be no neutrality in the face of genocide, no impartiality in the face of a campaign to exterminate part of a population."[8]

With the failures of the UN and member states widely acknowledged, attention turned to the effectiveness of the UN Security Council—the sole international body with the legal authority to authorize the use of military force to halt such atrocities. Focused work on these issues had already begun in the Security Council under the banner of the "protection of civilians in armed conflict."[9] The secretary-general issued a report to the Security Council in 1999 that included a list of forty recommendations, the final being the most controversial—that the Security Council, "in the face of massive and ongoing abuses, consider the imposition of appropriate enforcement action."[10] In response, the council expressed its willingness to respond "where civilians are being targeted or humanitarian assistance to civilians is being deliberately obstructed, including through the consideration of appropriate measures at the Council's disposal."[11]

Although the use of military force is always controversial, explicit Security Council authorization is commonly deemed to be the deciding factor in determining both the legality and legitimacy of the use of force. It is interesting to note, therefore, two largely overlooked cases in the 1990s where military intervention was undertaken, in the absence of Security Council authorization, without sparking widespread debate.[12] Both cases were in West Africa, endorsed by the Economic Community of West African States (ECOWAS), and carried out by the ECOWAS monitoring group (ECOMOG). The first intervention occurred in Liberia in August 1990 and was "retroactively" endorsed by the Security Council only in November 1992.[13] Similarly, a second intervention occurred in Sierra Leone in late August 1997 with Security Council authorization coming only in October 1997.[14]

The issue, it seems, is not simply Security Council authorization. For, these precedents notwithstanding, and in spite of the fact that the scale of the human tragedy paled in comparison to ongoing crises, it was Kosovo that thrust the question of humanitarian intervention onto the international stage. In response to repeated attacks against civilian populations by Serbian forces, in late March 1999, NATO began a seventy-eight-day bombing campaign designed to force Serbian forces to withdraw from Kosovo. The lack of explicit UN Security Council authorization for NATO's use of force sparked a diplomatic firestorm.[15] The weight of legal opinion suggested that the action had been unlawful.[16] An international commission to assess the NATO intervention concluded that the mission was illegal but nevertheless "legitimate."[17]

The legal and policy vacuum in which these events took place spawned a series of attempts to articulate a new doctrine of humanitarian intervention. Then British Prime Minister Tony Blair proposed a set of principles allowing for the use of force in extreme humanitarian crises and unsuccessfully pushed for their adoption within the Security Council.[18] Then Secretary-General Kofi Annan, adopting a more modest, though no less controversial, approach, highlighted the tension between "two sovereignties"—the sovereignty of nation-states and the sovereignty of people. Specifically, he asked, "If humanitarian intervention is, indeed, an unacceptable assault on sovereignty, how should we respond to a Rwanda, to a Srebrenica—to gross and systematic violations of human rights that affect every precept of our common humanity?"[19]

The Responsibility to Protect

In parallel with these efforts, the government of Canada sponsored the independent International Commission on Intervention and State Sovereignty (ICISS) to attempt to address the seemingly irreconcilable tensions between sovereign states' right to non-interference in their internal affairs and the humanitarian imperative to act in cases of mass atrocities.

The commission's report, launched in 2001, proposed a reorientation of the international debate. Although the question that formed its core mandate fell squarely within the traditional debate on humanitarian intervention, the commission concluded that it was a mistake to frame the debate along traditional lines: whether seeking to halt large-scale atrocities should be added to the list of legitimate grounds for external military intervention.[20] Rather, it chose to draw on a different tradition of thinking, one focused on human rights, humanitarian law, and humanitarian action. Thus, rather than endorsing a "right of humanitarian intervention," the commission articulated a "responsibility to protect."[21]

Starting not with the potential rights of outside powers but rather with the civilian populations facing death and displacement, the commission addressed the tension between sovereignty and intervention by focusing on the responsibilities entailed in being a sovereign state.[22] Foremost among these responsibilities, the commission argued, was the provision of physical safety for the civilian population. In cases where a state fails to provide effective protection, the principle of non-intervention must yield to a subsidiary responsibility to be borne by the broader community of states.

In addition to reorienting the debate from the perspective of the outside intervener toward the civilian populations at risk, the commission made several other important contributions to the debate. First, it situated any military response within a continuum of responsibilities, including the responsibility to prevent, to react, and to rebuild. Second, it defined a high threshold—mass killing or displacement, actual or imminent—for military intervention. Third, it rearticulated well-established just-war guidelines—right intentions, last resort, proportional means, and reasonable prospects—that should inform any consideration of the use of force in humanitarian crises. On the necessity of Security Council authorization, the commission called on the council to discharge its responsibilities effectively, noting that if it did not, others might on their own. Finally, the commission highlighted operational challenges in using military force to protect civilian populations including the need for clear mandates and robust rules of engagement.

The initial response to the commission's report was widespread skepticism. When the report was released, in the wake of the 9/11 attacks and the invasion of Afghanistan, international attention was diverted from responding to humanitarian crises to the emerging "war on terror." Prospects for international acceptance of the commission's recommendations diminished further with the 2003 invasion of Iraq, which was launched without Security Council authorization.[23] Worse still, when no weapons of mass destruction were found, attempts were made to justify the invasion on humanitarian grounds.[24] While such a case could perhaps have been made during Hussein's vicious assaults on the Kurdish population a decade earlier, employing a humanitarian justification, following the invasion, only deepened suspicions that this doctrine was merely a new-found rationale for great-power intervention.[25]

Opposition to external military intervention was particularly strong among the developing, and particularly post-colonial, world.[26] In 1999 and again in 2001, ministerial communiqués from the Non-Aligned Movement (NAM) rejected any so-called right of humanitarian intervention.[27] Similar resolutions in the UN General Assembly confirmed that a majority of countries were skeptical about the use of force to halt genocide and related crimes.[28] Canada's parallel efforts to launch a debate within the General Assembly to consider simply the findings of the responsibility to protect report foundered.

Yet, at the same time, cracks were beginning to show among the opposition. In Latin America, a region with long-standing concerns about external military intervention, efforts to issue a communiqué rejecting any right of humanitarian intervention failed in the face of opposition from Argentina and Chile.[29] While the essential elements of any new doctrine remained controversial, a growing number of countries were unwilling to endorse an absolutist vision of state sovereignty. African states, motivated by the legacy of the Rwandan genocide, pressed ahead furthest. Replacing the tradition of non-interference with a doctrine of "non-indifference," the Constitutive Act of the African Union, adopted in 2003, made explicit provision for military intervention "in respect of grave circumstances, namely: war crimes, genocide and crimes against humanity."[30]

Normative Progress

Given the considerable opposition to formal debate on the responsibility to protect in the UN, how then did the doctrine come to be endorsed by consensus at the UN in 2005? Two factors were principally responsible for this transformation. First, irrespective of the emphasis on the war on terror, humanitarian crises once again demonstrated the relevance of these ideas. Two cases were particularly significant: the war in the eastern Democratic Republic of the Congo, where estimates of conflict-related deaths were in the millions, and the conflict in the Darfur region of the Sudan, with more than two hundred thousand dead and 2.5 million displaced.[31]

Second, the call by then Secretary-General Kofi Annan for a summit of world leaders in 2005 to revive multilateral cooperation provided a venue for inter-governmental negotiations. A blue-ribbon panel, appointed by Annan to assess contemporary international threats in the lead-up to the summit, endorsed "the emerging norm that there is a collective responsibility to protect."[32] Building on this recommendation, and consistent with his own personal commitment to the concept, Annan encouraged member-states that were coming to the summit to embrace and act upon "the 'responsibility to protect' potential or actual victims of massive atrocities."[33]

Following intense negotiations, with numerous caveats in place, member-states acknowledged, by consensus, a responsibility to protect and agreed in paragraph 139 of the Summit Outcome Document to the following:

> The international community, through the United Nations, also has the responsibility to use appropriate diplomatic, humanitarian and other peaceful means, in accordance with Chapters VI and VIII of the Charter, to help to protect populations from genocide, war crimes, ethnic cleansing and crimes against humanity. *In this context, we are prepared to take collective action, in a timely and decisive manner, through the Security Council, in accordance with the Charter, including Chapter VII, on a case-by-case basis and in cooperation with relevant regional organizations as appropriate, should peaceful means be inadequate and national authorities are manifestly failing to protect their populations from genocide, war crimes, ethnic cleansing and crimes against humanity.* We stress the need for the General Assembly to continue consideration of the responsibility to protect populations from genocide, war crimes, ethnic cleansing and crimes against humanity and its implications, bearing in mind the principles of the Charter and international law.[34]

The adoption of this text at the largest-ever gathering of heads of state is noteworthy, but the actual commitment is best characterized as responsibility to protect "lite." The essential elements of the doctrine are: the recognition of each state's principal responsibility to provide protection; an acknowledgment of a subsidiary responsibility by the international community to respond where a state is "manifestly failing;" thresholds for international action; and the prospect of the use of force when other options have failed. Importantly, the document also clarifies the breadth of the Security Council's mandate to respond to humanitarian crises relative to that of the General Assembly. Specifically, the paragraph makes clear that the council can and should respond to atrocities that are committed against civilian populations even in the absence of wider threats to international peace and security, thus resolving a long-standing point of contention from some members of NAM regarding Security Council encroachment on the rights of the General Assembly.[35]

In other areas, the text remains vague. It does not explicitly link the right of non-intervention with the provision of effective protection for civilian populations. The existence and precise nature of the obligations of the UN and its member states remain unclear. The thresholds for action are somewhat ambiguous: ethnic cleansing has no legal definition, while isolated war crimes, perpetrated by individual combatants, would not seem to warrant robust international action. No guidelines are set out to govern the potential use of force in situations that meet the stated thresholds. And there is no mention of what should be done if one of the permanent members vetoes Security Council authorization.

Clearly more would need to be done to articulate a comprehensive doctrine. But progress in the short term is unlikely. The Security Council affirmed the World Summit conclusions in 2006.[36] Key council members, however, have been unwilling to agree on explicit guidelines for authorizing the use of force, to restrict the use of the veto when addressing humanitarian crises, or to accept any formal obligation to respond. Normative advances in the General Assembly are equally unlikely. Consensus at the World Summit does not signify universal acceptance. Some skeptics, including China, were focused, during the negotiations, not on the responsibility to protect but on the creation of the Human Rights Council. Intense lobbying was necessary to secure even the truncated version of the concept that exists in paragraph 139.[37] In the absence of the pressure-cooker atmosphere that surrounded the World Summit, it is unlikely that the language adopted in 2005 will receive assent again. Thus, calls for debate in the UN are as likely to come from those who wish to undermine the commitment as those who wish for it to be strengthened.

As the controversy surrounding the use of force for humanitarian ends remains a barrier to effective international action, a clear articulation of this doctrine remains an important goal. The commitment made at the 2005 summit rests on the collective failures during the 1990s. Further codification will rest on the responses to future crises—whether effective or not. The immediate agenda for proponents of the responsibility to protect, therefore, is to take this emerging doctrine and put it into practice.

Early Test-Cases

Any discussion of the challenges of implementing the responsibility to protect must begin with the crisis in Darfur. With widespread attacks against civilian populations, beginning in 2003, Darfur is often seen as the first "test-case."[38] Whether the attacks by the Khartoum-backed militia constitute genocide has been hotly debated. But there is no doubt that they meet a threshold for the responsibility to protect: crimes against humanity.[39]

The African Union (AU) deployed a force to Darfur, Sudan, in 2004, and by 2007, there were close to 7,000 troops on the ground. But the mission lacked both the mandate and the capacity to counter continuing attacks.[40] Following protracted negotiations, the Security Council authorized a UN-AU

Hybrid Peace Operation in 2007 with an explicit mandate to protect civilians, and the UN formally took control of the mission in early 2008.[41] Yet six years after the start of the crisis and in the wake of the deaths of hundreds of thousands and the forcible displacement of millions, the verdict is clear: the international community has failed, again.

The reasons for this failure are in part political, including effective Sudanese diplomacy, Chinese support within the Security Council for one of its key oil suppliers, the risk of undermining the peace agreement between North and South Sudan, and inconsistent leadership from the United States, Britain, and France. But the failure is also the result of the genuine difficulty in articulating a compelling alternative to seemingly endless negotiations with Khartoum. Darfur is a landlocked region in the Sahara desert about the same size as France. Long supply lines and complicated logistics make mounting a non-consensual military operation all but impossible.[42]

Yet the damage done to the responsibility to protect by the Darfur failure should not be overstated. First, test-cases are seldom indicative of the long-term acceptance of new normative standards, as early difficulties with such important developments as the abolition of slavery, the illegality of territorial gain through conquest, or the right of self-determination would suggest. The principles embodied in the responsibility to protect challenge some of the basic tenets of the post-Westphalian and post–World War II international order. That their acceptance and implementation is inconsistent and uneven should not come as a surprise.

Attention on Darfur has also obscured some signs for optimism. Two cases in central Africa suggest progress is being made on both the preventive and reactive dimensions of the responsibility to protect. Burundi illustrates how persistent international engagement can help prevent the outbreak of mass atrocities against civilians. With ethnic tensions similar to those in Rwanda, and a history of inter-ethnic violence, many thought that Burundi, too, could experience a large-scale genocide.[43] Yet the engagement by African nations, including the deployment of peacekeepers and mediation efforts by President Nelson Mandela, facilitated the implementation of a peace plan and may well have prevented genocidal attacks.[44]

Military operations under way since 2003 in the eastern Democratic Republic of the Congo illustrate how the use of military force can enhance the physical safety of civilian populations. With ethnically targeted killings escalating rapidly through the spring of 2003, a robust European Union (EU) force was deployed to halt the violence in the city of Bunia, the epicenter of the crisis. With a mandate to protect the refugee camps, secure the airport, and ensure the safety of UN staff and aid workers, the troops stopped the killings inside Bunia in a matter of days and quickly made the city a weapons-free zone (though atrocities continued in surrounding areas).[45]

When EU forces withdrew three months later, the UN deployed a brigade of 4,500 peacekeepers who, armed with heavy weapons and combat helicopters, were able and willing to undertake offensive military operations against militia factions.[46] The region has remained highly unstable and UN troops were often the target of attacks. But the brigades did manage to wrest control from the various militias and increase the level of security for the civilian population.[47]

Trends in contemporary peacekeeping also suggest that the prospects for implementing the responsibility to protect are improving. In stark contrast to the situation in the 1990s, the mandates of thirteen of the last fourteen peacekeeping missions provide authorization for the use of force to protect civilians who are threatened by violence.[48] Furthermore, successful military operations by Britain in Sierra Leone and by an Australian-led multinational force in East Timor, while not focused specifically on civilian protection, illustrate how robust national and multinational forces can quickly overwhelm vicious, but poorly trained, opponents.[49]

Implementation

The record on implementing the responsibility to protect may be more balanced than is often imagined. Nevertheless, putting this emerging doctrine into practice in future crises represents a major test for the UN and its member states.

The UN system, it seems, is taking this challenge seriously. It was widely expected that attention to the responsibility to protect within the UN Secretariat would decline with the departure of Annan at the end of 2006. Annan's commitment to the agenda was highly personal, born from his experience leading the Department of Peacekeeping Operations during the Rwanda debacle and maintained in the face of consistent opposition from the majority of his senior advisors. Furthermore, his successor was from Asia, a region more skeptical, on the whole, of the notion of the responsibility to protect.[50] Thus, Secretary-General Ban Ki-moon caught many observers off-guard with his prominent and persistent support of the concept. In public speeches and in statements to the Security Council, Ban Ki-moon has highlighted the need to make operational the responsibility to protect. For example, on the 2007 anniversary of the genocide in Rwanda he said:

> All the world's Governments have agreed in principle to the responsibility to protect. Our challenge now is to give real meaning to the concept, by taking steps to make it operational. Only then will it truly give hope to those facing genocide, war crimes, crimes against humanity and ethnic cleansing.[51]

And, he has done more than talk. Following the recommendations of the Advisory Committee on the Prevention of Genocide, created by Kofi Annan in 2006, Ban Ki-moon has converted the special adviser for the prevention of genocide to a full-time position and upgraded it to the level of under-secretary-general.[52] He has also created a new part-time position of special adviser on the responsibility to protect. A report from the secretary-general, released in early 2009, established a framework for operationalizing the agenda throughout the UN system.[53]

Policy commitment within the UN system is but one important ingredient in putting the principles of the responsibility to protect into practice. Three challenges loom particularly large: consistency of application, the capacity to forestall and halt atrocities, and the willingness of outsiders to act.

The most common critique of international actions in cases of genocide and crimes against humanity is their inconsistent application—they are only imposed against relatively weak states. Here it is important to acknowledge that the application of these standards will always be inconsistent—it is built into the doctrine. There simply are fewer levers available to dissuade powerful states from committing crimes against their own populations. In such cases, where preventive efforts fail and coercive measures are the only alternative, the precautionary principle of "a reasonable prospect of success" means by definition that there will be no military intervention. And this is not simply a question of the immunity of states that possess nuclear weapons. Interventions that require a direct assault on well-trained and well-equipped military forces would, in all likelihood, result in a greater loss of civilian life.

Rather than "going in fighting," it is always preferable to secure the consent of the host state. Consent, however, need not mean that the deployment of troops is willingly accepted; in some cases, it can be coerced. As the multinational mission to East Timor demonstrated, acquiescence under extreme diplomatic and economic pressure may be sufficient to avoid direct opposition from powerful military forces.[54] Again, though, the question of consistency arises as advocates for international action will invariably have greater leverage over some countries than over others.

A second prominent challenge is strengthening institutional capacity—civilian and military—to prevent atrocities in the early stages of a crisis and to intervene effectively to stop them if prevention fails. It is commonly argued that there is no lack of early warning, the problem is early action.[55] Yet the existence of memos and cables correctly predicting atrocities is not the equivalent of effective mechanisms for monitoring deteriorating situations and alerting key decision-makers.[56] The upgrading of the special adviser on the prevention of genocide and the creation of a dedicated post on the responsibility to protect in the UN are important first steps. But the creation of new bureaucratic entities is unlikely to generate sufficient coordination within the UN system. Implementing the responsibility to protect demands unprecedented collaboration between humanitarian and human agencies; it requires field-based information and peace and security institutions that are responsible for political negotiations and are capable of applying diplomatic and economic pressure.

Parallel efforts are under way in Washington, and in Europe, to expand the capacity to prevent and respond to genocide and related crimes. In Washington, a Genocide Prevention Task Force, co-chaired by former Secretary of State Madeleine Albright and former Secretary of Defense William Cohen, published in 2008 its recommendations on enhancing the U.S. government's capacity to respond to genocide and mass atrocities.[57] EU foreign policy representative Javier Solana highlighted the need for greater preventive capacity in his statement at the 2004 genocide prevention conference in Stockholm. He has subsequently supported a feasibility study for a European-based international center on the prevention of genocide.[58]

On the military side, the challenge is to enhance the capacity of soldiers to halt mass killings in non-permissive environments. These skills are needed not only to stop future genocides, they are becoming a part of regular peacekeeping, as mandates now routinely include authorization for the use of force to protect civilians under attack. Providing effective protection requires rules of engagement, a military doctrine, and pre-deployment training that all differ from traditional peacekeeping or war-fighting.[59] Enhancing military preparedness to protect humanitarian corridors, defend safe areas, disarm militias in refugee camps, and impose no-fly zones will improve the prospects for a mission's success.

The ultimate challenge is to ensure international action when it is needed most. For advocates of the responsibility to protect, the problem is not too many illegitimate interventions but too few legitimate ones.[60] What then is the barrier to more, legitimate interventions?

Public opinion, it would seem, is not the culprit that many presume. A recent international poll of twelve countries revealed their strong support for the concept of the responsibility to protect. "The most common response—a majority in eight countries and a plurality in four—is that the Security Council has not only a right but a responsibility to authorize the use of force" in cases of "severe human rights violations, such as genocide, even against the will of the government committing such abuses."[61] In an earlier public opinion poll of war-affected populations, two-thirds said there should be more international intervention on behalf of threatened civilians.[62]

An important missing ingredient is political leadership. Politicians are understandably reluctant to deploy military forces where the prospects of success are highly uncertain and the short-term political pay-off is modest. This is yet another tragedy of the war in Iraq. The responsibility to protect survived (just barely) the controversy surrounding the invasion in the absence of Security Council authorization. But it may not survive, at least in the near term, the risk aversion among political leaders that has resulted from the debacle of the failed peacebuilding and reconstruction in Iraq.

The concept of the responsibility to protect has brought greater precision to the international debate about international action to halt mass atrocities and greater clarity on the steps that are necessary to put those principles into practice. In spite of the highly political and frequently inconsistent application of this emerging doctrine, anecdotal evidence suggests that international action can and does have a positive effect. Wider implementation, however, will depend on the convictions of political leaders and on the public pressure placed on them to protect people—through prevention or intervention—facing the gravest of crimes.

Notes

1. Gary Bass, *Freedom's Battle: The Origins of Humanitarian Intervention* (New York, 2008), 18–19; Ian Brownlie, *International Law and the Use of Force by States* (New York, 1963), 338.

2. Brownlie, *International Law*, 710.

3. For an overview of these three cases, see Nicholas J. Wheeler, *Saving Strangers: Humanitarian Intervention in International Society* (New York, 2002), 55–111. See also Thomas Franck and Nigel Rodley, "After Bangladesh: The Law of Humanitarian Intervention by Military Force," *American Journal of International Law*, LXVII (1973), 275–305; Farook Hassan, "RealPolitik in International Law: After Tanzanian-Ugandan Conflict: 'Humanitarian Intervention' Reexamined," *Willamette Law Review*, XVII (1981), 859–912; Michael J. Bazyler, "Reexamining the Doctrine of

Humanitarian Intervention in Light of the Atrocities in Kampuchea and Ethiopia," *Stanford Journal of International Law*, XXIII (1987), 547–619.

4. For an early attempt to establish new international standards in the wake of the crisis in East Pakistan, see International Law Association, *The International Protection of Human Rights by General International Law: The Third Interim Report of the Subcommittee on the International Protection of Human Rights* (New Delhi, 1974).

5. See, for example, Michael Doyle and Nicholas Sambanis, *Making War and Building Peace: United Nations Peace Operations* (Princeton, 2006); Stephen John Stedman, Donald Rothchild, and Elizabeth Cousens (eds.), *Ending Civil Wars: The Implementation of Peace Agreements* (Boulder, 2002).

6. See Thomas Weiss and Don Hubert, *The Responsibility to Protect: Research, Bibliography and Background* (Ottawa, 2001), 79–126; idem, *Humanitarian Action in War: Aid, Protection and Impartiality in a Policy Vacuum*, Adelphi Paper No. 305 (London, 1996).

7. United Nations (UN), *Report of the Secretary-General Pursuant to General Assembly Resolution 53/35: The Fall of Srebrenica*, UN Doc. A/54/549 (New York, 1999), paras. 502 and 505.

8. UN, *Report of the Independent Inquiry into the Actions of the United Nations during the 1994 Genocide in Rwanda*, UN Doc. S/1999/1257 (New York, 1999), 50.

9. For an overview of this effort, see Elissa Golberg and Don Hubert, "The Security Council and the Protection of Civilians," in Rob McRae and Don Hubert (eds.), *Human Security and the New Diplomacy* (Montreal, 2001), 223–230.

10. UN, *Report of the Secretary-General to the Security Council on the Protection of Civilians In Armed Conflict*, UN Doc. S/1999/957 (New York, 1999), 22.

11. UN Security Council, 4046th Meeting, Resolution 1265, UN Doc. S/RES/1265, 1999, para.10.

12. See, for example, Anthony Chukwuka Ofodile, "The Legality of ECOWAS Intervention in Liberia," *Columbia Journal of Transnational Law*, XXXII (1994), 381–418.

13. UN Security Council, 3138th Meeting, Resolution 788, UN Doc. S/RES/788, 1992, determined that the situation in Liberia constituted a threat to international peace and security and provided authorization for the ECOMOG force under Chapter VII. See Marc Weller (ed.), *Regional Peacekeeping and International Enforcement: The Liberian Crisis* (New York, 1994); Ofodile, "The Legality of ECOWAS Intervention in Liberia," 381–418.

14. UN Security Council, 3822nd Meeting, Resolution 1132, UN Doc. S/RES/1132, 1997, provided explicit authorization for ECOMOG under Chapter VII. See Akintunde Kabir Otubu, "Collective Intervention in International Law: ECOMOG/Sierra Leone in Retrospect," available at http://ssrn.com/abstract=1140203 (accessed 7 April 2009).

15. Two Security Council resolutions passed in advance of the NATO bombing, 1160 and 1199. Both invoked "coercive" powers through Chapter VII of the UN Charter but neither explicitly authorized the use of military force.

16. Antonio Cassese, "*Ex iniuria ius oritur*: Are We Moving towards International Legitimation of Forcible Humanitarian Countermeasures in the World Community?" *European Journal of International Law*, X (1999), 25. Cassese notes that ". . . from an ethical viewpoint resort to armed force was justified. Nevertheless, as a legal scholar I cannot avoid observing in the same breath that this moral action is contrary to current international law." For additional analyses of the legality of the Kosovo intervention, see Bruno Simma, "NATO, the UN and the Use of Force: Legal Aspects," *European Journal of International Law*, X (1999), 1–22; Jonathan Charney, "Anticipatory Humanitarian Intervention in Kosovo," *American Journal of International Law*, XCIII (1999), 834–841; John J. Merriam, "Kosovo and the Law of Humanitarian Intervention," *Case Western Reserve Journal of International Law*, XXXIII (2001), 111–154.

17. Independent International Commission on Kosovo, *Kosovo Report* (New York, 2000).

18. Tony Blair, "Doctrine of the International Community," speech, Chicago Economic Club, Chicago, IL, 22 April 1999.

19. Kofi Annan, "Two Concepts of Sovereignty," address to the Fifty-fourth Session of the General Assembly, reprinted in *The Question of Intervention: Statements of the Secretary-General* (New York, 1999), 39.

20. For a more recent attempt to construct such a list, see Lee Feinstein and Anne-Marie Slaughter, "A Duty to Prevent," *Foreign Affairs*, LXXXIII (2004), 136–151.

21. The International Commission on Intervention and State Sovereignty, *The Responsibility to Protect* (Ottawa, 2001).

22. The concept of "sovereignty as responsibility" was drawn from the work of Francis Deng, former special representative of the secretary-general on internally displaced persons. See Francis Deng and others, *Sovereignty as Responsibility: Conflict Management in Africa* (Washington, D.C., 1996).

23. For a bleak assessment of the prospects for endorsement of the responsibility to protect from a broadly sympathetic analyst, see Adam Roberts, "Law and the Use of Force after Iraq," *Survival*, XLV (2003), 31–56.

24. During a speech given in Sedgefield, England, in 2004, Blair defended the decision to invade Iraq saying, "We surely have a responsibility to act when a nation's people are subjected to a regime such as Saddam's."

25. See Kenneth Roth, "War in Iraq: Not a Humanitarian Intervention," Human Rights Watch World Report (New York, 2004), 13–35.

26. See Mohammed Ayoob, "Humanitarian Intervention and International Society," *Global Governance*, VII (2001), 225–231; Ramesh Thakur, "Developing Countries and the Intervention-Sovereignty Debate," in Richard M. Price and Mark W. Zacher (eds.), *The United Nations and Global Security* (New York, 2008).

27. "We reject the so-called 'right of humanitarian intervention' which has no legal basis in the UN Charter or in the general principles of international law," para. 171. Final Communiqué of the Meeting of Ministers for Foreign Affairs and Heads

of Delegation of the Non-Aligned Movement, held in New York, New York, 23 September 1999. A similar communiqué was issued in 2001.

28. See UN General Assembly, *Resolution on Human Rights and Unilateral Coercive Measures*, UN Doc. A/RES/54/172, 2000, and UN General Assembly, *Resolution on Human Rights and Unilateral Coercive Measures*, UN Doc. A/RES/55/110, 2001.

29. For a discussion of the Rio Group efforts to formulate a position on the NATO bombing in the Kosovo conflict, see Mónica Serrano, "Latin America: The Dilemmas of Intervention," in Albrecht Schnabel and Ramesh Thakur (eds.), *Kosovo and the Challenge of Humanitarian Intervention* (New York, 2000), 232–237; Jorge Heine, "The Responsibility to Protect: Humanitarian Intervention and the Principle of Non-Intervention in the Americas," in Ramesh Thakur, Andrew F. Cooper, and John English (eds.), *International Commissions and the Power of Ideas* (New York, 2005), 221–245.

30. *Constitutive Act of the African Union*, Article 4(h), 2000. See Ben Kioko, "The Right of Intervention under the African Union's Constitutive Act: From Non-Interference to Non-Intervention," *International Review of the Red Cross*, LXXXV (2003), 807–825; Paul D. Williams, "From Non-Intervention to Non-Indifference: The Origins and Development of the African Union's Security Culture," *African Affairs*, CVI (2007), 253–279. On the principle of non-indifference, see Alpha Oumar Konaré, "Security Is the African Union's Priority," *African Geopolitics*, XIII (2004).

31. An International Rescue Committee survey of excess mortality attributable to the conflict in the DRC estimates 3.9 million deaths, though less than 10 percent were directly due to violence. Benjamin Coghlan and others, "Mortality in the Democratic Republic of Congo: A Nationwide Survey," *Lancet*, CCCLXVII (2006), 44–51. In May 2005, the Centre for Research on the Epidemiology of Disasters (CRED) in Brussels estimated that from September 2003 to January 2005 excess deaths due to the conflict ranged from 63,000 to 146,000. Debarati Guha-Sapir, Olivier Degomme, and Mark Phelan, *Darfur: Counting the Deaths—Mortality Estimates from Multiple Survey Data* (Brussels, 2005). See also Evelyn Depoortere and others, "Violence and Mortality in West Darfur, Sudan (2003–04): Epidemiological Evidence from Four Surveys," *Lancet*, CCCLXIV (2004), 1315–1320.

32. UN, *A More Secure World: Our Shared Responsibility* (New York, 2004), 65–66.

33. UN General Assembly, *Resolution on the Situation of Human Rights in the Islamic Republic of Iran*, UN Doc. A/RES/59/205, 2005, 34–35.

34. UN General Assembly, Sixtieth Session, *Resolution on the 2005 World Summit Outcome*, UN Doc. A/RES/60/1, 2005, para. 139. Italics added.

35. For an example of NAM opposition to alleged Security Council encroachment see the address by the representative of India during the open debate in the UN: *Report of the Secretary-General to the Security Council on the Protection of Civilians in Armed Conflict*, resumption 1. After reviewing the functions and powers of the Security Council as set out in Article 24, the representative contested the legitimacy of the council's proposed role in all but seven of the forty recommendations contained in the secretary-general's report.

36. UN Security Council, 5430th Meeting, Resolution 1674, UN Doc. S/RES/1674, 2006.

37. Those lobbying in favor included Canada, Australia, New Zealand, members of the EU (particularly the UK and France), and there was strong support from Africa, including the NAM chairs Mauritius and South Africa. Vocal opponents included Iran, Egypt, Russia, Pakistan, Jamaica, and India.

38. See Gareth Evans, "Darfur and the Responsibility to Protect," *The Diplomat* (August–September 2004), available at www.crisisgroup.org/home/index.cfm?id=2915&l=1 (accessed 19 June 2009); Alex De Waal, "Darfur and the Failure of the Responsibility to Protect," *International Affairs,* LXXXIII (2007), 1039–1054; Paul Williams and Alex Bellamy, "The Responsibility to Protect and the Crisis in Darfur," *Security Dialogue,* XXXVI (2005) 27–47.

39. The UN Commission of Inquiry on Darfur concluded that while the specific intent of genocide may be lacking, the scale of the killings and displacement certainly met the threshold of crimes against humanity and war crimes. See International Commission of Inquiry on Darfur, *Report to the Secretary-General* (Geneva, 2005), 4. See also Gérard Prunier, *Darfur: The Ambiguous Genocide* (Ithaca, 2005); Alex de Waal, *Darfur: A New History of a Long War* (London, 2008, 2nd ed.); Don Cheadle and John Prendergast, *"Not on Our Watch": The Mission to End Genocide in Darfur and Beyond* (New York, 2007); M.W. Daly, *Darfur's Sorrow: A History of Destruction and Genocide* (New York, 2007).

40. See Seth Appiah-Mensah, "AU's Critical Assignment in Darfur: Challenges and Constraints," *African Security Review,* XIV (2005), 7–21. For an analysis that recognizes the weaknesses but claims that the AU has in fact been more effective than is commonly accepted, see William G. O'Neill and Violette Cassis, *Protecting Two Million Internally Displaced: The Successes and Shortcomings of the African Union in Darfur* (Washington, D.C., 2005).

41. UN Security Council, 5727th Meeting, Resolution 1769, UN Doc. S/RES/1769, 2007.

42. In response to suggestions that a no-fly zone be imposed to stop the Sudanese air force from supporting janjaweed attacks, General Henri Bentegeat, chairman of the EU's Military Committee, noted that the 500,000-square-km territory made such a plan unfeasible. "You would need at least 60 combat aircraft to enforce it correctly," he said. See Mark John, "Darfur No-fly Zone Unworkable—Top EU Soldier," *Reuters* (22 May 2007).

43. According to Secretary-General Annan, speaking on the situation in Burundi in 1996, "We have to move very quickly before everything blows up in our faces. . . . As it is, history will judge us rather severely for Rwanda. I don't think we can repeat that experience in Burundi. What we need and what we are seeking now is the political will to act." Quoted in Barbara Crossette, "UN Asks Intervention Force as Burundi Nears a Collapse," *New York Times* (25 July 1996), x.

44. For overviews of preventive efforts in Burundi, see Kristina A. Bentley and Roger Southall, *An African Peace Process: Mandela, South Africa and Burundi* (Cape

Town, 2005); Howard Wolpe and others, "Rebuilding Peace and State Capacity in War-Torn Burundi," *Roundtable*, XCIII (2004), 457–467.

45. See Stale Ulriksen, Catriona Gourlay, and Catriona Mace, "Operation Artemis: The Shape of Things to Come?" *International Peacekeeping*, XI (2004), 508–525.

46. See, for example, UN *Seventeenth Report of the Secretary-General on the UN Organization Mission in the Democratic Republic of the Congo*, UN Doc. S/2005/167 (New York, 2005), 3–7.

47. "For the period covered by the survey, the only region to record a significant reduction in mortality since 2004 was that encompassing the five eastern provinces. This improvement coincided with a reduction in the risk of violent death, as well as a more robust U.N. peacekeeping effort by MONUC, the international force in DR Congo." Benjamin Coghlan and others, *Mortality in the Democratic Republic of Congo: An Ongoing Crisis* (New York, 2008).

48. For a full list of Security Council Resolutions including protection of civilians mandates, see Victoria K. Holt and Tobias C. Berkman, *The Impossible Mandate: Military Preparedness, the Responsibility to Protect and Modern Peace Operations* (Washington, D.C., 2006).

49. On Operation Palliser, the British deployment of troops to Sierra Leone in May 2000, see Paul Williams, "Fighting for Freetown: British Military Intervention in Sierra Leone," *Contemporary Security Policy*, XXII (2001), 140–168. On INTERFET, the Australian-led coalition to East Timor in 1999–2000, see Michael G. Smith, *Peacekeeping in East Timor: The Path to Independence* (Boulder, 2002).

50. See Paul M. Evans, "Human Security and East Asia: In the Beginning," *Journal of East Asian Studies*, IV (2004), 263–284.

51. UN Secretary-General Ban Ki-moon, *Challenge Is to Make Responsibility to Protect Operational, Statement on the Anniversary of the Rwandan Genocide*, UN Doc. SG/SM/10934 (New York, 2007).

52. Francis Deng, former representative on internally displaced persons and originator of the concept of sovereignty as responsibility, was appointed as special adviser for the prevention of genocide on 29 May 2007.

53. UN, *Report of the Secretary General to UN General Assembly on Implementing the Responsibility to Protect*, UN Doc. A/63/667 (New York, 2009).

54. International pressure included a mission of UN Security Council representatives from Jakarta, the suspension of U.S. military cooperation with Indonesia, and the freezing of major International Monetary Fund and World Bank assistance programs. These measures resulted, in less than one week, in Indonesia's acceptance of a multinational force to provide security. See Nicholas J. Wheeler and Tim Dunne, "East Timor and the New Humanitarian Interventionism," *International Affairs*, LXXVII (2001), 815–823.

55. See for example the Carnegie Commission, *Preventing Deadly Conflict* (New York, 1997). In response to the claim that a lack of action was due to a lack of information, the commission stated that this "argument is simply unconvincing in an

age when major governments operate extensive, sophisticated early warning and intelligence networks worldwide," 43.

56. See Robert I. Rotberg, "Conclusions: NGOs, Early Warning, Early Action, and Preventive Diplomacy," in Rotberg (ed.), *Vigilance and Vengeance: NGOs Preventing Ethnic Conflict in Divided Societies* (Washington, D.C., 1996); Lawrence Woocher, "Early Warning for the Prevention of Genocide and Mass Atrocities," paper presented at the Conference of the International Studies Association, Chicago, IL, 28 February–3 March 2007.

57. Genocide Prevention Task Force, *Preventing Genocide: A Blueprint for U.S. Policymakers* (Washington, D.C., 2008).

58. The study was conducted in 2006 by the steering group, chaired by David Hamburg, including representatives of the Carter Center, the Folke Bernadotte Academy, the Madariaga European Foundation, and a personal representative of Javier Solana.

59. See Thomas Weiss and Don Hubert, "Conduct and Capacity," in their *The Responsibility to Protect: Research, Bibliography and Background* (Ottawa, 2001), 177–206; Victoria Holt, *The Impossible Mandate: Military Preparedness, the Responsibility to Protect and Modern Peace Operations* (Washington, D.C., 2006).

60. Michael Walzer, *Just and Unjust Wars* (New York, 2000, 3rd ed.), xiii.

61. The Chicago Council on Global Affairs, *World Public Opinion 2007* (Chicago, 2007). Italics added. Countries surveyed on intervention included Argentina, Armenia, China, France, India, Israel, Palestine, Poland, Russia, Thailand, Ukraine, and the United States.

62. International Committee of the Red Cross, *The People on War Report: ICRC Worldwide Consultation of the Rules of War* (Geneva, 1999).

EDWARD C. LUCK

6 Building a Norm: The Responsibility to Protect Experience

The responsibility to protect (R2P) is a big idea, no doubt about it.[1] But it is also an evolving and still contentious one, despite pledges that the heads of state and government made at the 2005 World Summit. They affirmed, unanimously, that they would protect their populations by preventing genocide, war crimes, ethnic cleansing, and crimes against humanity, as well as the incitement of such acts. Further, they agreed that the international community should assist and support states in exercising that responsibility and in building their domestic protection capacities. When national authorities are nevertheless "manifestly failing" to protect their populations from the four specific crimes and violations and peaceful means are inadequate, the world leaders confirmed that the international community would take collective action in a "timely and decisive manner" through the United Nations (UN) Security Council and in accordance with the Charter of the UN, and with the cooperation of regional organizations as appropriate.[2]

This chapter looks at a piece of the evolution of R2P: the efforts of UN Secretary-General Ban Ki-moon, a host of member states, and a cluster of determined advocates and non-governmental organizations (NGOs) to advance its conceptual, political, and operational development over the course of 2008 and 2009. During that period (and since), this author has served as the secretary-general's special adviser on these matters. This chapter seeks to shed some light on the strategic and tactical choices that were made then to forward the development and acceptance of R2P. At several points, the discussion addresses the origins and earlier development of R2P, both because recent efforts at the UN build on them and because even the concept's roots are disputed by some. In addition to telling the story of R2P's more recent adventures on the world stage, this chapter tests how well the classic model of norm development that Finnemore and Sikkink have posed holds up in this case.[3]

At the outset, three things should be said. One, in a formal and technical sense R2P has not yet achieved—and may never achieve—the status of a binding legal norm. Two, to this author at least, the lack of that credential need not condition its effectiveness in terms of affecting the behavior of states and armed groups and the decisions of international bodies. Critics and advocates alike should understand that R2P is a political concept, albeit one based on well-established legal principles and norms. R2P's relevance and power derive from its capacity to help to spur political will for implementing widely accepted and long codified international standards. It promises, in other words, to help to generate what is too often the missing ingredient in international normative development: the will and a strategy for implementation, what the secretary-general calls turning words into deeds. In remarkably short order, compared to the historical development of the human rights, humanitarian, and refugee norms on which it is based, however, R2P is becoming a standard for the kind of proper behavior that is increasingly expected from both states and non-state actors. Three, rather than adding to or distracting from those established norms, R2P seeks to amplify and multiply the voices calling for their implementation and, if necessary, their enforcement.

Despite these distinctions, which matter in inter-governmental discourse, in the academic realm, political scientists regularly equate norms and standards. For example, Finnemore and Sikkink assert that "there is general agreement on the definition of a norm as a standard of appropriate behavior for actors with a given identity."[4] This discussion adopts this looser notion of norm and norm development, using "norm" and "standard" interchangeably, as well as referring to R2P as a concept or principle. On the other hand, in the inter-governmental debates about R2P, there has been far less acceptance of R2P as a legal norm than as a generally accepted standard of behavior. This reluctance reflects, as discussed below, the acute concern in some quarters about how R2P standards might be enforced, by whom, and under whose authority.

The Model

In an influential 1998 article Finnemore and Sikkink laid out a largely persuasive model of how international norms develop. Basically, they argued "that norms evolve in a patterned 'life cycle' and that different behavioral

Figure 6-1. *The "Life Cycle"*

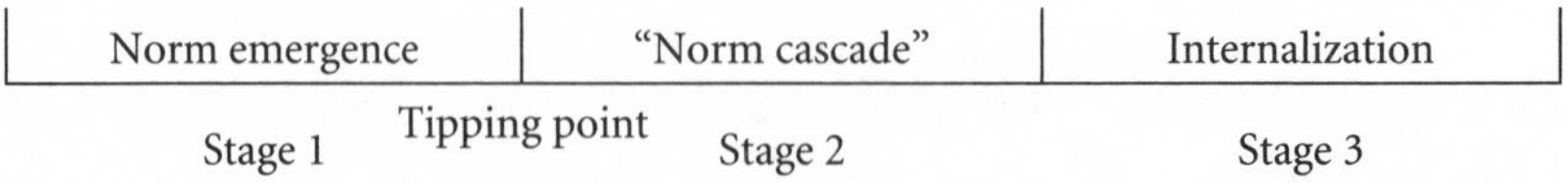

Norm emergence	"Norm cascade"	Internalization
Stage 1	Tipping point Stage 2	Stage 3

logics dominate different segments of the life cycle."[5] They offered the figure above (here figure 6-1) and the table opposite (table 6-1) to illustrate the "norm life cycle."[6]

Regarding the first stage, they suggested that "two elements seem common in the successful creation of most new norms: norm entrepreneurs and organizational platforms from which entrepreneurs act."[7] As one would expect, their historical review featured international organizations as prime platforms for such efforts. They hypothesized, as well, that after some critical mass of states has adopted a new norm, a "threshold or tipping point" is reached.[8] The second stage, a "norm cascade," follows, propelled by an international socialization process.[9] Such a process involves "peer pressure" within regions as states seek "legitimation, conformity, and esteem."[10] Eventually, in stage three, the norm becomes "internalized" in state practice and is largely "taken-for-granted."[11] This stage is presumably the ultimate goal of the norm entrepreneurs. At that stage, it is worth noting for R2P purposes, international enforcement would become unnecessary in all but rejectionist states.

What Finnemore and Sikkink described, in essence, is a political process. It is a process that transcends national boundaries, even as its success ultimately depends on decisions made in multiple capitals. It involves a creative and interactive mix of states, international organizations (global and regional), and civil society. As discussed below, the R2P experience coincides with this model in important ways and several of the characteristics that they identified can be seen readily in recent events and developments. However, R2P's experience to date also raises questions about how certain, sequential, chronological, and unidirectional a contested norm's "life cycle" is likely to be. Even at this writing, this author is not sure where to place R2P's development along the three-stage progression, despite a number of encouraging developments. There have been more stops, starts, detours, and regeneration in R2P's young life than any chart could properly depict. Indeed, the refinement of the concept itself at critical points has both allowed the developmental process to proceed and modified, in significant ways, the shape and content of what was being considered. That said, models are meant to simplify complex processes and this model succeeds admirably in that regard.

Table 6-1. *The Behavioral Logics in the "Life Cycle"*

	Stage 1 *Norm emergence*	*Stage 2* *Norm cascade*	*Stage 3* *Internalization*
Actors	Norm entrepreneurs with organizational platforms	States, international organizations, networks	Law, professions, bureaucracy
Motives	Altruism, empathy, ideational, commitment	Legitimacy, reputation, esteem	Conformity
Dominant mechanisms	Persuasion	Socialization, institutionalization, demonstration	Habit, institutionalization

Stage One: Norm Emergence

The model's two key ingredients for the successful completion of stage one—norm entrepreneurs and organizational platforms—did indeed play critical roles in the emergence of R2P as a "hot" issue on the international agenda. But identifying the prime movers behind R2P does not end the story, because the origins and intellectual roots of R2P are subject to some dispute and occasional reinterpretation. This dispute exists in part because transformative ideas may be claimed by more than one father or mother, and in part because the concept, as accepted by UN member states in 2005, differs in important respects from what was first proposed in the landmark 2001 report of the International Commission on Intervention and State Sovereignty (ICISS). In coining the phrase "responsibility to protect," the commission sought to address some of the sovereignty concerns that surfaced in the divisive General Assembly debate in 1999 on humanitarian intervention.[12] A major impetus for that debate had been the world body's failure to prevent or respond effectively to the repeated mass atrocities of the 1990s in places such as Somalia, Rwanda, Bosnia (Srebrenica), and Kosovo. Those theories of humanitarian intervention, in turn, drew, in the 1980s, from Bernard Kouchner's pioneering advocacy of the notion of the right to interfere (*le droit d'ingérence*) in humanitarian emergencies. Likewise, in arguing that "the primary responsibility for the protection of its people lies with the state itself" and that "sovereignty as responsibility has become the minimum content of good international citizenship," the commission drew heavily from the work of Francis Deng and his colleagues at the Brookings Institution in the mid-1990s on sovereignty as responsibility in Africa.[13]

This layered history, with variations on the central theme with each new decade and set of norm entrepreneurs, makes it difficult either to allocate credit to a single person or group or to assert that the concept emerged at any particular point. Yet clearly the most energetic and determined proponent of R2P has been Gareth Evans, the former foreign minister of Australia and co-chair, with Mohamed Sahnoun of Algeria, of the ICISS Commission. He is widely credited with coming up with the phrase "responsibility to protect."[14] Several other members of the commission have also remained active advocates, as has Lloyd Axworthy, the former Canadian foreign minister who was instrumental in the establishment of the commission at the time of the Kosovo crisis. The idea has not lacked articulate high-level advocates, as former Secretary-General Kofi Annan and his High-level Panel on Threats, Challenges and Change endorsed the commission's core recommendations.[15] Annan, in fact, asserted that there was an "emerging norm that there is a collective responsibility to protect."[16] He included a robust set of R2P proposals in his *In Larger Freedom* report to the 2005 World Summit, one of the largest gatherings of heads of state and government ever.

So, in the remarkably brief span of four years from its first articulation, R2P attracted both an impeccable array of norm entrepreneurs and the attention of the most prominent forum imaginable. One would have been excused for thinking that the proverbial "tipping point" had been reached and the promised "norm cascade" of the second stage would soon follow. But the model fails to incorporate the interactive and sometimes even dysfunctional nature of international politics, assuming an overly linear conception of progress. It seemed that as R2P was gaining its glittering chorus of advocates, the opposition, with keen memories of the General Assembly's humanitarian intervention debate just a half dozen years before, began to dig in that much deeper. Hegel might well have detected his dialectical process of thesis-antithesis-synthesis at work in this posing of opposites before the search for common ground. Indeed, the sharp criticisms of R2P that a number of developing and non-aligned countries expressed in the months preceding the 2005 World Summit gave little reason to be optimistic about its eventual adoption.[17]

Given this unpromising political context, it is all the more remarkable that the summit nevertheless reached consensus regarding the language to endorse R2P. Certainly this accord was due in part to the hard work of norm entrepreneurs, ranging from friendly member states to then

Secretary-General Annan and members of the ICISS Commission. But important substantive changes in the R2P vision were also incorporated to gain wider support among the membership. These modifications were essential because few governments felt any sense of ownership of the ideas that Annan put forward. The ICISS report, while impressive in many ways, was the product of an independent blue-ribbon panel. Though the commission had held hearings in various parts of the world, no inter-governmental body had debated or tempered its proposals. The same could be said of the High-level Panel on Threats, Challenges and Change and its endorsement of the ICISS conclusions and recommendations. Norm entrepreneurs, in other words, may get an idea to the conference table and even influence the subsequent deliberations, but they cannot substitute for governments and their interactions. So it is instructive to compare and contrast the ICISS proposals and the language that the summit actually adopted four years later. Three distinctions between the ICISS's and the summit's approaches stand out.

One, according to Jean Ping, president of the General Assembly in the months leading up to the summit and subsequently chairman of the African Union Commission, the critical breakthrough came when Munir Akram, then permanent representative of Pakistan to the UN, suggested that R2P should be "linked" to a specific set of atrocity crimes.[18] This distinction would address, to some extent, the concerns of many states, including some smaller developed, as well as developing, countries, that major military powers could use R2P as a pretext for intervening militarily in places such as Iraq. The ICISS report had not defined precisely or consistently from what people were to be protected. In its prescribed principles for military intervention, the commission spoke of "the just cause threshold," namely "there must be serious and irreparable harm occurring to human beings, or imminently likely to occur, of the following kind:

A. "Large scale loss of life, actual or apprehended, with genocidal intent or not, which is the product either of deliberate state action, or state neglect or inability to act, or a failed state situation; or

B. Large scale 'ethnic cleansing', actual or apprehended, whether carried out by killing, forced expulsion, acts of terror or rape."[19]

The report's foreword, however, underlined "that sovereign states have a responsibility to protect their own citizens from avoidable catastrophe—from mass murder and rape, from starvation."[20] One of the "basic principles" enunciated by the commission was that "where a population is suffering serious harm, as a result of internal war, insurgency, repression or state failure, and the state in question is unwilling or unable to halt or avert it, the principle of non-intervention yields to the international responsibility to protect."[21]

The independent commission, of course, was laying out important principles about the nature of state and international responsibility, not negotiating a legal or political document. Faced with the latter task, the subsequent World Summit had to be more precise about when R2P would or would not apply. Paragraphs 138 to 140 of the Summit Outcome Document sought to define both the scope of R2P crimes and the prevention and protection responsibilities of states and international organizations. The summit agreed, unanimously, that the scope of R2P would be limited to cases of genocide, war crimes, ethnic cleansing, and crimes against humanity. As the secretary-general's 2009 report noted,

> It should be underscored that the provisions of paragraphs 138 and 139 of the Summit Outcome are firmly anchored in well-established principles of international law. Under conventional and customary international law, States have obligations to prevent and punish genocide, war crimes and crimes against humanity. Ethnic cleansing is not a crime in its own right under international law, but acts of ethnic cleansing may constitute one of the other three crimes.[22]

In innumerable consultations with member states about the secretary-general's strategy for advancing R2P, this author found it necessary to reassure them that his approach was narrow but deep—narrow in terms of not going an inch beyond the four specified crimes but deep in terms of the number of tools the UN system and its partners should bring to the tasks of prevention and protection.

Early in my work as Special Adviser, in May 2008, Cyclone Nargis struck Myanmar (Burma). Some prominent personalities, including Foreign Minister Kouchner of France, urged international intervention to speed the delivery of relief to the beleaguered population there under a R2P rubric.[23] Evans contended that the situation had not yet reached R2P proportions, but that the government of Myanmar's persistent refusal to facilitate international relief efforts over time could amount to a crime against humanity and therefore invoke a R2P response.[24] This author asserted that this was not a R2P situation in terms of what had been agreed upon at the 2005 Summit and most member states, including importantly Myanmar's neighbors in the Association of Southeast Asian Nations (ASEAN), seemed to agree. Taking this stance was more than a political calculation, however. Existing standards for human rights, humanitarian delivery and access, and the treatment of internally displaced persons already applied to this kind of situation and it was not clear what invoking R2P would add to the chorus.[25] It was critical at that early stage of R2P development, moreover, to avoid falling into the UN's usual trap of making straightforward concepts incoherent, unintelligible, and unusable by stretching them to cover more and more issues and concerns. The secretary-general wanted to make R2P operational, not just appealing, and this required discipline, constraint, and consistency in its application.

A second critical difference between the ICISS report of 2001 and the Summit Outcome Document of 2005 is in their treatment of what both agreed would be an extreme measure: the coercive use of force in a R2P contingency. Many diplomats, particularly from the developing world, saw the ICISS report as a more attractive façade for unilateral humanitarian intervention; the notion that they thought they had squelched in the 1999 General Assembly debate. When this author started to work on R2P for the secretary-general, he was surprised that several leading representatives of developing countries told him that they had "killed" or "buried" R2P at the 2005 Summit. What they meant, it turned out, was that they once again had resisted the adoption of humanitarian intervention as a unilateral, coercive, and largely military doctrine. While the ICISS report stressed the importance of prevention, these diplomats perceived it to be a reincarnation of the right to intervene militarily in such situations. The opening sentence in the foreword did not help to dispel this impression: "This report is about the so-called 'right of humanitarian intervention': the question of when, if ever, it is appropriate for states to take coercive—and in particular military—action against another state for the purpose of protecting people at risk in that other state."[26] The report's careful and detailed presentation of "principles for military intervention," as well as its seeming focus on the Security Council as the prime international actor, added to the sense that there was little difference between R2P and humanitarian intervention. This seeming similarity was a theme that the opponents of R2P revived repeatedly during the 2009 General Assembly debate.

The assembled heads of state and government in 2005 did not deny the possibility that coercive action might be necessary in extreme R2P cases, but they put it in the context of the UN Charter, a multilateral decision-making authority, and the wider tools available to the world body for peaceful settlement. "In this context," they stated, "we are prepared to take collective action, in a timely and decisive manner, through the Security Council, in accordance with the Charter, including Chapter VII, on a case-by-case basis and in cooperation with relevant regional organizations as appropriate, should peaceful means be inadequate and national authorities are manifestly failing to protect their populations from genocide, war crimes, ethnic cleansing and crimes against humanity."[27] The key phrase here is "timely and decisive" action, whether it is of a military or non-military, a coercive or non-coercive, character. The secretary-general's strategy, in that regard, stresses "the value of prevention and, when it fails, of early and flexible response tailored to the circumstances of each case."[28] No option should automatically be ruled in or out. And no two cases are identical. As he stressed on various occasions, it would be morally unacceptable to base one's strategy only on responding to mass crimes after the bodies have started to pile up and when only extreme measures would make a difference.[29] Likewise, good policymaking depends on keeping multiple options open, not relying on a single tool or scenario to do the trick in all cases.

The third difference that stood out between the 2001 and 2005 interpretations of R2P lies in how they described the range of policy measures for advancing prevention and protection goals. The ICISS report described three sets of responsibilities: 1) the responsibility to prevent; 2) the responsibility to react; and 3) the responsibility to rebuild. It referred to these as "integral and essential components" and to the need for "conceptual, normative and operational linkages between assistance, intervention and reconstruction."[30] The need to rebuild, it noted at several points, would be particularly acute after a coercive military intervention.[31] The distinctions among these three responsibilities were cast along functional lines, not in terms of whose responsibility it would be to perform each function; though clearly the responsibility to react would fall to the international community and particularly to the Security Council.

The 2005 Outcome Document, on the other hand, focused more on who was responsible for what. Paragraph 138 stated, in unambiguous terms, that:

> Each individual State has the responsibility to protect its populations from genocide, war crimes, ethnic cleansing and crimes against humanity. This responsibility entails the prevention of such crimes, including their incitement, through appropriate and necessary means. We accept that responsibility and will act in accordance with it.

In the secretary-general's strategy, this was to become the first of three R2P pillars of equal length and strength.[32] This pledge of state responsibility, undertaken at the heads of state and government level, would have to serve as the bedrock of R2P, because the international community could rarely expect to be able to be a substitute for the state. The second pillar, relating to the international responsibility to help, assist, and support the state in meeting this core responsibility, appears in various ways in paragraphs 138 and 139, but is not stated clearly and precisely at any single point in the document. This author had to derive the second pillar through a deconstruction of these paragraphs word by word and phrase by phrase, as well as through conversations with delegates about what their intent had been in 2005. The secretary-general's pillar two strategy encompasses not only R2P-oriented development, human rights, governance, peacebuilding, rule of law, and security sector reform efforts, but also two types of consent-based military activities. One such effort is preventive peacekeeping deployments, as in the former Yugoslav Republic of Macedonia (FYROM) and in Burundi.[33] The second is military assistance, including Chapter VII enforcement missions, to help beleaguered governments confronted by armed groups that control portions of their territory and are committing R2P crimes, as in Sierra Leone.

It has been the third, response, pillar of the secretary-general's strategy that has attracted the most attention and concern among some of the member states.[34] Carefully drawn from the last sentence of paragraph 138 on early warning and the whole of paragraph 139, the third pillar of the strategy seeks to make the fullest possible use of the wide range of tools, procedures, and arrangements described in Chapters VI, VII, and VIII of the UN Charter. The discussion of military options is quite robust in the secretary-general's report, but occupies a less prominent place than it does in the ICISS report because of the increased attention to other possible measures. While substantial attention is given to the Security Council and its decision-making processes, the important roles of the General Assembly, the secretary-general, and regional and sub-regional organizations are also described in some detail.

Was the 2005 consensus regarding R2P a step forward or backward in terms of establishing a strong norm or standard compared to the way R2P was initially framed in the 2001 ICISS report? If the 2005 Summit was a "tipping point," which way did it tip: toward a reinforced or diluted norm? Some R2P proponents initially derided the summit language as "R2P-lite." They pointed to the caveat-heavy reference to collective action in paragraph 139, as well as to the invocation of a "continuing consideration" role for the General Assembly. On the other hand, Secretary-General Annan, among others, called the R2P language "an historic breakthrough."[35] Given the summit delegates' inability to find any common language on some other high visibility issues, such as disarmament, the R2P consensus stands out as one of the more conspicuous successes from the summit. The 2001 conception of R2P, it should be recalled, was negotiated among blue-ribbon panelists, not government officials, among a handful of leading internationalists, not scores of representatives of truly diverse countries.

Assessments of whether 2005 represented forward or backward movement depend in large part on whether the core of R2P is considered to be states' commitment to prevention and protection or the legitimation of a military response to mass atrocity crimes. Those still wedded to notions of humanitarian intervention might have had some reason for disappointment. But for those of us who welcomed the ICISS report as a compelling way to assuage some of the dilemmas that the rather sterile humanitarian intervention debate posed at the end of the century, the language in the 2005 document offered a further encouraging step toward a R2P conception that was sustainable politically, flexible tactically, and feasible operationally. The ICISS report, after all, underscored that it sought to shift the terms of the debate from the responsibility of the international community to those of the state toward its people and from those considering intervention to those needing assistance and protection.[36]

In several ways, moreover, the language that was used in 2005 added elements that were missing in 2001. For instance, the Outcome Document spoke of a state's responsibilities to the populations on its territory, not just to its citizens; such a distinction is critical when addressing identity-based crimes. At the summit, the heads of state and government pledged to prevent the incitement of as well as the commission of the four crimes. For operational purposes, this is a significant addition, as the secretary-general and his representatives have been able to persuade the parties to stop their incitement of violence in Côte d'Ivoire in 2004 and Kenya in 2008, among other places. Paragraph 138 of the Outcome Document includes an unambiguous endorsement of a UN early warning mechanism, something that is critical to an effective prevention strategy but was once quite controversial among the member states. The 2005 Outcome Document also recognizes the important role that regional bodies can play in prevention and protection efforts, a point that the secretary-general's report seizes on with some enthusiasm. Finally, paragraph 139 calls on the General Assembly to "continue consideration" of R2P, something some advocates fret about but a critical step in the further development of R2P as a global standard. So, at least in this author's view, it was a rush to judgment to call the language used in 2005 "R2P-lite." That language provided, instead, a remarkably solid and broad foundation on which to begin to build effective strategy, policy, and mechanisms for the prevention of and protection against the worst atrocity crimes.

Stage Two: "Norm Cascade"

As noted earlier, two years after the World Summit political support for R2P had ebbed, with some prominent representatives of developing countries claiming at that point that they had "killed" the concept at the summit. If the summit were to have served as a "tipping point" leading to a "norm cascade," as the Finnemore-Sikkink model would have predicted, then there was little evidence that it had worked, at least not to that point. Clearly the transition from their stage one to stage two does not happen automatically or inexorably in every case. In the case of R2P, for one, a lot of conceptual and political work would be required to spur anything resembling a "norm cascade." As suggested above, there is no reason to assume—as the model seems to—that normative progress necessarily follows a linear or unidirectional path. It is a political process, not a physical one. Even a cascade of water, of course, can be manipulated in any direction: speeding, slowing, curbing, or diverting the flow.

Though their model so far has fit the course of R2P development awkwardly at best, the terms that Finnemore and Sikkink used to describe the generic normative development process seem much more apt. The political strategy that Secretary-General Ban Ki-moon has pursued, with the critical help of like-minded member states and NGOs, indeed has resembled an international socialization process. Surely, as they had hypothesized, this has involved "peer pressure" within and across regions as states have sought "legitimation, conformity, and esteem."[37] With a contested norm, such as R2P, its supporters first need to ensure that association with the norm is seen as legitimizing rather than delegitimizing for most states. This involves reframing the debate. This feat has to be accomplished, of course, when those opposing the norm are trying to frame the debate along very different lines.

In crafting the secretary-general's strategy for advancing R2P, this author was acutely aware of the need to seize the high road in terms of laying out its intellectual and political lineage and to project a clear image of which historical situations compelled its development. In the secretary-general's 2009 report, *Implementing the Responsibility to Protect,* that this author drafted as his Special Adviser on these matters, he laid out his understanding of the origins of R2P. Citing the experiences of the Holocaust, Cambodia, Rwanda, and Srebrenica, he concluded that "the brutal legacy of the twentieth century speaks bitterly and graphically of the profound failures of individual States to live up to their most basic and compelling responsibilities, as well as the collective inadequacies of international institutions. . . . Could we not find the will and the capacity in the new century to do better?"[38] He underscored that countries in the North as well as in the South, and with different social systems and levels of development, had experienced the trauma of mass domestic violence.[39] This issue was, in other words, a universal problem that the world's only virtually universal political body had to address, as well as through regional, sub-regional, and national efforts.

Over the course of 2008 and the first half of 2009, as the battle lines were drawn for the 2009 General Assembly debate on the secretary-general's report, the origins of the concept of R2P were acutely contested. Was it, as some charged, a northern notion that had been imposed on the global South as a rationale for armed intervention in weaker countries? Or, as Secretary-General Ban has contended, did it emerge "from the soil, spirit, experience and institutions of Africa?"[40] For both substantive and political reasons, the secretary-general regularly invoked the notion of sovereignty as responsibility that had been developed by Deng and his colleagues more than a dozen years before. Both ECOWAS and the African Union (AU) had endorsed R2P-like principles before the 2001 ICISS Commission coined the phrase. The AU stressed *non-indifference* in such situations, unlike its predecessor, the Organization of African Unity (OAU) that had emphasized non-interference.

The secretary-general, however, was not the only player to appreciate that prevailing political perceptions about where it came from, how it was developed, and whose purposes it was meant to serve shape the legitimacy and viability of an international principle. Seeking to articulate quite a different history was one of the most prominent R2P skeptics, the president of the sixty-third Session of the General Assembly, Miguel D'Escoto Brockmann, a former Sandinista Foreign Minister of Nicaragua. "Is it more likely," he asked, "that the R[2]P principle would be applied only by the strong against the weak?" In his view, "recent disastrous interventions give developing countries strong reason to fear that laudable motives can end up being misused, as so often in the past, to justify interventions against weaker states."[41] Some developing countries, such as Venezuela, Cuba, Nicaragua, Iran, the Sudan, and North Korea, echoed this line in the 2009 General Assembly debate on R2P.[42] What was most striking, however, especially given the way that the president of the General Assembly had tried to frame the debate, was that most developing countries, particularly smaller ones and almost all African countries, agreed with the secretary-general about the African origins of R2P.[43] Egypt, speaking as chair of the Non-Aligned Movement (NAM), explicitly endorsed the secretary-general's account of the role of the AU and the African experience in the development of R2P.[44]

From the outset of my work on R2P, three things were clear to this author. One, by early 2008 support for the principle of R2P was regressing, not progressing among member states. Permanent damage would have been done both to the prospects for turning R2P from words to deeds and to the UN's credibility if steps were not taken to reverse the tide. Two, only an assertive strategy aimed at the UN membership as a whole could hope to restore the 2005 consensus. This, in turn, would require bringing the issue to the General Assembly, which had never addressed R2P directly. The focus of the debate, moreover, should be the secretary-general's clearly articulated implementation strategy. He would have to define, indeed redefine, the terms of the debate. It was, in other words, time to press the restart button, not to rest on the laurels of 2005. Many of the "friends" of R2P questioned the wisdom of taking such a risk, given push-back on the part of key developing countries in recent years on a range of human rights and humanitarian issues. The risks of moving forward were real, but, in this author's view, the downside risk of doing nothing was even greater.

Three, it was evident that if the presumption persisted that R2P was a North-South issue, then its political fate was sealed, whether or not the assembly took up the matter. The key variable lay in the attitude of the developing, not the developed, world. Mass atrocities can, and have, occurred in every part of the world. But in recent decades the frequency and depth of devastation of such traumas have been greater in smaller and more fragile developing countries. These countries have every reason to want more effective international efforts at prevention and protection, as long as these are undertaken under proper UN or regional authority and call on the full range of UN tools under Chapters VI, VII, and VIII of the UN Charter. So the goal was to spur latent support in developing countries by carefully listening to their concerns and expectations and by incorporating them as fully as possible in the secretary-general's report, while maintaining solid, but not dominant, support from the developed world. By and large, this approach appears to have worked well, as the 2009 General Assembly debate was more upbeat than most expected, and the subsequent consensus adoption of a R2P resolution, albeit of a modest and largely procedural sort, far exceeded anyone's expectations.[45] Characteristically, Guatemala, hardly a global power, but a country that still bears the deep and lasting scars of past atrocity crimes, drafted and negotiated the resolution.

R2P may be a global standard, but the politics of forwarding it tends to be regional, as Finnemore and Sikkink would have predicted. The UN's 192 member states are largely organized around regional groups. Some large trans-regional groups, such as the NAM and the Office of the Islamic Conference (OIC) also matter politically.[46] This author's consultations with the NAM were both extensive and instructive. Since the support of African countries, especially sub-Saharan ones, had been critical to achieving the 2005 results and R2P's African roots were an essential dimension of the secretary-general's narrative, the first step was to help to renew the sense of African ownership of the issue that had largely been lost since 2005. Rwanda, whose horrific 1994 genocide epitomized all that R2P seeks to prevent, was particularly active in encouraging the revival of African enthusiasm for the concept. The results were gratifying.

Latin American and Caribbean countries, with their strong traditions of respect for sovereignty, law, and human rights, generally supported R2P in 2005. The group, however, was more divided on a number of political and ideological questions by 2008 and 2009. While most of the region spoke favorably at the 2009 debate, five of the eight member states that offered an explanation of position on the consensus resolution were from the region.[47]

In 2008, at the outset of the preparation of the secretary-general's report and the General Assembly debate, it was widely expected that the biggest opposition to R2P would come from Asia. Fortunately, that did not prove to be the case. This author thought it best to focus initially on the ASEAN countries, both because of their numbers and because there had been some encouraging political developments in the region. Indonesia, for instance, as the most populous country in the region with the world's largest Islamic population, had become much more hospitable to democratic and humanitarian values than before. What this author and others in New York did not understand well, however, was how well-developed was civil society interest in R2P in the region.[48] Some of this interest, apparently, could be attributed to the regional outreach efforts of the ICISS Commission many years before. In any case, the ASEAN countries were largely supportive of R2P at the 2009 debate, perhaps lending credence to the Finnemore-Sikkink emphasis on peer pressure. Others engaged the leadership of India, the last to come aboard in 2005, at a high level. Both of these Asian governments—Indonesia and India—took a more positive stance in 2009 than in 2005, though China remained cautious.

Whether any of these encouraging developments qualify as a "norm cascade" remains to be seen. But the core proposition put forward by Finnemore and Sikkink—that the attitudes of neighbors and peers affect national elites—seems on target. It was striking, in this regard, to see so many of the world's so-called rising powers move to the R2P camp, as the principle took on the status of a global standard of proper behavior. R2P, one hopes, will continue to rise with them.

Conclusion

At the center of this narrative is the intimate interplay between politics, at several levels, and the evolution of norms and standards that some wish could be above narrow and parochial political concerns. As the still young history of R2P vividly illustrates, the development of international norms and standards, similar to law, is an inherently and predominantly political process. The most effective advocates and norm entrepreneurs have understood this reality and have played the political game skillfully. Those who wait for others to see the rationality or morality of their position, who expect the attractiveness of the emerging norm or standard to do the work, are likely to be disappointed. The development of norms is really the story of the expansion of political support for particular sets of ideas and values.

Norms and standards, especially in their formative years, are likely to be somewhat contested. The more that they bite, in terms of affecting state behavior, the more contentious they are likely to be. As theorists of compliance with international law have long recognized, there is a wide set of legal norms that are not controversial for the simple reason that they only confirm and perpetuate existing patterns of behavior and interests.[49] Such coordination or cooperation rules may play essential social and governance functions, but they are not of great political or policy interest. Nor does their path have much in common with the more arduous road travelled by more demanding and far-reaching standards such as R2P. The latter's course is apt to be uneven, circuitous, and uncertain. It is not quick or short. Persistence pays, as the end goal of gaining something close to an international consensus, not only on the principle but also on a feasible implementation strategy, is worth sustained effort over a number of years.

There is reason for optimism about recent progress in the normative development of R2P. It should be borne in mind, however, that neither an encouraging debate, a consensus resolution, nor even a summit-level declaration constitutes a consolidated norm. R2P-like language is appearing in all sorts of international statements, resolutions, and conventions. This trend is largely encouraging, though it shows lingering caution about invoking the actual phrase "responsibility to protect." Efforts are under way to embed R2P in the UN bureaucracy through a joint office on genocide prevention and R2P, an early warning and assessment capacity, and inter-departmental, inter-agency machinery for rapidly developing system-wide policy options in emergency situations. Operational departments, programs, and agencies are being asked to identify ways that they can mainstream R2P principles and objectives into their ongoing work. The General Assembly is beginning to consider how best to focus and carry out its "continuing consideration" role. And the secretary-general has asked this author to work with independent scholars on the preparation of case studies of good and best R2P practices, particularly in the realm of prevention and capacity-building.

The third stage—internalizing R2P standards in state policy and practice—is both the most critical and the most difficult phase to measure. Researchers tell us that the incidence of genocide has declined over the past fifteen years, but neither the causes nor the sustainability of this encouraging trend are evident.[50] R2P is both a reflection of and a stimulus for such changes in state behavior. The ultimate test of R2P will be in capitals and on the ground, not in international meeting halls. If, a decade from now, atrocity crimes are markedly less frequent and, when they occur, the international response is more ready, vigorous, and effective than it has been in the past, then all of the normative work of the past ten years can be declared a success. The goal can be no less than to moderate the actions of both states and armed groups. The progress to date in clarifying, building, and spreading R2P standards—as real as it has been—constitutes only the initial steps of a long journey. There is reason to believe, nevertheless, that we have now embarked on the right track.

Notes

1. Most public groups and authors have preferred the acronym R2P, but the UN has consistently used RtoP both because it seems more accurate and because it helps to distinguish the UN's approach to the concept from the various forms and meanings that independent authors, groups, and commissions have given it.

2. UN General Assembly, Sixtieth Session, *2005 World Summit Outcome*, UN Doc. A/RES/60/1, 2005, paras. 138 and 139.

3. Martha Finnemore and Kathryn Sikkink, "International Norm Dynamics and Political Change," *International Organization*, LII (1998), 887–917.

4. Ibid., 891.

5. Ibid., 888.

6. Ibid., 896 and 898, respectively.

7. Ibid., 896.

8. Ibid., 901.

9. They credit this phrase to Cass R. Sunstein. See his "Social Norms and Social Roles," in Cass R. Sunstein, *Free Markets and Social Justice* (New York, 1997), 32–69.

10. Finnemore and Sikkink, "International Norm Dynamics," 903.

11. Ibid., 904–905.

12. For Kofi Annan's address on 20 September 1999, see *Secretary-General's Annual Report to UN General Assembly*, Fifty-fourth Session, UN Doc. SG/SM/7136, 1999; for the subsequent debate, see UN General Assembly, UN Doc. A/54/PV.8 and PV.9, 1999. As this author has discussed elsewhere, it has not only been developing countries that have been concerned about sovereignty when it comes to R2P. While smaller or weaker countries tend to be worried about preserving their territorial sovereignty vis-à-vis larger and possibly predatory powers, militarily strong countries may be sensitive to any doctrine that implies an automaticity of response in such situations, as it could compromise their decision-making sovereignty. See Edward C. Luck, "Sovereignty, Choice, and the Responsibility to Protect," *Global Responsibility to Protect*, I (2009), 10–21.

13. Report of the International Commission on Intervention and State Sovereignty (ICISS), *The Responsibility to Protect* (Ottawa, 2001), 1; Ibid., 8; Francis M. Deng, Sadikiel Kimaro, Terrence Lyons, Donald Rothchild, and I. William Zartman, *Sovereignty as Responsibility: Conflict Management in Africa* (Washington, D.C., 1996).

14. For a full accounting of his views, see Gareth Evans, *The Responsibility to Protect: Ending Mass Atrocity Crimes Once and For All* (Washington, D.C., 2008).

15. Report of the Secretary-General, *In Larger Freedom: Towards Development, Security and Human Rights for All*, UN Doc. A/59/2005 (New York, 2005), 34–35, paras. 132 and 135; *Report of the Secretary-General's High-level Panel on Threats, Challenges and Change* (New York, 2004), 65–66, paras. 199–203.

16. *In Larger Freedom*, 35, para. 135.

17. Luck, "Sovereignty," 17–18.

18. International Peace Institute, the Office of the UN Special Adviser on the Prevention of Genocide, and the InterAfrica Group, *The Responsibility to Protect (RtoP) and Genocide Prevention in Africa* (New York, 2009), 12.

19. ICISS, *The Responsibility to Protect*, xii.

20. Ibid., xiii.

21. Ibid., xi.

22. UN, *Report of the Secretary-General on Implementing the Responsibility to Protect*, UN Doc. A/63/677 (New York, 2009), 5, para. 3.

23. See, for example, the remarks of Bernard Kouchner, in "Myanmar Faces Pressure to Allow Major Aid Effort," *New York Times* (8 May 2008); Lloyd Axworthy and Allan Rock, "Responsibility to Protect? Yes," *Globe and Mail* (9 May 2008); Ramesh

Thakur, "Should the UN Invoke the Responsibility to Protect?" *Globe and Mail* (8 May 2008); Ivo Daalder and Paul Stares, "The UN's Responsibility to Protect," *International Herald Tribune* (13 May 2008). For a balanced assessment, see Asia-Pacific Centre on the Responsibility to Protect, *Cyclone Nargis and the Responsibility to Protect*, Myanmar/Burma Briefing No. 2 (Brisbane, Australia, 2008).

24. Gareth Evans, "Facing Up to Our Responsibilities," *The Guardian* (12 May 2008).

25. Edward C. Luck, "International Disaster Assistance: Policy Options," briefing to the Subcommittee on International Development, Foreign Assistance, Economic Affairs and International Environmental Protection, U.S. Senate Committee on Foreign Relations, 17 June 2008.

26. ICISS, *The Responsibility to Protect*, vii.

27. UN, *2005 World Summit Outcome*, para. 139.

28. UN, *Implementing the Responsibility to Protect*, 2.

29. See, for example, address by the secretary-general in Berlin. See Secretary-General, "Secretary-General Defends, Clarifies 'Responsibility to Protect' at Berlin Event on 'Responsible Sovereignty: International Cooperation for a Changed World,'" UN Doc. SG/SM/11701, 2008.

30. ICISS, *The Responsibility to Protect*, 17.

31. Ibid., xi; 39–45.

32. UN, *Implementing the Responsibility to Protect*, 10–14.

33. The United Nations Preventive Deployment Force (UNPREDEP) in the Former Yugoslav Republic of Macedonia (FYROM) is mentioned in the ICISS report as well.

34. UN, *Implementing the Responsibility to Protect*, 22–28.

35. Address by Secretary-General Kofi Annan in Portugal. See Secretary-General, "World Summit Achieved Concrete, Significant Gains in Human Rights, Rule of Law, Secretary-General Says in Address to Universidade Nova De Lisboa," UN Doc. SG/SM/10161, 2005.

36. ICISS, *The Responsibility to Protect*, 16–18.

37. Finnemore and Sikkink, "International Norm Dynamics," 903.

38. UN, *Implementing the Responsibility to Protect*, 5, para. 5.

39. Ibid., 5–6, para. 6.

40. Secretary-General, "Upcoming Debate on Responsibility to Protect Not About History, but About Character of United Nations, Secretary-General Tells General Assembly," UN Doc. SG/SM/12374, 2009.

41. UN General Assembly, UN Doc. A/63/PV.101, 2009, 20.

42. For the statements that Venezuela and Cuba made, see UN General Assembly, UN Doc. A/63/PV. 99, 2009, 3–6; 21–23, respectively; for the statements that Iran, Nicaragua, and North Korea made, see UN General Assembly, UN Doc. A/63/PV.100, 2009, 10–11; 12–13; 17–18, respectively; and for the statement that the Sudan made, see UN General Assembly, UN Doc. A/63/PV.101, 2009, 10–11.

43. For a useful assessment of the debate by two active NGOs, see the Global Centre on the Responsibility to Protect, "Implementing the Responsibility to Protect, The 2009 General Assembly Debate: An Assessment" (2009), available at http://globalr2p.org/media/pdf/Meeting%20Summary%20Reflections%20on%20the%20UN%20General%20Assembly%20debate%20on%20R2P.pdf (accessed 21 January 2010); International Coalition on the Responsibility to Protect, "Report on the General Assembly Debate on the Responsibility to Protect," (2009), available at http://responsibilitytoprotect.org/ICRtoPGAdebate.pdf (accessed 21 January 2010). Unfortunately, the major press stories, written before the debate, predicted that it would be divisive given the PGA's negative stance.

44. "The Secretary-General has rightly noted in his report and presentation that the African Union is a pioneer in implementing the responsibility to protect due to its particular historical experience." See UN General Assembly, UN Doc. A/63/PV.97, 2009, 6.

45. UN General Assembly, Sixty-third Session, Resolution 308, UN Doc. A/RES/63/308, 2009.

46. The 130-member Group of 77 developing countries, which the Sudan chaired in 2009, is focused more on economic matters.

47. They included Venezuela, Cuba, Nicaragua, Bolivia, and Ecuador. The other three were the Sudan, Syria, and Iran. See UN General Assembly, UN Doc. A/63/PV.105, 2009, 2–7.

48. Particularly impressive has been the work of the Asia-Pacific Centre for the Responsibility to Protect (www.r2pasiapacific.org), which has received substantial support from the Australian government.

49. See, for example, George W. Downs and Andrea Trento, "The Compliance Gap: Some Conceptual Issues," in Edward C. Luck and Michael W. Doyle (eds.), *International Law and Organization: Closing the Compliance Gap* (Lanham, MD, 2004), 19–40.

50. Human Security Centre, *Human Security Report Brief 2006* (British Columbia, 2006), 14–15, available at www.humansecuritybrief.info/2006/contents/finalversion.pdf (accessed 21 January 2010); Conflict Data Program, Uppsala University, available at www.pcr.uu.se/research/UCDP/graphs/one-sided_fatalities_2007.pdf (accessed 21 January 2010).

CLAIRE APPLEGARTH *and* ANDREW BLOCK

7 *Acting against Atrocities: A Strategy for Supporters of R2P*

The advent of the "responsibility to protect" (R2P) was thought to signal the international community's commitment to ending genocide, war crimes, ethnic cleansing, and crimes against humanity once and for all. The emerging norm embodies the belief that all nations should prevent, react to, and assist in recovery from mass atrocity crimes wherever they may occur and by whomever they may be committed. Adopted by consensus at the United Nations' (UN) momentous World Summit in 2005, R2P served as a firm declaration that state sovereignty would no longer provide a shield behind which perpetrators of mass atrocities could hide, and promised to deliver on the solemn pledge of "Rwanda, never again."

More than four years after the World Summit, however, efforts to move this noble vision from words to action have stalled. Nations have stood by as atrocities unfolded in the Sudan and the Democratic Republic of the Congo, deferring action to weak regional bodies or patchy and under-resourced multilateral forces. Even where states have more firmly confronted such crimes, they have not staked their interventions on R2P's novel and universal frame of "sovereignty as responsibility," but rather on particular and often fickle national interests. R2P has neither galvanized a more robust international response in the face of atrocity crimes, nor provided a stronger platform for reinvigorating current actions in defense of the world's most vulnerable populations. A truly global acceptance of the norm would entail, above all, its utilization as a construct for conflict prevention, reaction, and intervention. By these measures, R2P remains an unfulfilled promise.

Yet there is little doubt that the concept's underlying moral message rings true with the international community. The UN and its member states have repeatedly recognized that the world's paralysis in the face of imminent genocide in Rwanda in the mid-1990s was inhuman. And no shortage of UN resolutions decries the suffering and eroding freedoms of peoples from Afghanistan to Zimbabwe. Where, then, lies the trouble with R2P? Why are nations still reluctant to immortalize the promise of "never again" through the rhetoric and the exercise of R2P?

One obvious hurdle to R2P's acceptance is the continued criticism of its staunch opponents. A small group of skeptical states have ably misconstrued R2P to mean humanitarian intervention. These skeptics, many of whom are noted outliers on other global agreements, denounce the concept as a tool of the world's most powerful states intended to justify military adventurism or political and economic interference in domestic affairs. Supporters counter that R2P emphasizes conflict prevention and capacity-building more than intervention. Even where intervention is warranted, they remind cynics that it in no way undermines a state's sovereign rights, which are protected in the UN Charter.

But R2P's uphill battle is not simply being fought against its adversaries' defiance. Were only a handful of opponents blocking consensus, committed states could likely still navigate around the opposition to achieve a near-global and perhaps even legally binding agreement on R2P, much as these same states have on other international human rights causes. Rather, the more troubling impediment to a global embrace of R2P is the disinterest and disorganization of the norm's supporters. Sympathetic states may pay lip service to the principle, but either disagree over the practical mechanisms of its implementation—on which its operational value depends—or lose traction in lobbying for reforms that seem to many states to be complicated, ill-defined, or unnecessary. While those states that are resistant to the notion of R2P will ultimately need to be brought on board, there is currently a larger role to be played by the principle's supporters. These nations must take the lead in finding and cementing consensus and in moving forward on an ambitious, actionable agenda.

To advance R2P, supportive states must work both with the UN and through their own national policy institutions. As states upgrade their ability to monitor, prevent, and respond to mass atrocity situations, the UN's decision-making and implementing organs are invested in improved prevention and response capacities.

Support for R2P may be lagging, but it is too soon to give up on the world's most promising normative advance in mass atrocity prevention. Indeed, recent developments show progress in raising the overall visibility and understanding of the norm. In 2009, the UN General Assembly convened to debate the concept for the first time since the 2005 World Summit. Greater-than-expected attendance and participation by member states caused the session to crowd into three days and created an atmosphere of curiosity and engagement. Moving forward from the 2009 debate, the UN, its member states, and their individual leaders all must capitalize on the current momentum to bring R2P, and the atrocious crimes it pledges to end, into the spotlight. And the idea of "never again" must remain the common denominator that bridges all divides in the debate.

The History of R2P: From "Right" to "Responsibility"

The notion of R2P was a direct response to the UN's sluggish intervention in the 1994 Rwandan genocide. For 100 days in the spring of that year, the world witnessed the slaughter of more than 800,000 people, while UN member states passively debated the merits and risks of involvement. The UN has since acknowledged its failure to galvanize the political will of its member states to intervene, prompting states to make "Rwanda, never again" a mantra for preventing mass atrocities.[1]

In 2000, on the heels of a more successful North Atlantic Treaty Organization (NATO) intervention to address an escalating conflict in Kosovo in 1999, Canada formed the International Commission on Intervention and State Sovereignty (ICISS) to tackle questions concerning the "right" of the international community to intervene on humanitarian grounds in the domestic affairs of sovereign states. The commission released a report of its findings in 2001, officially launching the R2P concept.[2]

According to the ICISS report, shifting the language of the debate from a "right to intervene" to a "responsibility to protect" would help to bridge the gap between humanitarian prevention and intervention activities, and would move the debate toward substantive dialogue. The report outlined the core elements of R2P, including the responsibilities to prevent, to react, and to rebuild, and it firmly associated R2P with four major types of atrocities: genocide, war crimes, ethnic cleansing, and crimes against humanity.

Since the ICISS report's release, the UN has become the primary forum for the discussion of R2P. Former Secretary-General Kofi Annan encouraged member states to consider seriously the ICISS report, and made genocide prevention a cornerstone of his tenure. In its report, *A More Secure World: Our Shared Responsibility*, the UN's 2004 High-level Panel on Threats, Challenges, and Change endorsed "the emerging norm that there is a collective international R2P."[3]

The 2005 UN World Summit, the world's largest-ever meeting of heads of state, was the first and most high-profile global debate on R2P and served to lay bare the full spectrum of state views.[4] The summit's Outcome Document, which affirmed that R2P was associated with the four atrocities, was hailed by many observers as an important and positive step forward. Paragraphs 138 and 139 of that document, which address R2P, have provided the almost exclusive basis for further consideration.[5]

Outside of the UN General Assembly, R2P has made other substantive advances. The Security Council, in 2006, made its first reference to R2P in Resolution 1674 on the protection of civilians in armed conflict, and Secretary-General Ban Ki-moon appointed a Special Adviser on the Prevention of Genocide and a Special Adviser to the Secretary-General who was tasked with promoting R2P.[6] And on January 12, 2009, the secretary-general released a highly anticipated report entitled *Implementing the Responsibility to Protect*, which provided the basis for a future debate in the UN General Assembly.[7] After months of delay and closed-door discussions between the Special Adviser on R2P and UN member states, that debate finally occurred in July 2009.

The State of the Debate: R2P in 2009

The July 2009 landmark proceedings on R2P in the UN General Assembly displayed both fervent commitment to the concept's utility and persistent wariness of its exact tools and parameters. A core group of states voiced strong support, echoing the secretary-general's warm embrace of R2P just two days earlier. A growing number of states that were previously lukewarm toward the concept also appeared to endorse more fully its fundamental tenets. Still, the General Assembly made little substantive progress in further embedding the principle in UN practice or otherwise translating words into actions. And a handful of determined skeptics missed no opportunity to associate R2P with terms such as "humanitarian intervention" and even "neocolonialism."

Thinly disguised antagonism between high-profile leaders from both the pro- and anti-R2P sides added tension to the debate, with the president of the UN General Assembly questioning whether the UN was "ready" for R2P at all and circulating a highly critical concept note before the debate's opening.[8] He convened a panel of speakers that included outspoken opponents, who joined the skeptical states in attempting to infuse the discussion with an air of cynicism. But in a statement delivered two days before the debate,

Secretary-General Ban Ki-moon pleaded for nations to "never forget why we are here," and to be reminded of the twentieth century atrocities that had led to R2P's adoption. He further urged nations to "resist those who try to change the subject or turn our common effort to curb the worst atrocities in human history into a struggle over ideology, geography or economics."[9]

At the debate's conclusion, observers were quick to encourage an optimistic view of the proceedings for fear of allowing opponents to dominate any messaging campaign. The intensity of government interest, observers claimed, exceeded expectations and lengthened the time allotted for the debate. Ninety-four governments and regional blocs delivered addresses to the UN General Assembly. Many were steadfast supporters—members of the so-called "Friends of R2P" (hereinafter "friends")—with some notable new voices joining the chorus in advocating for a stronger norm for the prevention of mass atrocities.

While R2P advocates should champion these successes, the 2009 debate also confirmed the disorganization of the supporters and the need for them to take a stronger leadership role than they had previously. The Friends of R2P have not yet adequately coordinated their policies and strategies in support of a common understanding of R2P, nor ensured that their own national governments embrace the norm. Lack of coordination in the supporters' positions impeded their ability to present a coherent vision of implementation for R2P, leaving the principle vulnerable to further attack.

Leading up to the debate, supporter states channeled their diplomatic energies into finding and cementing consensus around the basics of R2P, specifically the landmark language adopted in the final Outcome Document from the 2005 World Summit, in hopes of moving steadfastly toward an implementation agenda. The importance of the UN General Assembly's opinion to move R2P toward international acceptance and visibility justified these short-term efforts. But with the UN General Assembly's debate now passed and true consensus still lacking, states face a void in strategic thinking on the longer-term evolution of R2P. The concept's normative and substantive development will ultimately rely on a broad diplomatic campaign involving particular state efforts to move it forward, both inside and outside the UN.

Mapping States' Views on R2P

The 2005 World Summit Outcome Document continues to provide the conceptual basis for discussions of R2P. In the document, states agreed on the applicability of R2P to genocide, war crimes, ethnic cleansing, and crimes against humanity. They further affirmed that "each individual State has the responsibility to protect its populations," with assistance from the international community "as appropriate." The international community, in turn, was delegated the responsibility "to use appropriate diplomatic, humanitarian, and other peaceful means . . . to help to protect populations" if a state were "manifestly failing" to do so on its own.[10]

In 2005, observers heralded the Outcome Document's recognition of the four atrocities as a meaningful achievement, and noted its normative value if not its substantive contribution. This normative success gains greater meaning because R2P was preserved in the final document while other issues had to be abandoned for lack of consensus.[11] As a fundamental, shared value, the notion of "never again" thus provides some coherence to the R2P debate.

But the Outcome Document does not specify R2P's value as distinct from existing international political and legal protection principles. Admittedly, the Outcome Document uses "responsibility" as a stronger restatement of twenty-first century humanitarian doctrine. Even so, it told states what their responsibilities were but was silent on how to fulfill them. As a result, the document's two short paragraphs leave room for differing interpretations of these responsibilities and for mismatched levels of commitment. The secretary-general's January 2009 report gave more guidance in this regard, but did not lay to rest the major areas of contention, which again resurfaced in the July 2009 UN General Assembly debate.

A handful of conceptual sticking points frustrate efforts to define R2P and move it forward. One area of contention relates to the scope of R2P, particularly as to whether it should apply to situations of mass human suffering other than the four atrocities defined by the 2005 Outcome Document. While some supporters would go further, adding humanitarian crises brought about by natural disasters to the scope of R2P, many observers agree that R2P should be limited to the four atrocities.

States vary more considerably, however, in the emphasis they place on the different stages of conflict and atrocities that would qualify for action under R2P. The secretary-general's 2009 report divides R2P activities into three "pillars": member states' responsibility to protect their own populations; the international community's obligation to provide states with the capacity that states need to fulfill this responsibility; and the international community's obligation to respond to mass atrocities when and if such acts occur. While supporters are united in their embrace of the first pillar, some states place greater emphasis on the second pillar, wishing to draw attention to development aid and other capacity-building tools for preventing mass atrocities.

Others see greater value in the interventionist third pillar, contending that development aid may be too far upstream from conflict to protect civilians and asserting that the "teeth" of R2P lie in encouraging appropriate bodies, such as the Security Council, to authorize intervention in a state that it is "manifestly failing" to protect its own population.

Beyond the arguments regarding scope, there is further disagreement about what tools should be part of the R2P "toolbag." Evans, former president of the International Crisis Group, and former co-chair of ICISS, defines the tools of R2P more broadly than do some scholars.[12] In his view, the universe of tools consists of four categories: political and diplomatic measures, economic and social measures, constitutional and legal measures, and security sector measures. Each of these measures, in turn, consists of long-term, structural instruments (such as promoting good governance) and immediate-term, direct instruments (such as political sanctions).

When R2P supporters peer into the toolbag, however, they often disagree on exactly what it is that they see. In particular, the use of coercive measures, including sanctions and military deployment, is a persistent source of debate. For some wary countries, the 2003 U.S.- and UK-led invasion of Iraq and Russia's 2008 incursion into Georgia are evidence that the rhetoric of protection is just that—rhetoric. For the opponents, embracing the use of force as part of R2P is simply humanitarian intervention by another name. States' wariness also traces its roots back to the "right to intervene," espoused by Doctors Without Borders founder and current French Foreign Minister Bernard Kouchner during his governmental tenure in the early 1990s, which inflamed sensitivities about sovereign rights.[13]

Supporters, however, point out that R2P merely preserves the option of military intervention that already exists under Chapter VII of the UN Charter. In its 2001 report, ICISS introduced the following five criteria to further refine and restrict the "use of force": just cause, right intention, last resort, proportional means, and reasonable prospects.[14] Supporters of these criteria see them as providing a check against unilateral military action and an assurance to militarily weaker nations that more powerful states will not use R2P as a means of exploiting power imbalances. Opponents of the criteria fear that prohibiting armed intervention where it might be necessary may put an improper "ceiling" on the use of force, or that using force when other options would be more appropriate may install an improper "floor" for the term.[15]

States' contentions over R2P's institutional context provide an illuminating glimpse into the perennial power differential between the UN General Assembly and Security Council. Discussions about R2P have reinforced existing tensions between the two bodies regarding their respective roles in driving UN action. For example, the 2005 Outcome Document notes in paragraph 139 that member states "stress the need for the General Assembly to continue consideration of the responsibility to protect populations" from the four crimes described in the text. This "continu[ing] consideration" clause has allowed many smaller states to argue that the UN General Assembly should have a gatekeeper's role in R2P, with the authority to refer or not to refer matters to the Security Council. Opponents counter that such an arrangement strips the Security Council of its exclusive powers and thus violates the UN Charter. Some observers also note that the UN General Assembly is already empowered to act under the "Uniting for Peace" resolution.[16] While the Security Council is the primary body charged with authorizing military or other punitive action, the UN General Assembly is permitted to do so with a two-thirds majority in instances where the Security Council fails to act due to disagreement among its permanent five (P-5) members.

The P-5's veto power and the UN General Assembly-Security Council power differential help to explain the moderate positions on R2P adopted by members of the P-5 with otherwise weak human rights records—notably China and Russia. Although these states might not normally endorse a human rights norm, they are less wary of R2P than of other such norms, given that they can veto unfavorable Security Council actions involving R2P. By contrast, states in the General Assembly with similarly weak adherence to human rights that have allied with China or Russia on other international issues often oppose R2P, fearing their inability to contest an unwanted Security Council decision. The power imbalance also explains the P-5's resistance to a proposal asking that its members refrain from using their veto in cases of mass atrocities. Supporters of this proposal claim such a step is necessary to facilitate action, while detractors argue that veto authority should not be restricted.

Against this backdrop, the R2P debate also provides a unique window into historic antagonisms between the global North and the global South. R2P's misinterpretation as humanitarian intervention has enabled some less-developed states of the global South to rally in opposition against R2P, casting it as an imperialist tool of the global North. Consequently, rejection or support for R2P has frequently splintered along geographical or political lines. Principal R2P opponents often are members of the Non-Aligned Movement (NAM) and the Group of 77 (G-77). The European Union (EU), with growing support from some nations of the African Union (AU) and the Organization of American States (OAS), has established itself at the forefront of the friends group.[17] Members of the Association of Southeast Asian

Nations (ASEAN) generally fall in the middle, offering lukewarm support for R2P while holding fast to sovereign values. Of course, the dominant voices within these blocs do not always accurately reflect their members' preferences, and to ascribe a uniform position to each group would greatly oversimplify the spectrum of views and varying levels of support that differentiate the countries in these blocs.

The Obstructionist Camp: R2P as "A Reincarnation of Humanitarian Intervention"

A small but outspoken group of states has adopted a soundly rejectionist posture toward R2P from its earliest introduction, rallying opposition by citing an array of deep-seated suspicions. To some in this group, R2P is seen to contravene the right to sovereignty preserved in the UN Charter and thus to violate international law. In the 2005 negotiations regarding the Outcome Document, Algeria, Belarus, Cuba, Russia, Syria, and Venezuela all attacked R2P on the grounds that it had no legal basis in the UN Charter.[18] The NAM argued that R2P was merely "a reincarnation of humanitarian intervention."[19] Some members of this obstructionist camp rejected the notion that R2P could even be acknowledged as a "concept" or claimed, as did Venezuela, that it only served the interests of powerful states.[20] Cuba reiterated that R2P would "only facilitate interference, pressure and intervention in the domestic affairs of our States by the superpowers and their allies," and Zimbabwe thought R2P needed "careful scrutiny in order to test the motives of [its] proponents."[21] In 2005 and 2009, further defenses of sovereignty or denunciations of R2P as overly vague came from Iran and Pakistan, among others.[22]

States that are slightly less critical than the above opponents, most notably Egypt, have asserted that responsibility of any form rests primarily with the state. Once discussion of the pillars was introduced into the R2P debate after 2005, Egypt turned this position into a firm emphasis on the first and second pillars and an unswerving call for the "sequencing" of R2P actions between pillars two and three. In this view, the international community should exhaust all efforts to protect populations through the capacity-building mandated by pillar two before using the instruments of response provided for in pillar three. This position is thought by others effectively to neuter the ability of the international community to take any third pillar (coercive) actions.[23]

Some of the staunchest early opponents of R2P merely reiterated their opposition in the 2009 debate and intervening discussions since 2005. Cuba still led the charge against what it viewed as an illegal concept, with no basis in international law, that merely provides an "indiscriminate humanitarian blanket" for military intervention.[24] The Sudan warned that allowing the Security Council to deliberate on R2P matters would be "like giving a wolf the responsibility to adopt a lamb," and North Korea continued to instill fears of humanitarian intervention.[25] Significantly, however, not all obstructionist positions were as static as they once seemed, and observers noted successes in softening the rhetoric of some dissenters. Key states such as Vietnam and Egypt, speaking on behalf of the NAM, were notably warmer to R2P in 2009 than that they had been previously, and even adopted much of the same language as the friends. Others welcomed key facets of the secretary-general's report even if they remained hesitant to accept a resolution embracing the norm in the General Assembly.

This shrinking group of rejectionist states is unsurprising when viewed in the larger context of state relations and historical attitudes toward humanitarian and human rights causes. It is likely that some of the most vocal members of this camp have simply seized the R2P debate as an opportunity to assert leadership among their counterparts in the NAM and across the developing world. By some counts, the obstructionist camp as of late 2009 consisted of fewer than a dozen states.[26]

The Skeptical Middle: A Call for "Great Prudence"

Some governments appear still to mistrust R2P, but have refrained from openly rejecting it as a project of the West. China, a permanent member of the Security Council, but also the subject of criticism for human rights abuses, cautiously called for further discussion on R2P in 2005 and has consistently deferred matters of peace and security to the Security Council. China has warned that responsibility "lies primarily with the Governments of the countries concerned" and called for "great prudence" in approaching and applying the concept.[27] Nevertheless, China concedes some responsibility for the international community to provide "constructive help and support" to countries to fulfill their sovereign responsibilities.[28]

Russia, aside from its early questioning of R2P's legal basis, has spoken mostly in favor of the status quo, arguing that the Security Council already has adequate authority to react to international crises.[29] Echoing China's rhetoric, Russia in 2006 called for "the greatest prudence when dealing with documents and concepts worked out without coordination with all [UN] Member States."[30] India too has expressed skepticism, preferring to emphasize the Chapter VI role of the Security Council in peaceful settlements of disputes and other conflict prevention measures; India has used R2P as a platform to advocate for Security Council reform.[31] But India commented in a statement in 2009 that the 2005 Outcome Document provided a "cautious go-ahead" on R2P that should not be forgotten.[32]

Southeast Asia holds an additional concentration of states that remain hesitant on R2P. In the past, these states have included Indonesia, the Philippines, Thailand, and a more outspoken Vietnam, all of which staunchly defended sovereign values in 2005. The traditional defense of the norm of non-interference throughout this region has characterized attitudes toward R2P. Analysis by the Asia-Pacific Centre for the Responsibility to Protect contends that states in the region are not so much opposed "to the principle itself "as they are to "the possibility for the principle to be abused to justify expanded coercive interference."[33] Accordingly, they seek to shift the locus of debate to the UN General Assembly while cautioning against Security Council use of R2P.

As noted for the obstructionist states, not all views expressed by states of the skeptical middle are immovable. Indeed, many states' favorable reactions to the secretary-general's report and subsequent endorsements of its pillar framework and scope at the 2009 debate have given fresh cause for optimism.

The Likely Supporters: A Silent Majority?

A large number of states can be classified as relatively inactive supporters of R2P. Members of this group welcomed the notion as agreed on in 2005 but have failed to make R2P a cornerstone of their UN statements or to advocate strongly that it become the basis for distinct reforms. Some of these states became more vocal in their advocacy in the 2009 debate, but other potential supporters remain immobilized.

Many states in sub-Saharan Africa generally embrace R2P, albeit some more emphatically than others. The strongest African supporters are by and large those states with tragic histories of mass atrocities, such as Rwanda and Sierra Leone. Other, politically influential African states have also shown consistent support and engagement, including Ghana and Nigeria. In addition to these states, the other sub-Saharan African states that delivered supportive statements at the July 2009 debate were Benin, Botswana, Cameroon, The Gambia, Kenya, Lesotho, Mali, South Africa, Swaziland, and Tanzania.[34] The AU, in a 2005 document outlining a common position on the UN's Report of the High-level Panel on Threats, Challenges, and Change, underscored the need for regional organizations to be "empowered to take actions" under R2P in current crises in their regions, with the possibility of the UN Security Council even approving an intervention "after the fact."[35]

The growing interest of sub-Saharan Africa in R2P is consistent with the region's damaging intrastate conflicts, as well as with some countries' perceptions that they can benefit from capacity-building initiatives under a R2P conflict prevention approach. Approval of R2P also flows from the AU's shift from a staunch policy of non-interference in sovereign affairs to an acceptance of non-indifference toward the plight of other African nations.[36]

A number of Latin American and Caribbean nations also fall under this classification of likely or silently supportive states. Notably, some Middle Eastern and North African countries, among the most silent on R2P, may also prove persuadable. In 2009, for example, Jordan, Morocco, and Qatar took the floor at the General Assembly's plenary debate to speak favorably of the secretary-general's report and of R2P implementation. The willingness of these states and that of many Latin American nations to deliver approving remarks at the 2009 debate signals their growing interest and amenability to being engaged in a pro-R2P campaign.

Last, Japan has long stood out as a strong potential ally of R2P, having championed the notion of "human security," which has tangible policy overlaps with R2P. But while Japan has repeatedly expressed approval of R2P, it continues to favor the prism of human security in its advocacy of human rights, development, and conflict prevention.[37]

The Consistent Supporters and Friends: Active but Fragmented

The staunchly pro-R2P camp comprises many "middle power" nations that have historically defended multilateral agreements on similar human security and transnational challenges. Within this grouping, however, there is still a range of interests in advancing and implementing R2P, with some states assuming more overt leadership roles than others. Furthermore, the conceptual points of contention outlined earlier still divide states within this group. Even where dedication to R2P and conceptual understanding are aligned, strategic differences on how to promote the concept continue to impede progress.

It is important to note that observers of the R2P debate use the term "Friends of R2P" in reference to different groups of states. In some experts' estimations, there are as many as seventy pro-R2P countries.[38] For the purpose of this analysis, *supporters* are distinguished from *friends*, the first comprising a large grouping of consistently pro-R2P voices, and the latter referring to the smaller, more established subset of the pro-R2P camp.

Within the official friends group, the true champions of R2P actively market and promote the norm, missing few opportunities to push for its consideration at the UN. Spearheading this activist work is Canada, the initiator of the ICISS consultations and a firm ally of the civil society groups that played a pivotal role in shaping the concept at the start. Australia, Belgium, France, Mexico, the Netherlands, Rwanda, the United Kingdom, and a handful of other European nations have joined Canada in its robust promotion strategies. These states stand out as leaders on R2P for their involvement in one or more outwardly supportive activities, such as chairing friends' meetings, hosting informational R2P luncheons or seminars, and pursuing extensive diplomatic outreach on R2P to other member states' missions.

The less activist contingency of the friends includes those states that have nonetheless expressed tireless and unequivocal backing for R2P. These states include Ghana, New Zealand, many members of the EU, and Latin American nations such as Argentina, Chile, Costa Rica, Guatemala, and Panama.[39] A newer addition to this list is South Africa, formerly skeptical but now actively engaged with R2P.[40]

Despite consistent endorsements, however, there are still lingering conceptual differences inhibiting a consistent message from the Friends of R2P. France gained the reputation of an outlier in the EU bloc after France's Foreign Minister Kouchner suggested that the humanitarian disaster following Cyclone Nargis in Myanmar (Burma) be understood as a R2P situation. Most states rebuked the suggestion, saying R2P should be preserved only for strict mass atrocity crimes. Bangladesh regards itself as a strong supporter, but identifies the value-added of R2P as its provision of assistance for capacity-building rather than the license it gives to the international community to intervene in mass atrocities.[41] South Korea, a steadfast R2P supporter, has similarly emphasized preventive measures over third pillar actions.[42]

But the third pillar is central to other countries' support of R2P. Ghana endorsed a more interventionist interpretation of R2P in 2006, suggesting that it "behooves the United Nations to intervene and protect innocent populations."[43] Other nations, particularly within the EU, have more quietly advocated for retaining the option of military intervention than Ghana has.

The United States: A Strategic Wild Card

The United States' position on R2P has proven to be more context-specific than consistently supportive, shifting to reflect the views of each U.S. administration and U.S. policy toward particular situations. Under the direction of U.S. Ambassador to the UN John Bolton in 2005, the United States emphasized the role of the Security Council in determining R2P situations, but never approached the effusive support expressed by Canada and others.

Under the administration of President Obama, newly minted Ambassador Susan Rice has grown progressively bolder in her embrace of R2P. In Rice's first statement to the Security Council in January 2009, she said she merely looked forward to the secretary-general's report on R2P and the subsequent debate.[44] Controversially, in that statement, Rice mentioned R2P immediately following condemnation of the humanitarian situation in Darfur, implicitly linking the concept with the ongoing abuses in the Sudan despite the hesitancy of some states to affix the R2P label to the situation in Darfur. In a June 2009 statement at a seminar organized by the International Peace Institute, Rice elaborated extensively on U.S. support for R2P. She defended R2P as distinct from humanitarian intervention and elucidated areas for action to embed the notion in practice, including strengthened early warning, preventive diplomacy, peacekeeping, and sanctions.

As of late 2009, however, it remains unclear precisely what role the United States will play or who within the government will take the lead. While some friends fear that R2P may come to be perceived as an American initiative (and therefore a tool of Western intervention), others rightly point out that the United States can help to create buy-in within other governments, effectively coordinating plans and programs, and bring ambivalent or reticent countries on board.

An Action Plan for Overcoming Current Challenges

The obstacles to acceptance and implementation of R2P are multidimensional and interlocked. Evans adopts a useful framework for evaluating the diplomatic landscape, drawing attention to three broad challenges: conceptual, institutional, and political.[45] Developing an action plan to overcome these challenges is critical to building consensus and coordination among R2P supporters. As the driving force behind operationalizing R2P, it is essential that these supporters work toward the same set of goals.

The conceptual challenge, according to Evans, is to guarantee that "the scope and limits" of R2P are understood, agreed upon, and promoted uniformly by its supporters. Fundamental differences in the actors' understandings of R2P, or even differing emphases within its pillars, widen the grounds for its rejection and frustrate efforts to seek consensus on an implementation agenda.

A second roadblock to R2P's progression is institutional deficiency within multilateral bodies and relevant domestic entities. For Evans, building "institutional preparedness" entails creating adequate preventive, reactive, and reconstructive capacity, particularly within international and regional institutions that can contribute the most resources and deliver the most legitimate decisions on R2P situations. National bodies are equally crucial focal points for institutional reform and capacity-building, as national activities strengthen multilateral institutions while also encouraging individual states to implement R2P and build a repertoire of best practices.

Last, the political challenge of R2P, in Evans's view, is the struggle to mobilize nations to act in situations of concern. This ingredient has consistently frustrated the human rights community, which rebukes states' reluctance to respond in a timely or decisive manner to clear humanitarian crises. Deficient will to intervene is widely cited as the source of the international community's failure to prevent genocide in Rwanda, despite early warning signs of atrocities. Political will derives from clarifying the tenets and obligations of R2P, as well as from building proper institutional capabilities at the UN and within member states.

Each of these three challenges—conceptual, institutional, and political—will be detailed in turn, accompanied by a series of recommendations to address them. In each case, the action plan focuses on creating structures that facilitate R2P's eventual implementation, while leaving particular policy content to states to determine individually.

Action One: Achieving Conceptual Clarity

The July 2009 UN General Assembly debate confirmed that advances have been made in clarifying the conceptual underpinnings of R2P. Progress was marked by the large number of affirmative statements on R2P that delivered a more consistent message on the scope and value of the norm. Still, strengthening consensus around the 2005 Outcome Document and paving the way for an implementation agenda for R2P requires greater coordination among the widening network of pro-R2P states.

Achieving conceptual clarity would heighten commitment to the concept among its supporters, pressure reluctant or outlying actors to conform with the consensus view, and make room for supporters to take steps toward implementation. Because dialogue on R2P, as of late 2009, has its strongest footing in the UN, the recommendations here focus on making dialogue among supporters more effective within that forum. Subsequent sections in this chapter include proposals for moving the R2P debate outside the UN over the long term as another means of strengthening global consensus.

Historical examples abound of multilateral state and civil society campaigns to advocate for or cement emerging norms, whether legal or political.

A small group of committed states and civil society groups that spearheaded an international initiative in the early 1990s, which grew into the International Campaign to Ban Landmines (ICBL), achieved a global treaty prohibiting that weapon in 1997.[46] That experience demonstrated the value of persistent messaging around a cohesive vision and a set of goals that are supported by a wide range of actors. State capitals have not yet been adequately involved in the R2P conversation, however. Many UN missions report receiving little guidance on R2P from their foreign ministries or other relevant national authorities. Capitals perceive R2P as a UN concept, and effectively outsource the topic to their diplomats in New York. This approach condemns R2P to irrelevance for critical actors within member state governments that ultimately have to understand and exercise the principle. R2P will move from words to action only if capitals and missions coordinate their planning and strategies.

Closer coordination between a government and New York provides two benefits. First, it creates high-level buy-in and channels more of the country's time, effort, and diplomatic capital toward reaching a common conceptual understanding of R2P that can then be made actionable at the UN and other multilateral forums. Second, it ensures that governments will be more proactive in determining how to mainstream R2P into their country's own institutions.

Some missions have been hesitant to engage their capitals fully until R2P's uncertain future becomes clear. This was particularly true in the months leading up to the July 2009 debate, when several postponements diminished its sense of urgency and allowed missions to delay earnest debate preparations. If supporters want to move R2P from rhetoric to practice, they must adopt the opposite approach and involve capitals in the discussion straight away. Leaders will have to put in the legwork that a project of this magnitude requires, demonstrating that they are personally invested in the success of these initiatives.

In addition to boosting their local capitals' participation, R2P supporters must look to bolster the effectiveness of the friends' group at the UN. This forum, intended to coordinate R2P supporters' policies and plans, comprises a cross-section of regions with differing levels of political and economic development, demonstrating that support for R2P is global and not simply limited to a handful of prosperous states. It is important that this forum retain its open and non-exclusive character in order to welcome new adherents while limiting the persuasive power of ambivalent or reticent opponents.

The group has not met its full potential. To make the friends' group more effective than it has been thus far, meetings should become a regular venue for finding conceptual common ground on R2P, coordinating messaging around particular R2P situations or the concept more broadly, determining agreement on next steps, and sharing information on national-level R2P activities. As one example of insufficient coordination, the friends did not meet to discuss the secretary-general's January 2009 report on R2P until March. Allowing six weeks to pass before discussing such a landmark document undermines the friends' ability to forge a unified front. Observers have commented that the NAM has been more cohesive and disciplined in its messaging than have the friends, putting the friends on the defensive.

Although the short-term importance of friends' meetings is readily apparent, the forum could eventually be used as a vessel for addressing other situations on the Security Council's and General Assembly's agendas that fall under the rubric of R2P. Friends' meetings do not have to restrict discussion to a strategic plan for R2P, but can provide an opportunity for its supporters to coalesce around common positions on country situations that involve the four atrocities. Broadening the agenda, so long as discussion remains centered on a common understanding of R2P, would make the notion of friends' meetings more attractive to mission representatives juggling competing demands on their time and interests.

The friends must also be more active in drafting proposals for moving R2P forward. Observers suggest that, as of now, the group serves principally as a conduit for information from the secretary-general or his special adviser to member states. The group should not only digest information passively, but also be an incubator for ideas. One means of encouraging a more forward-looking posture would be to welcome the input of experts, whether on topics relating to R2P or on at-risk regions. Absent experts' attendance, it is incumbent upon mission representatives to seek the information and analysis required to engage in productive discussion.

In addition to working to gain collective conceptual clarity on R2P, the friends should be prepared to propose concrete measures for institutionalizing R2P in UN agencies. Proposals presented in the secretary-general's 2009 report were largely lost in the July 2009 debate, which ended without solid commitments on any front. States should push the UN General Assembly's Fifth Committee to provide a budget for the activities of the special adviser and his office on R2P, to advance the proposals on early warning, and to achieve a continuous process of consideration of R2P at the UN. Friends should move the discussion back into the Security Council and other UN fora that are central to R2P implementation.

Supporters might consider creating an additional forum for core friends' states that would complement the work of the wider group but allow for more intensive strategizing on R2P. The most active states would compose this group, and would stay in closer and more regular contact with each other than the official Friends of R2P body and the wider group of supportive states. Meetings would take place outside UN buildings and the body would not assume an official UN title. The value of this core group would be in its ability to engage in more frequent and more thoughtful pre-planning with the goal not of subverting the friends' gatherings, but rather giving direction to friends' meetings to make them more efficient and ambitious than they have been so far.

Additionally, a core planning group can discreetly engage key nations whose support for R2P is uncertain. Russia and China sit at the top of this list. As members of the P-5, their support is critical if the Security Council is to have any hope of backing its words with action. It is also necessary to ensure that other rising powers, such as India and South Africa, feel that their concerns have been addressed. A smaller group of core supporters is well placed to explore privately these countries' needs in advance of further open debate.

Aside from undertaking institutional reforms, the friends must reconsider their marketing strategy toward ambivalent states. In order to bridge the North-South divide that broadly characterizes much of the opposition within the General Assembly, friends' countries of the global South should take the lead in rallying further support at the UN. Most friends' missions are already sensitive to the need for greater southern state engagement, and have quietly begun looking to outspoken R2P proponents in Africa and Latin America to be vocal supporters. Mexico hosted a high-level meeting on R2P in early March 2009 in a move to bring other Latin American counterparts on board, and the Asia-Pacific Centre for the Responsibility to Protect has provided support to Indonesia, Japan, and the Philippines to promote domestic consensus on R2P and national implementation plans that will advance a constructive Asian dialogue on R2P.[47]

Northern friends' countries can do more to encourage southern leadership on R2P. They might ask regional blocs such as the AU to sponsor subsequent friends' meetings at the UN and host informal awareness-raising gatherings, much in the fashion of the events already sponsored by northern missions. Draft resolutions introduced at the UN General Assembly should also be sponsored by less-developed countries so as not to alarm other NAM members or active skeptics. Giving "ownership" of R2P to states of the global South helps to alleviate prior concerns over R2P's supposed imperialist front.

Advances in implementing the R2P agenda will occur incrementally, but widening and deepening agreement on the "common denominator" understanding enshrined in the 2005 Outcome Document is an essential first step. Engaging capitals in the discussion and improving the effectiveness of the Friends of R2P are key elements of this strategy. Supporters' efforts to achieve consensus should continue to target the UN so as to engage the widest range of states and to bring to bear the legitimacy and moral authority of the UN in approving new international norms. The UN cannot be R2P's final destination, however. As R2P is clarified, efforts to elaborate and implement R2P through channels outside the UN must be pursued with equal vigor.

Action Two: Making Institutions More Effective

As states continue to converge on the core tenets of R2P and to consider its more specific obligations, the political space to implement R2P is growing. Implementation requires that structures and processes be reformed to support decision-making for mass atrocity situations, which in turn calls for states and international bodies to conduct a thorough review of their current R2P-related activities.

The secretary-general's report has framed the implementation agenda at the UN by proposing initial modifications to the UN's early warning capabilities, and it has indicated more specific proposals to come. Some states have also begun to incorporate the language of R2P into their national strategy documents, mainstream R2P into policy agendas, and encourage high-level public officials to make references to R2P. Still, state activities taken under the rubric of R2P are the exception, not the rule, and many supportive governments have left nearly all deliberation on R2P to their nations' missions to the UN.

To understand the challenge of institutionalizing R2P, there is an important distinction to be made between institutionalization and operationalization. Institutionalization requires evaluating management structures and decision-making processes to facilitate good policymaking. Operationalization refers to particular policies, decisions, and actions taken to implement R2P's vision, sometimes in the context of specific country situations. While operationalization of R2P may ultimately be a better barometer for R2P's success, institutionalization is a prerequisite for identifying and mobilizing appropriate actors and resources.

Incorporating R2P's perspective into strategic planning documents is a crucial preliminary step in encouraging an entire-government approach to mass atrocity prevention and response. Many nations already have lower-level action plans to guide their human rights, development, conflict prevention, or humanitarian work, but they lack high-level, cross-sectoral strategies. Recognizing R2P as a national priority would help to align programs and policies across the bureaucracy under a R2P agenda, taking into account the capabilities of international aid and the diplomacy, military, and intelligence sectors. Mainstreaming R2P into national strategic documents should occur both in those documents that have a national scope as well as in the guiding strategies or doctrines of individual agencies or ministries where appropriate. Critically, budgets must be aligned with the priorities established in the strategic documents to ensure that resources match objectives.

One example of a government's integration of R2P into high-profile, national strategic documents is France's inclusion of R2P in a 2008 revision of its Defense and National Security White Paper.[48] On a regional level, the EU has also integrated language on R2P into its late 2008 *Report on the Implementation of the European Security Strategy*.[49] The U.S. Institute of Peace—a congressionally chartered think-tank—has published a genocide prevention strategy targeted at the American foreign policy establishment. Although the report addresses only genocide and not R2P more broadly, it provides a useful template for conducting an institutional review. The authors identify six areas that governments must address: leadership, early warning, early prevention to engage before the crisis, preventive diplomacy to halt and reverse escalation, employing military options, and strengthening norms and institutions through international action.[50] This report was not commissioned by the government but has generated considerable buzz among U.S. policymakers.

An example of an attempt to integrate preparedness into military doctrine is found in the Mass Atrocity Response Operations (MARO) Project, a collaborative effort between the Carr Center for Human Rights Policy at Harvard Kennedy School and the U.S. Army Peacekeeping and Stability Operations Institute. Among the items in the project's toolkit is an Annotated Planning Framework, meant to guide military planners to address areas such as "mission analysis, mission planning parameters, critical variables, main operating tasks, end states for parties to the conflict, and courses of action development, comparison, and recommendation."[51] In the future, MARO plans to add table-top exercises, a handbook, and a user's guide to its planning tools.

An R2P implementation plan should also ask agencies and bodies internally to review the impact of existing activities and the opportunities for their expansion or revision better to support R2P objectives. As activities are documented, it is important that member states carefully consider how R2P's institutional requirements may differ from existing policies and programs on similar issue areas, such as genocide prevention. States must appreciate the broader mandate of R2P.

To aid in this process, member states should look to the activities listed in the secretary-general's report for guidance on identifying the kinds of initiatives to consider as part of R2P and for ideas on improving their own related work. For example, some of the activities suggested under the first pillar—targeted at states seeking to strengthen their ability to protect their own populations—include researching the causes of violence, strengthening the national judicial processes, and establishing national mechanisms to support post-conflict peacebuilding. Similarly, the report suggests actions under pillar two that member states may take to improve other states' abilities to protect, while the text of pillar three provides guidance to the international community on appropriate responses to a state's failure to fulfill its responsibilities.

Most governments already engage in R2P-type activities without applying the R2P label. States may participate, for example, in bilateral or multilateral capacity-building initiatives, preventive diplomacy, peacekeeping operations, sanctions regimes, or other forms of conflict prevention and response activities. Many states are simply reluctant to re-label existing work on R2P absent a stronger consensus within the UN, or they view a re-branding of current work to be unnecessary. But the R2P label adds value to ongoing human rights, humanitarian, military, and foreign policy practices. The secretary-general's report, in its annex on early warning and assessment, argues for the logic of the R2P label, albeit in the context of UN activities:

> First, adding the perspective of the responsibility to protect to existing perspectives would help the United Nations to anticipate situations likely to involve the perpetration of such crimes and violations by enhancing its ability to identify precursors, recognize patterns, and share, assess and act on relevant information. . . . Second, such a unifying perspective would facilitate system-wide coherence by encouraging

more regular dialogue, information-sharing and common analysis among disparate programmes and agencies.[52]

Governments should use R2P as a lens through which they analyze and organize different work-streams, ultimately tying together existing programs and policies to form a unique R2P agenda. Although R2P is no silver bullet for transforming bureaucratic practice into policy successes, linking relevant programs to one another and to the ultimate objectives espoused by R2P will make it clear which tools are available for use in mass atrocity situations. Furthermore, aligning programs or policies with R2P legitimizes and heightens the profile of such work.

Mainstreaming R2P into national government policy and practice may also require prioritizing among the R2P tools available. States should be able to determine their own sources of leverage with respect to different humanitarian situations, and devise a system by which to select the appropriate tools for various contingencies in the context of their own capabilities and national interests. As this work continues, a database of best practices will arise, feeding into an evaluative process for the programs and policies that generated such practices.

In addition to mainstreaming R2P into policy documents, the principle needs a clear home in domestic government structures. Ideally, both an institution and a particular person within that institution should be designated as the lead coordinators of R2P activities, overseeing the integration of the principle across the government. A national coordinator could set a national plan of action to mainstream R2P into the appropriate agencies, bring together the necessary stakeholders in precursor discussions, and define metrics for successful implementation. This process then allows particular departments and people to be held accountable for moving the agenda forward. As an international network of high-level officials tasked with advancing R2P takes shape, it will also give rise to a natural constituency with an interest in mobilizing international action to confront R2P situations, making it more likely that the UN's response will be timely and effective.

Given the delayed recognition of R2P at the national level, few governments have advanced to the stage of appointing individuals or agencies as their coordinators. The Canadian government has such a person, whose portfolio of issue areas includes related humanitarian work. The UN missions of the Friends of R2P also commonly have political affairs officers whose responsibilities and knowledge-bases include R2P. For many governments, the appointment of special advisers for areas of strategic concern is already a common mechanism that ensures ongoing monitoring of and reporting on critical national security and foreign policy topics. The designation of such a person becomes even more crucial given the wide range of national actors, resources, and activities that are essential to R2P and that may not otherwise be incorporated into a coherent, interagency program. A government's R2P point-person should also work to educate members of the legislative branch on R2P and enlist their help to make it a national priority.

Part of the work of this designated coordinator must be to enact a standing interagency and cross-sectoral process for evaluating R2P situations. This process could take several forms, depending on the structure of the implementing government and foreign policy decision-making bodies. Individual governments should look within their own institutions for existing models of such a system. One example is a standing interagency mechanism for mass atrocity prevention that was recommended to the U.S. government in the Genocide Prevention Task Force's final report, which proposed a committee co-chaired by the U.S. National Security Council and State Department.[53] Regardless of the form of this structure, its key elements should include regular meetings, representation from all relevant agencies, processes for producing standardized assessments and reporting on situations, and a direct line of communication to decision-makers who have the ability to act quickly in response to identified situations of concern. This last element is perhaps the most crucial; lower-level government officials will need to have immediate access to national leaders who can mobilize assets in the event of developing crises.

The above recommendations underscore the importance of high-level leadership in actively promoting R2P. When supportive heads of state or other key officials speak publicly about their commitment to R2P, there are two audiences listening: the government's own bureaucracy and members of the international community. To the bureaucracy, this rhetoric signals that R2P is a political priority and that the leadership expects lower-level government officials to dedicate time and resources to put R2P into action. Such statements also make other governments aware that R2P is an important item on the global agenda and that their cooperation in meeting R2P's objectives is highly valued. Furthermore, high-profile rhetoric serves as a tool of public diplomacy, bringing the support for R2P directly to the world's people and civil society groups.

The opening meeting of the sixty-third session of the General Assembly marked a turning point in some nations' rhetoric on R2P, as a growing number of foreign ministers from supportive countries made strong affirmative references to R2P. The July 2009 debate again heard such statements, albeit generally from lower-level representatives. Still, these references occurred in speeches at the UN, to an audience already relatively sensitized to R2P's value. Officials should infuse high-level rhetoric on R2P into speeches and press conferences before national publics and foreign constituencies and directly into bilateral dialogue. To achieve progress, leaders must take responsibility for ensuring that R2P features prominently—and consistently—on the global agenda.

States that support R2P need to do some internal housekeeping alongside calling for action in the UN. By creating an interagency process, assigning R2P to a specific unit of government, and integrating the R2P perspective into current and proposed policies and budgets, these countries can ensure that grave human rights abuses are addressed on an ongoing basis across a variety of institutional settings. Change starts at home.

Action Three: Sustaining Political Will over Time

The political will required to mobilize the international community to address genocide, war crimes, ethnic cleansing, and crimes against humanity is always in short supply. From a purely political standpoint, some amount of stonewalling will always come from certain corners. In any particular situation that is ripe for action under R2P, some states or regions will feel unfairly targeted, will try to block action in order to gain concessions, or will see value in assuming a leadership role in the opposition movement.

Mobilizing even pro-R2P states to act is often challenging, as any particular use of R2P is a highly political decision. Where states fail to understand mass atrocities abroad as direct threats to their national interests, they will be unwilling to engage in prevention or response activities. Prevention—let alone intervention—may require intensive and long-term resource commitments, including time and attention from senior policymakers. In any given case, there are strong incentives to channel these resources elsewhere. R2P's supporters must acknowledge these disincentives to mobilize and prepare now to counteract them. States need to have a long-term perspective, creating structures and adopting policies that will ensure that R2P is a central part of the international agenda.

The conversation about R2P is trapped in New York. Many governments see R2P as solely the preserve of the UN, with member states' missions driving the debate and national leaders under-engaged. In light of this situation, supporters must expand the discussion directly into capitals. A new, capital-to-capital partnership in support of R2P would embody these efforts. A R2P partnership would not sidestep the UN, but rather tackle issues that require government officials to engage directly with one another.

The International Partnership on Avian and Pandemic Influenza (IPAPI), formed in 2005, provides a model for this type of intergovernmental cooperation. The centerpiece of IPAPI is an annual Senior Officials Meeting in which key officers from dozens of countries and a handful of NGOs gather to develop "a plan of action for coordinating national activities, evaluating national capabilities and filling gaps."[54] Similarly, the primary purpose of the R2P partnership would be to build state capacity and coordinate planning to address mass atrocity monitoring, prevention, and response. The relationships built at the annual meeting would catalyze intergovernmental cooperation throughout the year. Also during this time, a core group within the partnership would retain contact to drive broad planning, coordination, and strategy.

Specific outcomes of the partnership in these first two areas may include such initiatives as increased early warning systems, information sharing, coordinated aid programs, and partnerships to build a civilian advisory corps. Regarding peace operations, potential avenues for cooperation include the establishment of joint scenario planning teams, shared efforts in building specialized capabilities, and joint strategic planning.[55] For each of these efforts, the UN can contribute substantive area expertise to the partnership.

Supporters should announce the launch of the partnership in a capital with some significance for the R2P concept. An announcement in Skopje or Nairobi may draw attention to instances in which international cooperation was effective in preventing mass atrocities, while holding a kick-off event in Kigali might symbolize the international community's pledge to work harder than it has to fulfill the promise of "never again." The partnership's annual meeting could rotate to a different region each year.

Aside from creating new institutions, R2P's supporters must leverage the assets of existing international bodies. In particular, advocates should look to regional and sub-regional groups and multilateral fora (such as the Group of Eight [G8]) in forging cooperation on R2P. As a first step, member states must put R2P on the official agenda of such a body's regular meetings. Simply raising R2P in passing is not enough—there must be sustained discussions focused specifically on this topic.

Once R2P is on the agenda, the opportunities for ongoing collaboration are broad. Such fora provide space for member states to clarify their understanding of R2P, share best practices on mainstreaming R2P, and rally political support for R2P principles. Additionally, these bodies should explore ways to integrate R2P into their collective programs in areas such as foreign aid, early warning systems, diplomacy, and military cooperation. As with the new capital-to-capital R2P partnership, non-UN fora should look to the UN as a source of expertise on R2P and as a potential partner in launching new, related initiatives.

Ultimately, the R2P dialogue must move out of the boardroom and into the public square. Engaging publics directly on R2P is a key part of building a global constituency in support of R2P's vision. By educating citizens about R2P and enlisting their support for the concept, governments will find it difficult to sit idly by in the face of mass atrocities. Such engagement should take place domestically, as well as abroad through the country's diplomatic posts.

Public outreach may come in forms as varied as speeches by senior officials and diplomats, opinion pieces published in local and national newspapers, or high-profile events featuring survivors of atrocities. Mainstream media are critical to the success of such a campaign, but so too is effective use of internet-based "new media." Such outlets include online newspapers, blogs, social networking applications, and video-sharing sites. Creating a central website for R2P that gives visitors easy access to these virtual tools and invites them to create and disseminate their own content would be especially effective in achieving mass engagement.

A promising example of the use of internet-based tools in advancing R2P's objectives is found in a project called Ushahidi.[56] Meaning "testimony" in Swahili, Ushahidi's platform was first used in the midst of post-election violence in Kenya in 2008. Witnesses to the violence sent reports of what they were seeing to Ushahidi's website, where managers then produced maps that served as visual representations of the crisis as it spread. The ability to monitor crises in real time has far-reaching implications for improving crisis response. The genius of Ushahidi lies in its ability to harness the power of widely available technology and channel it toward humanitarian ends, and it is a model that R2P's supporters should explore further as efforts to engage global publics proceed.[57]

Investing in public diplomacy also requires the creation of a space for civil society to act. From the start, civil society groups have played a critical role in advancing R2P's agenda. These groups can reach out to actors that supportive states cannot engage, or make the blunt statements that states are hesitant to utter. Civil society organizations and networks are also the most direct link to national publics, building constituencies that understand and accept R2P, and thus adding another layer of pressure on states. Civil society's ability to mobilize the public is all the more crucial considering that they sometimes constitute the only source of new perspectives or pressure for change in countries where governments have proved immovable.

A large number of NGOs target national government policymakers in their home countries, while a few have assumed coordinating roles for this widening web of actors, looking to channel disparate activist efforts into coherent policy recommendations. One such coordinating NGO, the New York-based Global Centre for the Responsibility to Protect, has developed close working relationships with friends' countries and has been instrumental in consolidating consensus around R2P. Another key group, the World Federalist Movement–Institute for Global Policy (WFM–IGP), launched an International Coalition for R2P (ICR2P) in 2009, comprised of eight organizations strategically located in Africa, Asia, Latin America, and North America.[58]

Pro-R2P states must ensure a favorable political environment for the continuance of these groups' work and to expand their number and reach. To date, civil society endeavors have received financial support from only a handful of countries. But supporters' initiatives can extend well beyond funding by inviting civil society to participate in fora where governments themselves engage in dialogue on R2P, whether at the UN, other international venues, or on a national stage. Indeed, the Canadian-sponsored ICISS report that first introduced R2P was in many ways a product of civil society; many of the commission's members hailed from non-governmental institutions and academia, and the report was a consultative endeavor in which commission members sought input from government and non-governmental actors worldwide.

The political will to act is never guaranteed, but supporters of R2P can take steps to increase the odds that the international community will do what is necessary to prevent and respond to human rights abuses. Creating a capital-to-capital partnership and intensifying work within existing multilateral bodies are key components. Supporters must undertake efforts to engage the public and civil society in reinforcing the mandate and vision of R2P in order to complement and enhance official diplomatic activity. A coordinated push across all organizations and institutions is the best means to generate and sustain political resolve over time.

It is critical to understand that R2P remains unfulfilled not because a small handful of skeptical states continue to decry its normative authority, but because even supporters remain divided on how best to advance R2P. Fulfilling the promise of "never again" requires stronger leadership from and the sustained interest of supportive states—and from the Friends of R2P in particular—to take R2P from principle to practice. Clarifying the R2P concept, mainstreaming it into international and national structures, and engaging non-governmental actors are the elements that underlie a successful implementation agenda.

Notes

1. "UN Admits Rwanda Genocide Failures," *BBC News* (15 April 2000), available at http://news.bbc. co.uk/1/hi/world/africa/714025.stm (accessed 1 February 2009).

2. International Commission on Intervention and State Sovereignty (ICISS), *The Responsibility to Protect: Report of the International Commission on Intervention and State Sovereignty* (Ottawa, 2001).

3. United Nations (UN), *A More Secure World: Our Shared Responsibility, Report of the Secretary-General's High-Level Panel on Threats, Challenges, and Change,* UN Doc. A/59/565 (New York, 2004), para. 203.

4. UN, "The 2005 World Summit: An Overview," United Nations 2005 World Summit High-Level Plenary Meeting, 14–16 September 2005, available at www.un.org/ga/documents/overview2005summit.pdf (accessed 1 February 2009).

5. See UN General Assembly, Sixtieth Session, *2005 World Summit Outcome*, UN Doc. A/RES/60/1, 2005, paras 138–140.

6. UN Security Council, 5430th Meeting, Resolution 1674, UN Doc. S/RES/1674, 2006, para 4. Although it is widely understood that this Special Adviser to the Secretary-General is responsible for advising on R2P, states did not agree to use R2P in the title of the position and so it remains unassociated.

7. See UN, *Report of the Secretary-General on Implementing the Responsibility to Protect*, UN Doc. A/63/677 (New York, 2009).

8. UN, "Delegates Seek to End Global Paralysis in Face of Atrocities as General Assembly Holds Interactive Dialogue on R2P," (2009), available at www.un.org/News/Press/docs//2009/ga10847.doc.htm (accessed 26 July 2009).

9. Neil McFarquhar, "Memo from the United Nations: When to Step in to Stop War Crimes Causes Fissures," *New York Times* (22 July 2009), available at www.nytimes.com/2009/07/23/world/23nation.html?em (accessed 23 July 2009).

10. UN, *2005 World Summit Outcome.*

11. Edward Luck, Special Adviser to the Secretary-General, keynote address, Harvard Law School Human Rights Journal 2009 Symposium on the Responsibility to Protect, Cambridge, MA, 20 February 2009.

12. See Gareth Evans, *The Responsibility to Protect: Ending Mass Atrocity Crimes Once and For All* (Washington, D.C., 2008).

13. Caroline Wyatt, "Profile: Bernard Kouchner," *BBC News* (18 May 2007), available at http://news.bbc.co.uk/2/hi/europe/6666707.stm (accessed 2 February 2009).

14. ICISS, *The Responsibility to Protect*, 32–37.

15. Phone interview between authors and an official from a pro-R2P country (28 January 2009).

16. See UN General Assembly, Resolution 377A, UN Doc. A/RES 377(V) A, 1950.

17. The Group of 77 or G-77 is a group of seventy-seven developing states within the UN, "which provides the means for the countries of the South to articulate and promote their collective economic interests and enhance their joint negotiating capacity on all major international economic issues within the United Nations system, and promote South-South cooperation for development." See www.g77.org (accessed 20 October 2009).

18. Responsibility to Protect–Engaging Civil Society (R2PCS), "State-by-State Positions on the Responsibility to Protect," (2005), available at www.responsibilitytoprotect.org/index.php?module=uploads&func=download&fileId=134; R2PCS, "Chart on Government Positions on R2P," (2005), available at www.responsibilitytoprotect.org/index.php/government_statements/295?theme=alt1 (both accessed 5 March 2009).

19. Ibid.

20. R2PCS, "Chart on Government Positions on R2P."

21. R2PCS, "2005 World Summit Excerpts: The Responsibility to Protect," (2005), available at www.responsibilitytoprotect.org/index.php?module=uploads&func=download&fileId=167 (accessed 5 March 2009).

22. R2PCS, "Chart on Government Positions on R2P."

23. Interview between authors and an official from a pro-R2P country (6 February 2009).

24. UN, "More than 40 Delegates Express Strong Skepticism, Full Support as General Assembly Continues Debate on Responsibility to Protect," (2009), available at www.un.org/News/Press/docs/2009/ga10849.doc.htm (accessed 29 July 2009).

25. UN, "Delegates Weigh Legal Merits of Responsibility to Protect Concept as General Assembly Concludes Debate," (2009), available at www.un.org/News/Press/docs/2009/ga10850.doc.htm (accessed 29 July 2009).

26. Interview between authors and a UN official (25 March 2009).

27. R2PCS, "Government Statements on R2P, Asia-Pacific 2005–2007," (2008), available at www.responsbility toprotect.org (accessed 5 March 2009); Global Centre for the Responsibility to Protect (GCR2P), "Excerpts of R2P Related Comments from UN Member States: Security Council Open Debate: Protection of Civilians in Armed Conflict," (2008), available at www.responsibilitytoprotect.org/index.php?module=uploads&func=download&fileId=547 (accessed 5 March 2009).

28. Ibid.

29. R2PCS, "State-by-State Positions of the R2P."

30. R2PCS, "Excerpted Statements on the Open Debate on the Protection of Civilians in Armed Conflict," (2006), available at www.responsibilitytoprotect.org/index.php?module=uploads&func=download&fileId=311 (accessed 5 March 2009).

31. Communication with civil society representative (27 February 2009).

32. UN, "More than 40 Delegates Express Strong Skepticism."

33. Asia-Pacific Centre for the Responsibility to Protect, *The Responsibility to Protect in Southeast Asia* (Brisbane, Australia, 2009), 3.

34. International Coalition for the Responsibility to Protect, "Report on the General Assembly Plenary Debate on the Responsibility to Protect," (2009), available at www.responsibilitytoprotect.org/index.php/about-rtop/the-un-and-rtop (accessed 17 September 2009).

35. African Union Executive Council 7th Extraordinary Session, *The Common African Position on the Proposed Reform of the United Nations: The Ezulwini Consensus* (Addis Ababa, 2005), 6.

36. For more discussion of African views on non-indifference and intervention, see Fund for Peace, *Neighbors on Alert: Regional Views on Humanitarian Intervention, Summary Report of the Regional Responses to Internal War Program* (Washington, D.C., 2003).

37. Asia-Pacific Centre for the Responsibility to Protect, *Japan and the Republic of Korea on the Responsibility to Protect* (Brisbane, Australia, 2008), 7, available at www.r2pasiapacific.org/images/stories/food/japan%20and%20korea%20on%20r2p.pdf (accessed 14 March 2009).

38. Interview between authors and a civil society group representative (27 February 2009); UN official interview (25 March 2009).

39. "Group of Friends," unpublished civil society document on Friends group members, received 24 February 2009.

40. UN official interview (25 March 2009).

41. Communication with civil society representative (27 February 2009).

42. Asia-Pacific Centre for the Responsibility to Protect, *Japan and the Republic of Korea on the Responsibility to Protect*, 19–20.

43. R2PCS, "Government Statements on R2P: Africa 2005–2007."

44. R2PCS, "U.S. Ambassador to the UN Susan Rice Voices U.S. Support for R2P," (2009), available at www.responsibilitytoprotect.org/index.php/government_statements/2109?theme=alt1 (accessed 10 February 2009).

45. Gareth Evans, *The Responsibility to Protect: Ending Mass Atrocity Crimes Once and for All* (Washington, D.C., 2008), 54.

46. International Campaign to Ban Landmines, "Campaign History," available at www.icbl.org/campaign/history (accessed 2 February 2009).

47. Asia-Pacific Centre for the Responsibility to Protect, "R2P in Asia-Pacific National Programs," available at www.r2pasiapacific.org/index.php?option=com_content&task=view&id=80&Itemid=95 (accessed 10 March 2009).

48. President of the Republic of France, *The French White Paper on Defence and National Security* (Paris, 2008).

49. European Union, *Report on the Implementation of the European Security Strategy–Providing Security in a Changing World*, S407/08 (Brussels, 2008).

50. Madeleine K. Albright and William S. Cohen, *Preventing Genocide: The Report of the Genocide Prevention Task Force* (Washington, D.C., 2008).

51. Harvard Kennedy School of Government, Carr Center for Human Rights Policy and U.S. Army Peacekeeping and Stability Operations Institute, *Mass Atrocity Response Operations Annotated Planning Framework Version 2.0* (Cambridge, MA, 2008).

52. UN, *Report of the Secretary-General on Implementing the Responsibility to Protect*, Annex 1, para. 4.

53. Albright and Cohen, *Preventing Genocide*, 8.

54. U.S. Department of Health and Human Services (HHS), "HHS Pandemic Influenza Plan," (2005), available at www.hhs.gov/pandemicflu/plan/appendixh.html (accessed 15 March 2009).

55. Bruce Jones, Carlos Pascual, and Stephen John Stedman, *Power and Responsibility* (Washington, D.C., 2008).

56. More information may be found at ushahidi.com. In addition, the Harvard Humanitarian Initiative (HHI) is engaged in a project seeking to expand the use of crisis mapping; details are available at http://hhi.harvard.edu/programs-and-research/crisis-mapping-and-early-warning.

57. See also chapter 1, note 40, and chapter 10 in this volume.

58. R2PCS, "Launch of the International Coalition for the Responsibility to Protect," (2009), available at http://responsibilitytoprotect.org/index.php/civil_society_statements/2144?theme=alt1 (accessed 30 January 2009).

SARAH SEWALL

8

From Prevention to Response: Using Military Force to Oppose Mass Atrocities

Prevention is a compelling concept. As it pertains to the subject of this volume, the prevention of mass atrocities or crimes against humanity, it appears to be an unalloyed good. Individuals, states, non-governmental organizations (NGOs), and international and regional institutions that advocate against genocide and in support of the "Responsibility to Protect" (R2P) increasingly cast their arguments and craft their solutions as contributing to prevention. This approach presents as sensible and prudent, non-violent and economical. Focusing on prevention allows humanitarian advocates to skirt key controversies and political pitfalls and garners widespread support.

This chapter, however, questions the seductiveness of prevention as the catch-all solution for mass atrocities. An exclusive focus on prevention poses subtle risks. By encompassing so much on the non-kinetic spectrum, prevention can dilute efforts to prioritize and harness limited tools for maximum effect.

Further, prevention in the debate as of late 2009 is often used to create a firewall around non-military activities. But when the subtext is *preventing consideration of the use of armed force,* the prevention debate undermines its own goals. Prevention should include the use of military force as a prevention tool while non-military prevention efforts should accompany any actual use of force to stop ongoing massacres.

Fundamentally, though, prevention alone is insufficient as a strategy for civilian protection because it obscures the need to reckon with the possibility

Some material in this chapter is drawn from Sarah Sewall, "Do The Right Thing: A Genocide Policy That Works," *Boston Review,* September/October 2009. The author would like to thank Mia Bruch, Ya'ara Barnoon, and Sally Chin for research and editing support.

of failure. Much work remains to be done to master the appropriate responses to mass killings when they begin. For maximum value, then, the concept of prevention must be reconceived and married with response strategies.

This chapter argues that the United States and the international community should proactively respond to the outbreak of widespread civilian massacres with military force as well as other tools of national and international power. After briefly reviewing conceptual and practical efforts to prevent and halt mass atrocities during this century, I explain the risks and shortfalls inherent in the current vogue of focusing on prevention. I argue that prevention alone risks becoming a contributor to political and operational paralysis.

The chapter urges systematic and coordinated preparation for a Mass Atrocity Response Operation (MARO) in the event that prevention fails. I show how MARO planning can in fact support non-violent prevention efforts to forestall the outbreak of mass killings. I also highlight some unique requirements of a MARO in response to widespread killings. Finally, I explain why a MARO may emerge in unexpected contexts, not simply in a stand-alone crisis that triggers a R2P debate.

Given the obvious need for non-violent efforts to prevent mass killing, it may seem churlish to challenge the prevention lexicon. But staying in the "safe lane" of prevention can have significant costs. Focusing on the ideal of *preventing* mass atrocities should not blind key international actors that more *response* may nonetheless be required.

The Origins of Genocide Prevention

In the first half of the twentieth century, Raphael Lemkin launched a one-man effort to fix a problem that no one had named. An immigrant to the United States from Eastern Europe, Lemkin coined the word "genocide" in 1944 to describe "a coordinated plan of different actions aiming at the destruction of essential foundations of the life of national groups, with the aim of annihilating the groups themselves."[1] After World War II, his relentless advocacy led to the United Nations' (UN) 1948 Convention on the Prevention and Punishment of the Crime of Genocide.

It was a startling achievement. Yet its promise has essentially lain dormant through six decades of state-sponsored violence against persecuted groups. An artifact of aspiration, the Genocide Convention's main function has been to chastise the 140 nations that signed it for their hypocritical promise to prevent and punish mass extermination.

With the end of the Cold War, it seemed that the convention's moment might have arrived. The United States and its Western allies suddenly enjoyed a security surplus. Internationalism was in vogue. And in fits and starts, an unprecedented series of events unfolded, hinting that the moral impulse behind the convention had begun to reawaken.

In 1991, after the first Gulf War, the United States installed no-fly zones to protect threatened minorities in northern and, ultimately, southern Iraq. Yet just three years later, the United States and UN stood by as 800,000 were slaughtered in Rwanda. In the early 1990s, a feckless peacekeeping mission in Bosnia failed to prevent genocide, but military coercion ultimately led to a political settlement.

In 1998, President Clinton offered a public apology for the United States' failure to intervene in Rwanda. That same year, 120 nations agreed to create an International Criminal Court to prosecute those accused of genocide (among other crimes). While most states viewed NATO's 1999 bombing campaign to stop Serbian persecution of Kosovars as illegal under international law, that breach of state sovereignty was nonetheless forgiven, or at least tolerated, largely on overriding moral grounds.

Together, these acts of commission and omission helped forge consensus around a new concept: a "Responsibility to Protect" civilians that extended across state boundaries. This expansive concept was historical heresy. Ever since the Treaty of Westphalia in 1648, states had granted one another freedom of action within their borders. The goal of foreign relations was to safeguard existing regimes and promote international stability. But in 2001, a star-studded, Western government–backed commission proclaimed that sovereignty was no longer a given. R2P held that state sovereignty had become a conditional right.[2]

In recognizing R2P, the commission reconceived the rights of states and the obligations of the international community. The right to control the use of power within state boundaries was now paired with the responsibility to respect citizens' most fundamental human right—the right to exist. When governments systematically abuse their people, the international community has a responsibility to protect these victims despite the norm of state sovereignty. In 2005, the concept of R2P was endorsed by UN member states at the World Summit and reaffirmed by the UN Security Council in Resolution 1674 in 2006.[3]

What began as Lemkin's lonely crusade has evolved into a mass movement, with its own acronym, interest groups, and celebrity sponsors. Advocates across the globe—NGOs, faith groups, individual citizens—promote

R2P as a norm of foreign policy, most notably with regard to Darfur. But for all its fury, sincerity, and visibility, the R2P effort has gained little traction inside national governments, which are the agents ultimately charged with the tough business of halting mass atrocities. Moreover, R2P has faced an uncertain future in the UN Security Council, where states have come to equate it with a neo-imperialist program of regime change. Inertia and fears of politically motivated intervention, respectively, have stalled concrete progress toward making R2P an operational reality. In an effort to make R2P sound benign, great powers are remaining silent about armed intervention.[4] They risk throwing the baby out with the bathwater.

The Emerging "Political Pragmatism" of Prevention

The Genocide Prevention Task Force (GPTF), chaired by former Secretary of State Madeleine Albright and former Secretary of Defense William Cohen, is one of several more recent efforts to reinvigorate R2P. Its work illustrates the difficult tradeoffs between seeking political relevance and achieving practical effort with regard to mass violence against civilians. It underscores the limits of prevention.

Calculations of political feasibility seem to have shaped powerfully the final report of the GPTF.[5] Of course, political pragmatism is both a blessing and a curse. Even moderate recommendations would be important steps forward, given how assiduously genocide is ignored during national security decision-making processes. For example, strengthening a government's ability to identify the potential for mass atrocities and develop bureaucratic procedures to ensure debate about appropriate policy responses would begin to change the way policymakers think and act. Moreover, uncontroversial recommendations from a diverse, bipartisan group should easily find purchase in policy. By endorsing attainable steps, the task force refused to let the perfect become the enemy of the good.

The report's key concession to pragmatism was its focus on prevention of rather than response to mass killings.[6] Here, the report mirrors the direction in which others have begun to turn: the UN in its R2P debate, and leading states as they seek to avoid the label "interventionist." Focusing on prevention of, rather than response to, mass atrocities is understandable. By avoiding the harder questions of response, prevention supports the legitimization of R2P as a policy priority. But prevention *alone* is an ineffective strategy.

Historically, the requirements for action and the politics of inaction have clashed. To prevent the escalation of violence, states must take strong, early action. Yet national leaders face powerful political incentives to delay controversial decisions until the last possible moment. In the case of mass atrocities, the prevention curve and the political calculation curves are inversely related. We know that acting early is likely to be more effective and efficient. Yet time and time again, states and leaders avoid acting, delay choosing among uncertain and costly options, and wait until the costs of *not* acting become higher than those of acting.

This phenomenon is not unique to mass killings of civilians. But it helps to explain why doing the right thing remains difficult, even as states have begun to acknowledge past failures and a new generation has awakened to a fresh set of possibilities. A successful approach to combating mass atrocities must couple prevention with planning (and resourcing, training, and equipping) for action, including military action.

Defining Prevention: Everything and Nothing

As a concept, prevention is often simultaneously ill-defined and all-encompassing. Consider the task force admission that "there is no consensus as to the causes of genocide and mass atrocities, nor is there one commonly agreed-upon theory that sufficiently explains the key catalysts, motivations, or mechanisms that lead to them."[7] Addressing root causes in the form of prevention is often a sensible approach to public policy (as in the example of preventive health care). But if the causes of atrocities are unclear, how can the U.S. government and the international community prevent their effects?

We do not understand why so many states with severe differences and conflicts have managed to avoid mass violence. Without a sustained effort to prioritize needs, make detailed assessments of potential hotspots, and consider context-specific options for action, relying on a vague concept of prevention could lead the United States to spend billions on economic development or political reconciliation in places that are not at real risk—all in the name of genocide prevention. While such assistance might well be useful for development or political stability, it will certainly divert attention or drain resources from efforts to stop genocide. This approach to prevention suggests that the solution to mass atrocities lies with stable, economically viable states that respect the human rights of all citizens. What problem would this not solve? This is a tautology, not a strategy.

If the international community had unlimited resources to devote to global challenges, an ecumenical approach to genocide prevention would make sense. But since the difficulty of addressing mass atrocities lies in galvanizing action when it is most urgently needed, a generic prevention solution is likely to prove counterproductive. A vague and open-ended notion of prevention fails to recognize the special challenges that a mass atrocity situation presents for policymakers and military planners. It cannot serve as a substitute for a more concerted prevention strategy that confronts the complex challenges that mass atrocities pose in detail, before events overtake diffuse and unfocused prevention efforts.

The Consensus Trap

An emphasis on prevention is far less controversial than any discussion of military intervention—the "third rail" of genocide politics. The debates over intervention in both Kosovo and Darfur show that the international community remains divided in its opinion of R2P. Many developing countries fear R2P merely masks modern imperialist ambition. How, then, can they be convinced that R2P legitimately includes the use of force to protect civilians? Rather than confront this challenge, many (including the GPTF) simply downplay the potential military leadership of individual states (including the United States), taking refuge in failed multilateralism and historical patterns of inaction. The non-aligned nations' concerns with sovereignty dovetail neatly with advanced nations' reticence to contemplate acting alone. This divide leads both constituencies toward multilateralism for the wrong reasons.

Where multilateralism becomes a seeming prerequisite for action, defenders of state sovereignty gain a *de facto* veto over humanitarian response. Although multilateralism is often desirable, it should not become an excuse for inaction when moral outrages emerge and national interests are at stake. Sound policy requires contending with the realities and constraints of politics, but it may mean rejecting a multilateral impulse that has proven ineffective.

In the case of the United States in particular, constraining unilateral military options may actually undermine prospects for a preventive and multilateral approach to mass atrocities. At present, most states (and therefore collective organizations) are poorly equipped to take on genocide prevention, particularly if the actual use of force, rather than simply the presence of troops, is required. The United States is one of only a handful of nations that can lead a significant intervention requiring combined land and air forces. American advantages in high-technology capabilities such as surveillance and communications and in logistical support (including the ability to deploy forces quickly to a crisis area) render the United States both an enabler and security blanket for other nations' forces.

But a supporting role for other actors is not always going to be enough. If the effort is, or risks becoming, large and violent, success requires an effective lead nation. And if the crisis unfolds quickly, or if its demands escalate beyond expectation, the world's most capable military power may be the only force able to act in time. There is an inevitable slippery-slope problem in justifying intervention in the name of humanity. But we need only think back to the horror of Rwanda in 1994 to see that unilateral military intervention, while complex and costly, may have a place in the range of options for action.

Simply put, if prevention meant acting only when the rest of the world said to do so *and* before it got too hard, it would have clearly failed in most historical cases of widespread violence. A desire to avoid political controversy regarding military intervention threatens to erode the meaning of R2P unwittingly by pushing tough action, including military force, out of the equation entirely.

Plan B

Prevention advocates should also be wary of becoming just a little bit pregnant with military force. The task force rightly argues against an "all-or-nothing choice between taking no military action and launching a major intervention."[8] Indeed, the task force's most innovative work may be in the military options that it details for use in support of diplomatic prevention efforts. Yet the logic implies that U.S. policymakers can do more without the risk of becoming fully engaged militarily and responsible for outcomes on the ground.

This is a common flaw in civilian logic when trying to develop a military approach. Less forceful military options may not succeed without a clear national will to escalate. Some actions have concrete value in and of themselves (e.g., interdicting arms), but "signaling" actions, such as moving an aircraft carrier, are likely to be effective only if they reflect a credible threat. Bluffing is a strategy, but not a sound one.

The "signaling" example also reveals that the dichotomy between prevention and response is not only false but also unrealistic. Many preventive actions rely on military force, even if such force is deployed for demonstrative purposes. Such actions can only be successful if they emerge from systematic thinking about the specific requirements of mass atrocity situations. An emphasis on prevention without the use of force creates an unrealistic division between prevention and response. A strategy of prevention can only be effective if it is part of a continuum of planning that recognizes that prevention may fail and that escalation may be necessary. This requires careful thinking about the specific problems and unique demands of mass atrocities.

Mass Atrocity Response Operations (MARO)

Effective military intervention in the face of a large-scale, ongoing genocide requires more than military capability; it requires preparation for the unique challenges of ending mass atrocities. Treating prevention as the solution to mass atrocities, rather than as one part of a sophisticated and detailed planning process, perpetuates this lack of preparation rather than addresses it.

At the present moment, the world's leading military power is unprepared to halt ongoing mass atrocities. The U.S. military does not recognize mass atrocity response as a contingent requirement. *MARO* is a newly coined term for a specific type of military operation. A MARO aims primarily to halt the systematic and widespread killing of civilians.[9]

What distinguishes a MARO from other response mechanisms is its goal of ending violence against civilians—not as a means to an end (regime change, winning a counterinsurgency, enforcing a peace agreement, or as an adjunct of a peacetime humanitarian relief operation), but as a goal in and of itself.

As of late 2009, national forces are unable to carry out even the basic civilian protection tasks assigned in UN peacekeeping operations.[10] Stopping a Rwandan-type scenario would be far more challenging. This is not to argue that capable forces could not conduct an intervention. Certainly, the sheer capability of the U.S. military, as well as the professionalism of its uniformed men and women, provides an enormous margin within which political authorities can assign missions. Moreover, U.S. forces have managed past deployments for peace operations and counterinsurgencies despite a lack of institutional preparedness and support. In such cases, however, American troops have been less successful than they might have been. As in Operation Iraqi Freedom, they can muddle through, but often at a greater cost in lives and resources than if they had been prepared conceptually and operationally for the challenges that they would face.

Successful planning requires policymakers and military planners to recognize that a MARO is a different kind of operation from those recognized in the U.S. military's "spectrum of operations." It will have similar component parts. Like other operations, a MARO involves elements of offense, defense, and stability operations. Many MARO tasks will be familiar; for example, convoy escorts, direct fires, and detainee operations.[11] Concepts will also be common across the operational spectrum, including no-fly zones, protected enclaves, or separation of forces.[12] Yet the context of and purpose for these tasks or operational concepts differs dramatically and some requirements are unique to a MARO. Some of the salient features of a MARO include:

A Multiparty Dynamic

A mass atrocity situation is a multi-party affair, complicating planning and operations. At least three major groups of actors—the perpetrators of violence, the victims of violence, and the interveners—interact with unpredictable results. Perpetrators attack victims, and interveners seek to stop the killing of non-combatants. A fourth group—the bystanders—can also play a critical role depending upon whether they join in or dissuade the killing. Bystanders can come from within the country, just across the border, or farther afield. Mass atrocity situations involve many parties who may abruptly switch roles, and such situations can escalate rapidly.

But warfare has long been considered a two-party game: enemy and friendly forces. U.S. military war games and exercises have typically involved two actors: a red team (enemy) and blue team (American/coalition). The U.S. military has begun to add a "green" team to represent non-state actors, civilian governmental actors, or others with the capacity to affect the battlefield. While a welcome replication of complexity, this approach still fails to replicate the intricacy in a MARO. In fact, during mass atrocities the reaction of the "other" to the violence can determine the outcome.

As noted earlier, perpetrators attack victims while interveners seek to stop the killing of non-combatants. In fact, it is possible that multiple armed actors will commit mass atrocities against civilians rather than focus on fighting armed opponents. The number and types of perpetrators will be specific to the circumstance, but in any MARO there will be at least one armed group committing violence.

The victims, too, have a vote. The victim response is not likely to be strategic or coordinated but rather *ad hoc* and reactive, varying across geography and time. Victims' choices—fleeing, hiding, organizing to defend themselves, appealing to other citizens or nations to intervene on their behalf—affect the strategies of the perpetrator.

Victims' actions will also affect the MARO force, whose mission to stop the killing may then become a shield behind which victims can take revenge or a force that neighboring states or external actors fight for their own reasons.

Understanding these dynamics is critical as the intervening force begins to plan for an appropriate course of action. Such an action puts a premium on obtaining information about the motivations, strengths, and weaknesses of each of the relevant parties. Doing so may require a change in the type of information that the intelligence community gathers—psychological profiles of non-state actors, cultural assumptions and practices, conflict analysis, tracking of small arms flows—and an emphasis on open-source information from non-traditional providers ranging from NGOs to the diaspora community.

Certainly it suggests that greater capacities of the intelligence communities are needed to provide rapid assessments of the "human terrain" in otherwise low priority parts of the world. At the tactical level, the U.S. military is moving in this direction as a result of its missions morphing into counterinsurgencies and irregular warfare. Widening the intelligence community's collection investment strategies is necessary to support effectively a MARO.

Any particular plan to address mass atrocities is shaped by a variety of factors including available resources, speed of required response, degree of acceptable risk, etc. But a choice from among competing courses of action should also be informed by an analysis of the likely effect of intervention upon the calculations of other actors, and the subsequent third-order effects upon each other.

Illusion of Impartiality

An intervener may be acting for what it considers impartial reasons (e.g., defense of human rights), unrelated to the identities of the parties or the underlying conflicts. The intervener may be opposed to the *actions*—violence against civilians—rather than opposed to a particular party in the conflict. Indeed, if there were more than one party inflicting mass violence upon civilians, the intervener might oppose actions in an even-handed way, i.e., against all civilian attackers. Nonetheless, the perpetrators of violence and victims perceive an intervening force as anything but impartial even where all parties are restrained from using violence.

Humanitarian intervention will inevitably be hostile to the party committing the violence, effectively putting the interveners in alliance with the victims and against the perpetrators. The perpetrators may turn their vengeance against the interveners, transforming the mission's emphasis from civilian protection to enemy neutralization. Concomitantly, the victims may regard interveners as protectors, and they may also use the intervening forces as a means for extracting vengeance. Victims may use the implicit shield of protection offered by foreign intervention to carry out reprisals against perpetrators or those outside the victim group.

Other actors in and outside the region may come to see the interveners as threats to the pre-existing power balance, or as threats to their own aspirations to change the constellation of power. Examples might include countries allied with the interests of the perpetrators, or armed groups seeking to overthrow a government conducting mass killings. These actors may then decide to use force against the intervening party.

Thus, there is high potential for a MARO to metastasize quickly into a very different type of operation—counterinsurgency (COIN), civil war, non-combatant evacuation operation (NEO), or interstate conflict—and to dissolve its original distinctions between victim and perpetrator such that the intervener can no longer enjoy a morally or operationally pure role.

The Power of Witness

The nature of mass atrocities committed against civilians creates opportunities to use different tools and approaches to halt them. Because killing civilians is a criminal and shameful act, exposing these killings can have an impact quite different from recording the conduct of war among combatants. This difference creates new possibilities for prevention and deterrence, as well as suggests a great value in using non-kinetic tools during combat operations.

This approach is particularly important since not all aspects of U.S. military superiority will be particularly effective in a MARO situation. Perpetrators do not require either regular forces or high-tech weapons for mass murder. Many tactics and concepts that advanced Western military forces have refined—standoff destruction of massed forces, coercion of state leaders by jeopardizing their hold on national allegiances or institutions, and sanctions to deny weapons transfers—may be less useful during MAROs than they have been in other responses.

But witnessing or recording acts of genocide may be particularly valuable responses. Transparency can actually halt acts of violence if perpetrators decide that the risks of being subsequently held personally responsible (either as a matter of justice or physical violence) are significant. Transparency can convince "others" (neutrals, neighbors, allies) not to join in the violence against civilians for similar reasons. Witness shatters the illusion that "everyone's doing it" by demonstrating that outsiders have an interest in knowing precisely who is committing crimes.

Witness can shape international understanding regarding the nature of crimes and the need for action to stop or ameliorate their impact. While it is rarely the case that outside states and organizations are unaware of mass atrocities, they have historically been reluctant to believe sporadic reports, and have been unwilling to take action until sufficient consensus regarding the brutality and impact of the crimes has emerged. Witness can also be critical for obtaining evidence that can be used in future national or international processes for legal redress.

The Escalatory Dynamic

MARO planners must also factor in the escalatory dynamic of mass killings. Mass killing of civilians can intensify and expand very quickly once it begins. We have already discussed the shameful aspects of civilian slaughter. Perpetrators may consciously speed-up their killing in anticipation that they may be either discovered or stopped. The start of massacres (often coupled with a deliberate strategy to incite the population or allied actors) can unleash emotions and fears with exponential effect.

Such situations are particularly likely when the ranks of potential perpetrators are highly elastic. The number and capabilities of those carrying out the killings may expand as the result of a *de facto levée en masse* among citizens or because additional internal or external military or paramilitary forces join in the massacres.

There is no single pattern or explanation for the intensity or spread of mass killing. Genocides can also simmer slowly and flare episodically, as has been the case in Darfur. This constrained dynamic is more common where perpetrators have limited capability or believe that they can escape intervention so long as the level of violence stays below a particular threshold.

Yet the potential for a rapid escalation of violence raises acute challenges for an intervening force. States are generally slow to reach decisions about the use of force, particularly in situations that remain as controversial as humanitarian intervention. Even when states choose to intervene, they often prefer to respond tentatively, as explained in the above discussion of political constraints on military options.

The asymmetry between a rushed genocide and a hesitant political response has important and somewhat contradictory implications for intervention. As U.S. Air Force Officer Clint Hinote observes, "This asymmetry . . . works against those who want to stop mass atrocities. To be successful, a model of military intervention must account for it."[13]

The first obvious implication is the need for a rapid intervention. This type of intervention necessitates advance planning, even if it is more generic than what may be required for a particular crisis. A MARO may not allow months of iterative planning, lengthy assessments regarding transit or overflight, or the significant buildup of forces and equipment at staging bases. A MARO is most likely to require crisis planning, best served by adaptation of an existing military plan (known in military parlance as a deliberate or on-the-shelf plan).

A second implication for intervention is that the speed of response may assume a greater importance as an operational principle than do the mass and firepower of the response. This variation upends conventional military planning and points to the importance of using novel technologies and concepts, such as massing surveillance early on both to verify and deter mass atrocities. Overall, it is evident that a failure to plan in advance, or insistence upon employing force in routine ways only, may result in a MARO mission failure.

Moral Dilemmas

In a MARO, the difference between doing right and wrong is strategically crystalline and tactically elusive. Moral dilemmas are likely to be the least appreciated dimensions of MARO planning and operations, yet they may create the most significant political vulnerabilities for the intervening parties.

The categorization of persons is an *a priori* moral dilemma facing interveners. Where the distinctions between victims and perpetrators cannot be easily recognized or verified, how can interveners determine who belongs to which party? One can easily think of historical examples where the predominant dividing lines were unclear—Nazi Germany murdered not just Jews but homosexuals and other groups; Rwandan *genocidaires* killed moderate Hutu in addition to Tutsi. Even where the distinctions can be discerned, does the intervener accept and work with the divisions or refuse to honor them, crafting responses based solely on the actions or choices of individuals?

In practice, these choices affect everything else the intervening force undertakes. Will the categorization aid or abet the separation of groups of persons in safe zones or refugee camps? Will this penalize neutral parties or endanger dissenters within categories?

Interveners must not only anticipate these dilemmas, but prepare themselves for criticism from interested parties—such as neighboring countries, human rights groups, and diaspora communities. The potential ethical backlash can be debilitating. Instead of producing pride and satisfaction, a MARO operation may cause service members to question the morality of their actions and nations to second-guess their decisions to act.

A MARO is clearly different from many other types of operations in which military forces may engage. In many respects it is more challenging as well.

It requires advance thought and preparation, just as doctrine and education prepare forces for COIN and NEOs and other interventions. But the political emphasis on prevention makes military planning appear bellicose. Political leaders are reluctant to direct the military to prepare for a MARO, while military leaders, already fully occupied, say they will prepare for a MARO when civilian leaders direct them to do so. As a result, the United States may not be better prepared for the next Rwanda than it was in 1994.

Conclusion

Force is the ultimate arbiter of politics and sanction against crime. The United States may choose to galvanize or provide a humanitarian response—or it may find itself confronted with mass atrocities in the course of other operations. Either way, it behooves the U.S. military and other armed forces to be prepared, and ideally, to be prepared collectively. Such preparedness requires developing a common understanding of the special challenges of halting mass atrocities and developing concrete options for a MARO, because, ultimately, R2P may require military action.

Political will is routinely cited as the core problem in preventing genocide. But it is only half the battle. Political will without effective strategies and tactics offers the worst of both worlds: leaders accrue the costs of making bold decisions without reaping the rewards from successful missions. Familiar, rehearsed, well-understood strategies and tactics can, in turn, reduce the political barriers to action, greasing the skids of decision-making in governments and institutions that remain risk averse. Practical capability is intimately connected to political will, and both are essential for fully realizing all aspects of R2P.

As well intentioned as pragmatic preventionists are, their prescriptions do not address either requirement. By making prevention appear to be low-cost and uncontroversial, they do little to buttress political will for genocide prevention—which is precisely when concerted effort is required. And by ignoring the controversy of military intervention, preventionists fail to advocate preparing for the uniquely challenging missions that will inevitably emerge.

Mass atrocities—the systematic and widespread killing of civilians—come in many guises. They are not always free-standing crises requiring controversial decisions about whether to launch a humanitarian intervention. Large scale murder of civilians can grow out of an initially uncontested peacekeeping or humanitarian relief operation. The targeting of civilians, often an element of insurgency or civil war, can develop into a full-blown genocide or mass atrocities with violence on a scale that becomes unacceptable to outside parties. Military actions to halt the targeting of civilians may therefore develop from, or even coexist with, other operational concepts in the context of a larger campaign. It remains to be seen in what context halting mass atrocities will become the next military mission for a leading international power, but the challenge is virtually certain.

Prevention is critically important. In a perfect world, it will preclude the need for a MARO. But as a concept, prevention requires a more rigorous definition and empirical grounding; as a political strategy it begs the question of whether it will be supported to its logical conclusion; and as a practical matter, prevention deserves a backup plan in the event that it fails. The search for political consensus to support R2P should not become an end in itself, blinding supporters to the fundamental underlying purpose of the principle of protection.

Notes

1. Raphael Lemkin, *Axis Rule in Occupied Europe: Laws of Occupation, Analysis of Government, Proposals for Redress* (Washington, D.C., 1944), 79.

2. International Commission on Intervention and State Sovereignty, *The Responsibility to Protect*, (Ottawa, 2001), available at www.iciss.ca/pdf/Commission-Report.pdf (accessed 27 October 2009).

3. UN General Assembly, Sixtieth Session, *Follow Up to the Outcome of the Millennium Summit*, UN Doc. A/60/L.1, 2005, paras. 138–139.

4. See, for example, Claire Applegarth and Andrew Block, "Acting against Atrocities: A Strategy for Supporters of R2P," chapter 7 in this volume.

5. Genocide Prevention Task Force, *Preventing Genocide: A Blueprint for U.S. Policymakers* (Washington, D.C., 2008), available at http://media.usip.org/reports/genocide_taskforce_report.pdf (accessed 27 October 2009).

6. While the report discussed a range of options for using military force for genocide prevention, and called for the United States to address prevention as a unique military mission, it qualified these contributions in two important respects: it detailed only a very limited range of military options and largely avoids the possibility that U.S. leadership will be required in order to galvanize international will.

7. Genocide Prevention Task Force, *Preventing Genocide*, xxii.

8. Ibid., 73.

9. The MARO Project is a project of Harvard University's Carr Center for Human Rights Policy with support from the U.S. Army's Peacekeeping and Stability Operations Institute (PKSOI). It provides a conceptual basis and planning tools for military and non-military actors seeking to halt mass atrocity. More information

is available at www.hks.harvard.edu/cchrp/maro/index.php (accessed 28 January 2010). The term *MARO* is not yet incorporated in U.S. military doctrine.

10. The Stimson Center is conducting work on this issue. See www.stimson.org/home.cfm.

11. Stanley A. McChrystal, *Universal Joint Task List CJCSM 3500.04E* (Washington, D.C., 2008), available at www.dtic.mil/doctrine/jel/cjcsd/cjcsm/m350004c.pdf (accessed 27 October 2009).

12. This similarity was evident during Operation Iraqi Freedom, when the context changed from major combat operations to counterinsurgency. Although many of the tasks and concepts remained the same, U.S. forces were inadequately prepared to carry them out.

13. Clint Hinote, "Campaigning to Protect: Using Military Force to Stop Genocide and Mass Atrocities," (2008), 29, available at www.hks.harvard.edu/cchrp/maro/pdf/Clint_Hinote_Campaigning_to_Protect_Third%20Draft.pdf (accessed 27 October 2009).

SARAH E. KREPS

9

Social Networks and Technology in the Prevention of Crimes against Humanity

In a 2004 speech, then United Nations (UN) Secretary-General Kofi Annan lamented the "conspicuous gaps in our capacity to give early warning of genocide or comparable crimes, and to analyze or manage the information that we do receive."[1] Several years later, the early warning gap remains, but less conspicuously so. Improvements in technology have given the illusion that crimes against humanity might now be anticipated and prevented, but, in fact, most of these technologies—mobile phones, satellites, and unmanned aerial vehicles—are still better suited for identification and documentation than for early warning and prevention.

This chapter takes stock of those technologies and assesses whether or how they are oriented toward early warning of crimes against humanity. It grounds the discussion of technology—specifically mobile phones and satellites—in theories of social networks. In isolation, these technologies may help to document atrocities, but their power to mobilize is realized only when they intersect with the social networks that receive, disseminate, and act on this information.

The chapter gives an overview of the technology available for early warning, including mobile technology, satellites, and unmanned aerial drones, and illustrates their use both in theory and, where those technologies have been used, in practice. Next, the chapter discusses the pathways by which those technologies are effective, including their role in advocacy, recruitment of peacekeepers, and as deterrents for future crimes against humanity.

The author would like to thank Ariela Blatter, Lars Bromley, Patrick Meier, and the participants of the Harvard Crimes against Humanity workshop for their valuable comments on this manuscript.

It turns to the tradeoffs associated with these technologies, addressing international legal issues related to sovereignty and the relative willingness of non-governmental organizations (NGOs) to assist with the employment of some technologies but not of others. The chapter concludes with ideas for future research, including ways to focus more on early warning and prediction, since many of the technologies discussed here are largely restricted to identification and documentation.

The Organizing Power of Social Networks

Using technology for early warning is closely coupled with the idea of social networks. Without a large network of users, technology alone has limited impact on early warning. But, technology gives social networks a way to organize and a way to amplify their effects. This section briefly discusses the idea of social networks and its intersection with technology.

The concept of social networks is not new. In his travels to the United States, Tocqueville observed that "Americans form associations for no matter how small a matter" and that by organizing, individuals found a "powerful means of action."[2] The idea was that groups of people bound by a common purpose could bring more action than could acting alone. The power of associations was a double-edged sword, however. On the one hand, Tocqueville implied that it was no accident that the most democratic country was also the one with the most associations. On the other, associations that had no hope of becoming the majority could become violent; they could become rallying points for war rather than for persuasion.[3]

What has changed through the introduction of technology is that these associations or social networks now have more efficient ways to organize. As Portes has noted, social networks are "not a natural given and must be constructed" through investment strategies that seek to institutionalize the relationships among individuals.[4] Technology is a group-forming tool. It helps to construct those networks.[5] Providing an efficient means of social connectivity, mobile phones and the Internet facilitate the construction of relationships. Replying to all on an email, for example, can communicate to far more people far more quickly than writing individual letters.[6] The idea of "smart mobs"—groups that come together through technology—is that people with communication and computation devices can organize their behavior quickly, even if they do not know each other.[7]

As with associations in general, technology-based networks create a social paradox: they can provide a public good or be dangerous tools for coordinating large-scale harm. By organizing in large numbers, they are more likely to pressure governments to be accountable, and in this sense, they provide a public good. Mass text messages to mobile phones arguably produced the widespread protests in Manila that led to the collapse of President Joseph Ejercito Estrada's government in the Philippines. The power of technology and social networks can also "amplify the capabilities of people whose intentions are malignant," however, as we saw when the perpetrators of the Rwandan genocide incited violence by using the rudimentary technology of radio to foment brutality.[8]

The more diffused that technology becomes, the more powerful the "mobile many" become.[9] As the number of network-compatible users grows, the value of the network grows exponentially.[10] Its potential value becomes clear through data on technology users. Just a decade ago, accessibility to mobile phones was mostly limited to developed countries. Since then, developing countries have been enticed by the relative affordability of mobile phones, have skipped over landlines, and have directly gone to mobile technology. In 2001, Nigeria had 500,000 landlines. By 2007, it had 30 million mobile phone subscribers. A growing number of people have access, even in areas that lack stable peace; mobile phone companies have been eager to expand into new markets and have been willing to invest in networks in countries such as the Democratic Republic of the Congo. Jeffrey Sachs has called the cell phone "the single most transformative technology for development."[11]

The nexus of social networks and technology has considerable implications for crisis and conflict management. The next sections look at how two different types of technology—the mobile phone and satellites—come together with social networks to anticipate and act against the perpetration of crimes against humanity.

Mobile Technology

In addition to their growing availability, what makes mobile phones useful is that their products, such as text messages—also called short message service or SMS—are multi-directional. Unlike older hub-and-spoke forms of communication such as the radio, mobile phone communications are decentralized and a SMS can be sent to an entire network of users, which then can be further distributed to an additional network of users. The nature of SMS allows perpetrators to incite large-scale violence quickly—part of the paradox—but it also can be used to mobilize counter-measures. In January 2008, Kenyans received text messages to register their electoral dissent through violence, and ethnic violence spread quickly as 800 Kenyans were killed.[12] By the same logic, however, counter-responses were just as rapid. Rather than trying to shut down the SMS system, an approach that the government had considered, the Kenyan government kept the SMS system active, which allowed users to send messages of calm that helped to counter the bellicose messages.[13]

Beyond their palliative effect, mobile phones are vehicles for collective intelligence; each person with access to a mobile phone is a source of communication that is "visible, recordable, and/or transferable to other people over time."[14] By virtue of living in a conflict area, locals are in a position to act as citizen journalists, identifying, collecting, and distributing information on pre-conflict unrest, the early onset of violence, or post-conflict destabilization. This decentralized, peer-to-peer, indeed, even "leaderless" approach to conflict management contrasts with the centralized model of information dissemination in which government authorities have a monopoly on public relations messages, set the agenda for the media, and the media then plays a belated role in documenting the crisis.[15] It also contrasts with mainstream journalism, which tends to arrive in a conflict zone to document violence once it has commenced and leaves after it appears to have been resolved.

The social network function enters when the products of citizen journalism—text, photos, micro-blogging or even video sent by SMS—reach their audience. The products may be shared directly with groups that are in a position to offer a large-scale response to the crisis, whether governments or NGOs. Increasingly useful is for tactical level data to be incorporated into a wiki that would, for example, merge these data with a Google map, creating an integrated graphical representation of the location, type, and magnitude of violence.[16] The result, a data "mash-up," provides information about the spatial and temporal dynamics of violence and is more useful and actionable than highly aggregated macro-indices.

The potential of this technology, especially at the intersection of social networks, showed promise during Kenya's 2008 electoral violence. One particular platform, Ushahidi, was launched to "crowd-source" crisis information.[17] In other words, it provided a platform that coordinated data that were input from a large number of citizens. Using mobile phones or the web, citizens contributed data on riots, looting, rape, and displacements, which were then aggregated and served as a collective source of intelligence. This information was then overlaid on a Google map to show when and where specific violent acts had occurred. Citizens then gained situational awareness about geographical areas to avoid, and the government learned about where and in what manner to respond. Access to relatively inexpensive mobile technology and the availability of a few citizen bloggers offered a way to collect information on the violence. The result was a low-cost global campaign to address the crisis in Kenya.[18]

In analyzing the relative timeliness of this crowd-sourcing platform versus the mainstream media, Meier and Brodock made three observations. First, the mainstream media had been the first to document the casualty count. Second, however, citizen journalists were the first onsite and, therefore, the first to document the early episodes of violence well before the mainstream media began reporting on the violence.[19] Third, the nature of the mapping platform meant that citizen data could provide real-time updates and document and publicize violent episodes that were omitted in mainstream media accounts.[20]

Geospatial Technologies

Based on the premise that a picture may be worth a thousand words, governments and NGOs have increasingly relied on geospatial images as a tool for early warning. These images fall generally under the heading of remote sensing, which refers to "instrument-based techniques employed in the acquisition and measurement of spatially organized . . . data/information on some property(ies) . . . by applying one or more recording devices not in physical, intimate contact with the item(s) under surveillance."[21] Remote sensing collects data through a variety of instruments, including lasers, radar systems, and seismographs.

To identify crimes against humanity, an increasingly common tool is geospatial, overhead satellites that collect information on the ground. The general approach involves using publicly or commercially accessible high-resolution satellite imagery to document the scale and method of human rights abuses and the areas affected by such abuses. Mapping information from conflict zones—such as field data on dislocations, the destruction of villages, and ethnic cleansing—onto satellite imagery makes this application even more powerful.[22]

One version of geospatial technology are infrared sensors, used to track variations in energy signatures across a geographical area. To illustrate how these might be used to document crimes, one study collected infrared satellite images of Baghdad and detected power usage—reflected as a light signature that is a proxy for civilian activity—across neighborhoods. The weather satellite images taken in 2006 showed a drop in the light signature of 57 percent in a Sunni neighborhood in the East and 80 percent in a neighborhood in the West. Meanwhile, light in the Shia-dominated, impoverished Sadr City remained constant. The images were then mapped onto a daytime image of Baghdad and the areas where light signatures had declined corresponded with areas that had experienced neighborhood ethnic cleansing.[23] While the technology was unable to prevent the violence from occurring, the study showed how it could be useful in identifying and documenting it in future cases.

Another form of imagery that has promise but is not yet used widely is the normalized difference vegetation index, which distinguishes between healthy, stronger vegetation—which is associated with a particular energy signature—and barren terrain. This form of imagery is particularly effective where perpetrators of crimes have engaged in a "scorched earth" approach with respect to their target population. Satellite data from the genocide in Guatemala (1979–1986) showed that dramatic deforestation corresponded directly with the "Ixil Triangle" of settlements destroyed by the military. In the Rwandan case, changes in terrain on satellite imagery also showed degradation resulting from mass dislocation of Tutsi affected by the genocide. Information on known geographical distribution of genocide activity, mapped onto before and after satellite imagery, confirms that the changes in vegetation corresponded closely with patterns of genocide.[24]

These academic studies of satellite imagery show how this technology might be used to document genocide, but, in many cases, they have had limited utility because the studies have merely been used to demonstrate the concept *post hoc* rather than in real-time. In some cases, however, satellite imagery has been used in practice to identify and document ongoing crimes, with an eye toward cessation. The earliest case that used satellite images in this way was the U.S. Agency for International Development's (USAID) use of high-resolution imagery to verify claims of human rights abuses in Darfur at a time when there were unconfirmed reports of destroyed villages. Imagery came from a commercial source and helped to build a diplomatic case for more aggressive humanitarian efforts in Darfur.[25] Whether this usage had stemmed human rights abuses remains unclear.

Since the USAID program demonstrated the potential of using geospatial technology to document atrocities, NGOs have begun to collaborate with technical experts to replicate those successes. In one high visibility program, Crisis in Darfur, Google Earth partnered with the U.S. Holocaust Memorial Museum to map the crimes and disorder in Darfur. The program uses images from Google Earth's satellite and couples those with data from the Holocaust Museum, the U.S. Department of State, the UN, individual photographers, and NGOs to show the magnitude and location of the janjaweed militia and Sudanese forces' destruction in the region.[26] Despite the laudable goals of the project, the process of data collection was no small task, and the information became outdated soon after the launch, suggesting the need for real-time mapping that can provide a more dynamic picture of a conflict area.[27]

Eyes on Darfur, a partnership between Amnesty International and the American Association for the Advancement of Science (AAAS), uses low orbit, high-resolution commercial satellites to track troop movements, refugees, and destruction of villages, showing the human rights impact of the militia groups.[28] The project builds on the use of satellites that analyzed forced evictions in Zimbabwe in June 2005. Satellite images dramatically illustrated the destruction of the Porta Farm community in Zimbabwe and the relocation of political opponents of the regime.[29] It is now used to detect human rights violations in Darfur through imagery, but intends to expand to infrared technologies that could pick up variations in light by way of monitoring disturbances to habitation in conflict environments.[30]

Imagery for Mobilization, Deterrence, and Prosecution

The idea of using satellite technology in the human rights context turns on the basic argument that images are powerful tools. Whether in conjunction with social networks, or alone, these images may be effective in promoting advocacy and awareness, deterrence, and contributing to the legal prosecution of violations of human rights. This section addresses each of those intended effects in turn.

The first pathway by which overhead imagery may be effective returns to the idea of social networks as a tool for organization. If pictures say a thousand words, and millions of people have access to those pictures, then the mobilizing effects are potentially enormous. The logic that action requires mobilization and that mobilization requires a clear understanding of why action is necessary have motivated both the Google Earth-Holocaust Museum project and Eyes on Darfur. Images show the remnants of homes, schools, and mosques destroyed by militia groups, the locations of displaced people in camps, and villages that have been damaged or destroyed (i.e., the "after" picture). Eyes on Darfur goes a step further and presents a before-and-after view of areas in Darfur to show dramatically the effects of destruction. It then links those images with a site that generates an automatic letter to the U.S. Secretary of State urging faster and fuller deployment of the UN Africa Union Mission in Darfur (UNAMID). The crowd-sourcing element—Google Earth has about 200 million users—then has a multiplier effect on mobilization efforts. These projects have sought to change levels of awareness and mobilize advocacy that would be impossible absent both the images and the ability to broadcast them to a large number of persons.

Awareness helps to mobilize the general population, which can help to put conflicts such as Darfur on the international agenda. More directly, increased awareness could make it easier to mobilize states' contributions to peacekeeping operations. UNAMID, for example, has suffered from insufficient troops, poor logistical support, and little firepower, and the international community has had challenges in fulfilling the goal of a well-equipped, 26,000-person peacekeeping force.[31] Among the explanations for why contributions have been insufficient is a sense of apathy among possible troop-contributing countries, less out of insensitivity and more out of a lack of awareness of the situation's gravity. Documenting the scorched earth approach to villages in Darfur, for example, would clearly illustrate the need for a more robust peacekeeping force.[32] Images could demonstrate to troop-contributing countries why they need to act; similarly, they could mobilize domestic audiences to put pressure on their governments to provide more resources.

The second pathway by which satellite images could affect crimes against humanity is by creating a version of deterrence. Knowing that the region is essentially under international surveillance makes it considerably more difficult for the perpetrators of abuses to conduct those actions and believe that they are doing so in an information vacuum. On the contrary, the visual documentation of massacres creates a virtual fish bowl in which actions become transparent to a large number of outsiders. The publicity of these satellite-based programs coupled with the actual images that they deliver create more of a sense of accountability and, presumably, deterrence for Sudan's President Omar al-Bashir, for example, than if there were no documentation of these actions.[33]

Third, the images may ultimately serve as evidence of atrocities for legal proceedings. One problem, though, is that the images are less capable of attributing causality or assigning culpability, but they can, nonetheless, measure destruction and be a powerful way to document atrocities. Satellite imagery of dislocation in Zimbabwe showed that the effects were of such a scale that they had to have been the result of a concerted effort by a government-backed entity acting against political opponents. Zimbabwe Lawyers for Human Rights, a NGO, used imagery as evidence when prosecuting the human rights case in the African Court on Human and Peoples' Rights.[34] During the September 2007 military crackdown in Burma, the AAAS requested commercial satellite images that showed evidence of the military clashes with demonstrators. Rights groups then used the evidence to support lobbying efforts for a UN-sponsored intervention in Burma.[35]

While the use of satellite technology has helped to document past or existing atrocities, its current usage is less equipped to anticipate future atrocities. One reason is that the programs tend to be directed toward awareness of and mobilization for existing conflicts; as such, their partnerships with commercial satellites are similarly targeted. Their goal is not to mine a trove of global photographs but to hone in on a particular area that is known to have experienced conflict. The result is largely a downstream documentation of atrocities rather than an upstream prediction.

Unmanned Aerial Vehicles

Unmanned aerial vehicles (UAVs), as the name implies, are pilotless vehicles that fly either pre-programmed or by remote-control. In the context of crimes against humanity, their utility is largely in reconnaissance, in which they perform as remote sensing devices that can collect imagery, whether as video, color images, or radar imagery of moving targets on the ground. Whereas satellites are useful for illustrating the broad scope of the problem, UAVs can target an area of interest, dwell there for a period of time, and collect information on suspicious behavior.

As the next section on tradeoffs suggests, UAVs have the advantage of being less costly, intrusive, and controversial than sending in troops. They are, nonetheless, more intrusive than a satellite or mobile technology and might elicit less international or host-country support.[36] With those constraints in mind, potentially even more appealing is the use of nanotechnology materials or micro-nanotechnology mapped onto UAVs, which would enhance their stealth function. Nanotechnology implies creating materials built on a very small (nano) scale. MIT's Institute for Soldier Nanotechnologies is researching nano-scale materials that can "reproduce the light that would pass through as if the soldier were not there, creating an effect approaching invisibility."[37] In other words, these materials could alter the way a soldier reflects light to give the same impression as though he were not there. That same material, integrated into a UAV, could replicate that invisibility and convert a small UAV into one that is even more difficult to discern and target than a traditional UAV.

A related path is to use nanotechnology to make even smaller sensors and micro-aerial or even nano-aerial vehicles (MAVs and NAVs). MAVs are highly sensitive and GPS-guided, but they become increasingly unidentifiable because of the size but also the form that they can take, such as resembling a small bird and even a flying insect.[38] The next generation is the NAV, whose prototype is less than three inches and no more than one-third of an ounce; it can perform both indoor and outdoor missions and uses bio-mimicry to conceal its role in reconnaissance and surveillance.[39]

Tradeoffs with Technology

Previous sections have indirectly noted the tradeoffs of the technologies that may be employed to identify and document crimes against humanity; this section treats those issues more directly. Those tradeoffs suggest wisdom to their use under certain conditions and recommend against their use in others.

In this sense, it is analytically useful to think of these technologies on a non-intrusive–intrusive continuum, in which mobile phone technologies are on the non-intrusive end, in that they are available to and the most likely to be employed by local civilians rather than outside actors. On the other end are UAVs, which may be the most intrusive, have the trappings of military technology, and are controversial in that they require crossing into a state's sovereign territory. This latter characterization has implications for how they might be employed, both from technical and legal standpoints. Somewhere in the middle, though, closer to the non-intrusive end, is satellite technology, which is located at such a point that it does not infringe on a state's sovereignty, though it is also not permissive in that the target state has little say over whether it comes under satellite scrutiny.

The increasingly widespread use of mobile phone technology creates the potential for citizen-level communications that can quickly identify and disseminate information about crises. Though this community-based response is non-intrusive in terms of a state's sovereignty, it does require that enough individuals be in proximity to the violence that they can document and report it. As such, it comes with perils. For example, at some point, the level of violence could cross a threshold where even remaining in the area becomes hazardous; the result is likely displacement of people, and with that, displacement of any citizens available to report on the violence.

One way to document violence and displacement without individuals being exposed to crimes is to do so from a distance. Satellites have the advantage of offering a range of information without needing to be in direct contact with the conflict. While they do not technically violate another state's sovereignty, they are more intrusive than citizen-level data collection, since the source of geospatial information is through third-party collection rather than from the government or opposition group within the country. It is less intrusive than a UAV, but it is still able to produce detailed imagery of conflict, whereas mobile phone technology tends to be limited to reports of episodes rather than visual evidence.

Nonetheless, geospatial technology has some technological flaws that inhibit its utility in documenting atrocities. Commercial satellites are vulnerable to poor weather conditions. Many satellites cannot penetrate cloud-cover, so weather can be used or even manipulated to obscure suspicious activities. One way India was able to conduct its nuclear test in 1998 without the CIA satellites identifying preparations for the test was for engineers to time their activities to coincide with intense sandstorms. The presence of the sand clouds "effectively blind[ed] the two KH-11 'Keyhole' photo-imagery spy satellites."[40] Because satellites have difficulty in seeing through cloud cover, atrocities committed during a rainy season might go undocumented. Satellites are further impeded by dense ground cover. Efforts to analyze human rights abuses in Burma, for example, were obscured by the thick jungle, quickly regenerating vegetation, and cloud cover. Ultimately, the satellites were able to document thirty-one of seventy reported human rights abuse cases, but UAVs would have been able to target these locations irrespective of whether they were taking place in the middle of the jungle or during a cloudy day.[41]

A further challenge to satellite technology is the predictable timing of their revisit rates, which makes them easy for a perpetrator, looking to escape scrutiny, to evade. Indian nuclear scientists seeking to escape scrutiny in 1998 also timed their activities around the revisit rates of CIA satellites, which speaks to a structural problem associated with this technology. Satellites revolve hundreds of miles above the earth and, therefore, cannot dwell on a particular area. For example, the Landsat TM satellite can only detect changes every sixteen days because of its revisit rate. In most cases, the orbital elements are released publicly; only for more classified satellite assets is that information not publicly available, and in those cases, minimal technical means—the use of stopwatches, sky maps, and binoculars—are needed to track satellites.[42] Though it would be impossible to hide macro-level trends behind revisit rates, perpetrators could easily time particular atrocities for a time when a satellite is not overhead.

One of the most significant limitations of satellite technology is that human rights and development organizations rely on a limited number of satellites belonging to commercial firms. Those images not only tend to be costly to procure, which deters their broader use, but they are reliant on the orbit of those firms' satellites, which travel in a fixed, non-maneuverable path. When the organizations receive a tip on human rights abuses, they place an order for imagery on a specific set of coordinates. They must then wait for the satellite to pass overhead. If larger, competing orders supersede those of the human rights group, they wait even longer. Even if the satellite does take photos, clouds may block the image, which requires waiting until the satellite passes the target in its next cycle. Such data are therefore far from real-time. If a new conflict breaks out at a location that does not intersect with the orbital path of a particular satellite, then imagery data may not even be available, or will be slow to arrive.[43]

Because of these limitations related to weather patterns, timing, and commercial availability, the use of UAVs could offer a possible alternative or perhaps be supplemental to satellites under certain conditions. Because they are intrusive, UAVS are generally able to sidestep the challenges faced by satellites. They can fly below cloud cover, within dense vegetation, and even into buildings. That they can dwell over a particular area and obtain persistent coverage of ongoing conflict also may make them targets. Smaller UAVs are less likely to draw fire than the larger ones, and the nanotechnology reduces that problem even further. Moreover, because of their relative low cost, the loss of some UAVs is far from catastrophic, especially compared to the loss of a manned aircraft. One important tradeoff, however, is between size, range, and cost. Small UAVs, which are affordable, also have a limited range. Larger UAVs have a range of 500 miles but are extremely expensive.

Legal Issues

From a technical standpoint, each of these technologies contributes data that together help to provide a more complete picture of where and how crimes against humanity are being undertaken. Ideally, they would all be part of the response toolkit, but in practice, legal questions—specifically, the issue of intrusiveness and how it affects sovereignty—affect the conditions under which these technologies could be used and by whom.

For reasons already discussed, mobile phone technology is used at the citizen level, is non-intrusive, and, therefore, has no attendant legal obstacles. Even if satellites collect similar data and images as do UAVs, they do not technically violate any legal rules of sovereignty. Conventional law on airspace reflects maritime law, which defines a state's territorial limit at 12 nautical miles, or 22.4 kilometers.[44] Satellites do not violate a state's sovereignty because the low-earth orbit satellites operate at least 100 kilometers from the earth's surface. UAVs, however, violate sovereign airspace insofar as they operate well below the 22.4 kilometer threshold.

These legal issues first have a bearing on whether international authorization is needed. UAVs are less intrusive than deploying troops; nonetheless, they would require either the permission of the host state or authorization by the UN for their deployment. In contrast, satellites have the advantage that their images, in many cases, are commercially available (albeit costly) and, therefore, do not require additional international authorization.

In addition, since UAVs violate another state's sovereignty, many NGOs will not participate in or offer financial support to a particular genocide prevention or awareness mission when such technology is employed. The policy of Amnesty International, for example, is not to participate in a mission where sovereignty has been violated and authorization has not been granted.[45] The problem with such a policy, though, is that a state that is actively or tacitly involved in atrocities is unlikely to consent to an assertive peace enforcement mission. For example, a peacekeeping mission operating in Darfur prior to the passage of Resolution 1769 might have been legitimate but not legal. Employing a technology such as UAVs would therefore have been seen by some NGOs as a military instrument that violated the Sudan's sovereignty and, as such, these organizations would not have been able to offer their support. Absent state consent and UN authorization, the use of UAVs might mean less of a multidimensional mission with NGO involvement and more of a narrow military operation. The use of nanotechnology might make the appearance of violating sovereignty less flagrant, but would, nonetheless, cross the technical threshold of legality and possibly reduce NGO commitment.

Conclusion

Though these advanced technologies existed a decade ago, their application in identifying and documenting crimes against humanity did not. Often through the power of social networks, these applications have already demonstrated their potential for providing information about the location and nature of the violence. More information is not necessarily better, however. This perspective explains the appeal of technologies, such as mash-ups, that aggregate raw source data into a single presentation accessible to nonspecialists. The visual products are more likely to mobilize the public than are unfiltered raw data. They are also more helpful to elites, who often must make decisions with too much information and not enough time. A mashup is a way to distill information and inform decisions in order to commit resources more effectively.[46]

The relative novelty of these applications implies that there is more work to be done. A first step is to establish causality. Much of this chapter has regarded technology as a potential silver bullet for crimes against humanity. Large numbers of citizens are a source for information, and technology is an effective vehicle for organizing that information and mobilizing a response. This assumed link between technology and effective responses may, however, be a leap of faith. To date, there are virtually no studies that evaluate causality or whether the application of a particular technology stems human rights violations in practice. But, because some of these technologies are costly, it makes sense to understand whether and how they work before suggesting that such technologies be implemented more broadly.

A second step is to address the criticism that, in most cases, the new technologies are not structured to *anticipate* conflict. They do well in identifying and documenting the conflict, but the ideal goal should be conflict prevention, which in principle requires early warning and prediction. Satellites, for example, are useful in documenting conflict once it has reached a high enough level that a NGO is willing to invest in commercial satellite imagery, but they do not provide a way to predict new outbreaks.

Therefore, future research might assess how to merge academic models, technology, and networks in a way that would inform upstream prevention efforts rather than downstream identification and documentation once a conflict had begun. Statistical studies have identified, with a reasonable degree of accuracy, the factors that precede genocide or politicide, such as prior genocide, magnitude of political upheaval, and autocracy, to name a few.[47] Countries where these risk factors are present might be put on a watch list and be tracked geospatially through community-based mobile technologies. One problem with these factors is that few lend themselves to early, actionable responses since several—such as the "occurrence of prior mass atrocities"—are fixed. Resources are limited, so it is difficult to collect and analyze satellite images on all high-risk countries. Thus, more work needs to be done to incorporate patterns and risk factors into the evolution of technology. Despite their general focus on downstream efforts, however, the technological and social advances of the last decade should not be underestimated.

Notes

1. Secretary-General Kofi Annan, address to the Stockholm International Forum, Stockholm, Sweden, 26 January 2004, available at www.un.org/Pubs/chronicle/2004/issue1/0104p4.asp (accessed 18 April 2009).

2. Alexis de Tocqueville, *Democracy in America* (New York, 1969), 514.

3. Ibid., 194.

4. Alejandro Portes, "Social Capital: Its Origins and Applications in Modern Sociology," *Annual Review of Sociology*, XXIV (1998), 1–24.

5. Clay Shirky, *Here Comes Everybody: The Power of Organizing without Organizations* (New York, 2009).

6. Clay Shirky, "Here Comes Everybody," talk at Harvard Law School, Cambridge, Massachusetts, 28 February 2008, available at www.youtube.com/watch?v=A_0FgRKsqqU (accessed 11 April 2009).

7. Howard Rheingold, *Smart Mobs: The Next Social Revolution* (New York, 2002), xii.

8. Ibid., xiii, 157; Allan Thompson, *The Media and the Rwandan Genocide* (Ann Arbor, 2007).

9. Rheingold, *Smart Mobs*, 157–182.

10. Metcalfe's law says that the value increases by the square of its users. See George Gilder, "Metcalfe's Law and Legacy," *Forbes ASAP* (13 September 1993).

11. Jack Ewing, "Upwardly Mobile in Africa," *Business Week* (13 September 2007).

12. Shashank Bengali, "How Kenya's Election Was Rigged," *McClatchy* (31 January 2008).

13. Joshua Goldstein and Juliana Rotich, "Digitally Networked Technology in Kenya's 2007–2008 Post-Election Crisis," *Internet and Democracy Case Study Series* (Cambridge, MA, 2008), 5. That the Kenyan government considered shutting down cell towers correctly suggests a vulnerability, particularly in repressive regimes.

14. Leysia Palen and Sophia B. Kiu, "Citizen Communications in Crisis: Anticipating a Future of ICT-Supported Public Participation," CHI 2007 Proceedings, San Jose, California, 28 April–3 May 2007, 727–736.

15. The logic of decentralized networking is illustrated in Ori Brafman and Rod A. Beckstrom, *The Starfish and the Spider: The Unstoppable Power of Leaderless Organizations* (New York, 2006).

16. Tactical level data are data from the streets, rather than big-picture, strategic images that might come from satellites.

17. Crowd-sourcing is defined as "The act of taking a function traditionally performed by an employee and outsourcing it to an undefined, generally large group of people." It is a form of collective intelligence in which large groups of people contribute (usually virtually) to a specific task. See Chris Baker, "Crowdsourcing and Virtual Worlds," *Wired* (8 November 2006).

18. Goldstein and Rotich, "Digitally Networked Technology," 6.

19. See Patrick Meier and Kate Brodock, "Crisis Mapping Kenya's Election Violence: Comparing Mainstream News, Citizen Journalism and Ushahidi," (2008), available at http://irevolution.wordpress.com/2008/10/23/mapping-kenyas-election-violence/ (accessed 30 November 2008). See also discussion of this phenomenon in chapters 1, 7, and 10 of this book.

20. Meier and Brodock, "Crisis Mapping."

21. Remote Sensing Tutorial, available at http://rst.gsfc.nasa.gov/ (accessed 14 November 2008).

22. American Academy of Arts and Sciences, "Geospatial Technologies and Human Rights," available at http://shr.aaas.org/geotech/whatcanGISdo.shtml (accessed 15 November 2008).

23. John Agnew, "Baghdad Nights: Evaluating the US Military 'Surge' Using Nighttime Light Signatures," *Environment and Planning A*, XL (2008), 2285–2295. In this case, the satellite imagery was low resolution, which means the study is subject to other possible interpretations.

24. Russell Schimmer, "Indications of Genocide in the Bisesero Hills, Rwanda, 1994," GSP Working Paper No. 32 (New Haven, nd); Philip Verwimp, "Death and Survival during the 1994 Genocide in Rwanda," *Population Studies*, LVIII (2004), 233–245.

25. See www.usaid.gov/locations/sub-saharan_africa/sudan/satelliteimages.html and "Darfur Satellite Imagery," *Global Security* (24 June 2004), available at www.globalsecurity.org/military/world/war/sudan-imagery.htm (accessed 15 November 2008).

26. The project maps data from these organizations onto maps from Google Earth to provide a geographical depiction of where and how the crisis has unfolded. See www.ushmm.org/maps/projects/darfur/ (accessed 23 November 2008).

27. The Humanitarian Sensor Web, for example, incorporates real-time mapping and distributes information to UN field-based agencies. Author's correspondence with Patrick Meier, Harvard Humanitarian Initiative (14 November 2008).

28. Eyes on Darfur is a partnership between Amnesty International, AAAS's Geospatial Technologies, and Human Rights Project. See www.eyesondarfur.org/index.html. See also Kimberley Ebner, "Amnesty Uses Commercial Satellite Imagery to Monitor Darfur," *Jane's Defense Weekly* (13 June 2007).

29. See www.eyesondarfur.org/satellitetech.html (accessed 16 November 2008).

30. Nora Boustany, "Amnesty Launches 'Eyes on Darfur' Site," *Washington Post* (7 June 2007), A24.

31. Derek Kilner, "UN Continues Struggle with Peacekeeping in Darfur," *Voice of America* (10 June 2008).

32. Author's interview with Ariela Blatter, Amnesty International (4 October 2008).

33. "Google Earth, Holocaust Museum Focus in on Sudan's Darfur," *Associated Press* (11 April 2007).

34. Boustany, "Amnesty Launches 'Eyes on Darfur' Site," A24.

35. Duncan Graham-Rowe, "Satellites Capture Evidence of Burma Crackdown," *New Scientist* (28 September 2007).

36. Douglas Peifer, "Genocide and Airpower," *Strategic Studies Quarterly*, II (2008), 93–124.

37. Jun Wang and Peter J. Dortmans, *A Review of Selected Nanotechnology Topics and Their Potential Military Applications* (Edinburgh, South Australia, 2004), 18.

38. "Itsy-Bitsy Drone," *Defense Tech* (5 April 2005), available at www.defensetech.org/archives/001467.html (accessed 30 October 2008).

39. Jonathan Skillings, "AeroVironment Flies Ahead with 'Nano' Air Vehicle," *CNET* (27 May 2008); Ruijie He and Sho Sato, "Design of a Single-Motor Nano Aerial Vehicle with Gearless Torque-Canceling Mechanism," presentation to the Aerospace Sciences Meeting and Exhibit, Reno, Nevada, 7–10 January 2008.

40. "CIA Searching for Answers behind its India-Nuclear Failure," *Associated Press* (16 May 1998).

41. David Talbot, "Satellite Images Catch Human Rights Violations in Burma," *Technology Review* (28 September 2007).

42. Allen Thomson, "Satellite Vulnerability: A Post-Cold War Issue?" *Space Policy*, XI (1995), 19–30.

43. Author's email correspondence with Lars Bromley, American Academy of Arts and Sciences (26 October 2008).

44. UN Convention on the Law of the Sea, available at ww.un.org/Depts/los/convention_agreements/texts/unclos/closindx.htm (accessed 28 October 2008). See also "Legal Committee—33rd Session," International Civil Aviation Organization, Montreal, Canada, 22 April–2 May 2008, available at www.icao.int/icao/en/leb/mtgs/2008/lc33/docs/LC33_wp4_7e.pdf (accessed 18 April 2009).

45. Author's interview with Blatter (4 October 2008).

46. Kevin M. Cahill, *Emergency Relief Operations* (New York, 2002), 15.

47. Barbara Harff, "No Lessons Learned from the Holocaust? Assessing Risks of Genocide and Political Mass Murder since 1955," *American Political Science Review*, XCVII (2003), 57–73.

JENNIFER LEANING

10 The Use of Patterns in Crisis Mapping to Combat Mass Atrocity Crimes

For most of this decade a terrible conflict has played out in Darfur, yet the international community still has not managed to acquire a reliable estimate of how many people have been killed and under what circumstances. The government of the Sudan successfully blocked all usual means and methods of gathering population-based data on war-related morbidity and mortality in the region. Yet this decade has also seen an explosion in capacities and creative uses of technology to amass information from a variety of indirect sources. The potential now exists for mass atrocity crimes to be identified and tracked through the application of remote sensing and information communication technologies.

A key conceptual and computational bridge must be crossed, however, before that potential can be fully realized. Massive amounts of data can now be gathered but extracting meaning from that mass requires the development of analytical frameworks and computational models that are informed by the empirical ways that human observers make sense of their world. This chapter argues that an essential element in this extraction of meaning from data is the development and use of visual patterns.

The argument in this chapter builds on the suggestion, advanced by many elsewhere, that visualization enhances the capacity to engage with large data sets, apprehend their main findings, and derive from that visual depiction a sense of patterns.[1] The intent here is to revitalize the notion that through the use of patterns, informed and experienced observers can interrogate an "apparent" fact picture, generate deeply relevant questions from that interrogation, and through further research, drive closer to an understanding of what is actually going on, in a given place and time.

The specific focus of this chapter is to examine the potential of visual pattern recognition to expand our understanding of issues of human consequence in crisis settings, particularly major disasters and wars. This potential, once realized, could allow the humanitarian and policy worlds to recognize elements of evolving crises sooner and more coherently than we do now and thus support the development of more relevant and timely strategies than we have presently for mitigating the impact of these crises on human populations.

At the level of populations and population sub-groups, issues of human consequence include visual or visualized patterns of population movement and settlement, shelter options and conditions, population interaction with surface topography and terrain, population adjacency and access to sources of food and water, occurrence of and population response to threats and hazards (military, environmental, disease), and parameters of demographic and epidemiological stability and change.

More intimate aspects of human behavior may possibly be inferred from these population-based patterns, assuming aggregation of previous patterns and fine-grained political, historical, economic, and psychological analysis of what these patterns can tell us about individual and social perceptions, relationships, and choices.

The approach taken here draws eclectically from methods used in the empirical social and natural sciences, particularly those from demography, epidemiology, and geographical mapping techniques. It also invokes normative and analytical frameworks elaborated in law, political science, history, and social psychology, including international humanitarian and human rights law and constructs of human security.

Visualization as Analysis

Human beings apprehend information in visual modes and think about this information generatively in terms of visual adjacencies. These visual adjacencies of data points, which may be displayed in terms of time and geographical space, or in more abstracted relationships, form patterns in the mind's eye. The mind asks questions and raises hypotheses regarding these perceived adjacencies or patterns. These questions and hypotheses become more fully informed when experienced people provide information relating to context and offer interpretations of what is seen. Experienced people, by definition, have acquired a virtual library of patterns and can search, in the new array of data, for patterns that they may recognize from the past.

The use of patterns as a means of understanding the world of observed phenomena has a complex and eclectic history. The word itself, "pattern," straddles different concepts and methods. Advances in mathematics and computational capacities have played significant roles in mobilizing modes of displaying vast amounts of data in visual format and demonstrating the independent intellectual power of pattern formation and recognition. Computer-enhanced graphing and mapping technologies have brought the question of patterns into the mainstream. We can now gather data and information in many categories, levels, and formats and we can increasingly geo-code virtually any of these data. The challenge now is to "make sense" of this flood of input from the empirical world.

The validity of a project that seeks to "make sense" of data gathered through indirect means is based on three premises:

1) That aspects of human consequence—where human beings act or are acted upon—occur in settings that can be characterized in terms of time and place.

2) That these aspects can be identified and assessed by gathering data of various kinds and interpreting them through the use of standard and evolving techniques of inference, hypothesis generation, and hypothesis confirmation through iteration of results. These scientific methods, applied to qualitative or quantitative data, rely on probabilistic determinations of what is most likely to be the case, based on what we have seen before.[2]

3) That the opportunity to visualize these data, depicted in various modes once they have been gathered, leverages enhanced human powers of hypothesis generation and interpretation by strengthening the process of pattern recognition. Also, perhaps more important, visualization of data allows observers to apprehend, through immediate visualization of departures from the patterns that we expect to see, interesting new questions to address.

This chapter proceeds from these premises to argue that these aspects of human consequence, occurring in space and time, can be visualized directly through satellite or land-based imagery or displayed in graphical or mapping formats as reported in real time—prior to deliberate and methodological scientific data gathering and analysis. It is argued that the very act of visualizing these phenomena allows informed observers to discern patterns, raise questions about departure from patterns, and generate relevant hypotheses in advance of, or as a partial substitute for, standard approaches to data acquisition and assessment.

The History

John Snow, in his investigation of the cholera outbreak in London in 1854, was an early adopter of the use of maps to interrogate data.[3] He had compiled lists of deaths from cholera at the household level (number of deaths per day and per week) through the summer of that year and could have let his inquiry rest there. His genius was to incorporate the household data into the second dimension of geography, thus shifting the data to a map of the streets of London. The map, to his interpretive eye, revealed clusters of deaths around certain streets.

A number of possible explanations went through his mind and for various reasons were rejected as not fully accounting for the pattern that he was seeing. (His list of possibilities was wider than necessary since in those days before the germ theory had been established he was wrestling with a phenomenon—infectious disease—whose underlying dynamics were not yet understood.) Finally he hit on a water pump on Broad Street as the possible source of transmission. Deaths from cholera declined after the pump handle was removed, and his hypothesis, based on visualization of a pattern, was confirmed.

Snow is properly hailed as one of the foundational practitioners in public health (because he resorted to advocacy to get the pump handle removed on behalf of the public good) and as one of the founders of the field of epidemiology (where methods are developed to trace the distribution and determinants of conditions and events affecting a given population over a defined time).[4] He is less renowned—perhaps we now take it for granted—for his technical creativity and intuition in realizing that if he could see the data arrayed in space, he might learn something further.

Development of Visual Analysis

The rapid growth of "applied" social science in the years leading up to and during World War II enlisted qualitative and quantitative methods to arrive at "best fit" simplifications of reality. In the years after 1945, amid mounting concerns about accelerating world instability and militarization, social scientists in the U.S. and elsewhere endeavored to understand the behavior and actions of the great powers. Subjects of special interest were the pace of military growth, spending, and strategies; descriptions and interpretations of economic and political trends; and ways to discern social behavior under stress and social attitudes, particularly discontents and latent hostilities.[5] These efforts produced increasingly vast amounts of data and information, which demanded the development of analytical capacities and methods for making sense of the elements that were being gathered.

The search for ways in which data elements could be seen as related to each other, in some causal way or in some other important parameter, has been a long-standing aspect of scholarly activity, and this quest accelerated rapidly in the inter-war years. The field of war studies straddled at least three disciplines (history, sociology, and political science) and a focus on the use of quantitative methods and mathematical models emerged as inter- and intra-disciplinary debates.[6]

It is outside the scope of this chapter to attempt to recapitulate or assess these trends. It is relevant to note, however, that the methods of some of these early empiricists in the study of war did not include visualization, even in rudimentary forms such as charts or graphics. The results of their extensive data aggregation and quantitative modeling were not expressed in readily appreciable conceptual forms, hindering fruitful application in new settings. The opportunity for this crucial outcome—generating ideas that might form the basis for pattern formation, or aggregating data so that it suggested patterns—was not taken up. The failure to communicate visually was important in its own right but also reflective of a deeper incapacity, when one is faced with enormous amounts of data, to recognize how meaning is created and communicated.

An example of one such effort is the magisterial work, *A Study of War*, by Wright.[7] Undertaken in the years after World War I and first published in 1942, this book endeavored to gather all facts and ideas relevant to a general theory of how wars come about and how they might be prevented. It is a grand effort, filled with categories, themes, and subthemes; and it is packed with detailed tables of quantitative information. However, the book relies on few maps and its graphical depictions are infrequent and invariably hard to read. Deep in the appendices is a laboriously derived differential equation that presumably serves as the basis for his overall conclusion, expressed in abstract theoretical terms: the cause of war results from disequilibrium within and among nations in four major categories (technology, law, social organization, and attitudes). Wright's book serves many purposes, but it does not offer generalizations of practical and testable value to apply in dynamic settings of unfolding conflict.

From the 1940s to the 1970s, when the applied social science scholarship was advancing, one needs to look somewhat strenuously to find early instances of the use of graphics to convey an abundance of empirical information. In this period, computational capacities were becoming robust, but the means of displaying large amounts of quantitative or qualitative information in visual formats were not yet highly developed. According to Tufte, who speaks of the "graphically barren years from 1930 to 1970":

> Much of twentieth-century thinking about statistical graphics has been preoccupied with the question of how some amateurish chart might fool a naïve observer. Other important issues, such as the use of graphics for serious data analysis, were largely ignored. At the core of the preoccupation with deceptive graphics was the assumption that data graphics were mainly devices for showing the obvious to the ignorant. It is hard to imagine any doctrine more likely to stifle intellectual progress in a field.[8]

It is of course the power of ideas rather than the deftness of a graphic that determines the durability and influence of intellectual work. Yet, it is striking that two of the most influential scholars dealing with crises and war, Pitirim Sorokin and Raul Hilberg, both based in the evolving traditions of mid-twentieth century social science, did indeed grasp the need to convey their conceptualizations of processes and trends in visual formats.

Sorokin, a sociologist with protean empirical interests, and Hilberg, a documentary historian and political scientist, although contemporaries of Wright, each managed to avoid the turgidity and impenetrability of Wright's approach and certainly steered clear of the quantitative obscurantism of his disciple, Richard Barringer. Their research, compared to the efforts of Wright, was equally grounded in a broad and deep command of historical empirical detail, quantitative facts, and data sets. What distinguishes their work are three main features: a respect for the role of informed judgment and intuition in making sense of the data they amassed; a capacity to frame information in the service of generative ideas and hypotheses regarding relationships among and between events; and a recognition that to transmit complex ideas there is sometimes nothing better than a good visual portrayal of the pattern of relationships that had been discerned.

In this last aspect, their notion of pattern is one that is tied to what can be learned from visual depiction, not analytical depiction: it is a pattern of associational relationships, gathered inductively from masses of evidence and depicted in a graphical mode that empowers comprehension. Their patterns arise from what they see in the data, not from a theoretical relational model that data serve to validate.

In his classic study, *Man and Society in Calamity,* Sorokin sets out to assess the impact of different kinds of historical calamities on human populations.[9] His extensive research and previous writings (captured in twenty-six pages of notes), elegantly persuasive use of specific facts and lists, and eloquent generalizations combine to create a social panorama of centuries of distress that is at once convincing and deeply inquiring. Table 10-1, which encapsulates his research on the effects of famine on human behavior, conveys in a simple format an immense amount of information and brings to the surface a wide array of general observations that could form the basis for much more in-depth study.

The categories are robust and useful. His findings provide guideposts for the initial framing of any information we might receive from a given famine region. In his research on famine, he found cannibalism to be extremely rare, whereas violations of basic honesty and fairness were highly variable. So were we to find, in a current famine area, reports of widespread cannibalism, we might initially mark these reports as perhaps exaggerated, requiring further probing. Yet if observers noted that up to 70 percent of the population had lied about ration cards, we might consider that information unexceptional.

Sorokin explores widely but thinks in patterns. His book is thus highly accessible to experts and general readers alike and it has served as a foundational trove of ideas and hypotheses for those who have followed.

Hilberg was the first historian to make methodical and exhaustive use of the German and Allied archives relating to the Holocaust. His masterful work, *The History of the Destruction of the European Jews*, was begun in 1948 and first published in 1961. In the preface, Hilberg states:

> Only a generation ago, the incidents described in this book would have been considered improbable, infeasible, or even inconceivable. Now they have happened. The destruction of the Jews was a process of extremes. That, precisely, is why it is so important as a group phenomenon. That is why it can serve as a test of social and political theories. But to perform such tests, it is not enough to know that the Jews have been destroyed; one must also grasp how this deed was done. That is the story to be told in this book.[10]

Hilberg's approach was to distill the details from every document, testimony, and fragment of evidence that he could find to describe that "process of extremes." As a historian, he dealt with facts; as a political scientist, he sought patterns. A simple graphic (see figure 10-1) reveals, at the population level, the steps that the reigning authority took in what Hilberg defines as the "destruction process."

Here, in the most simple of figures, is the depiction, in space as well as in time (since the steps are sequential), of a path that has now become forbiddingly familiar. And, providing empirical evidence of the "concentration"

Table 10-1. *How Famine Influences Our Behavior*

Activities Induced by Starvation	*Percentage of Population Succumbing to Pressure of Starvation*	*Percentage of Population Resisting Such Pressure*
Cannibalism (in non-cannibalistic societies)	Less than one third of 1 per cent	More than 99 per cent
Murder of members of family and friends	Less than 1 per cent	More than 99 per cent
Murder of other members of one's group	Not more than 1 per cent	Not less than 99 per cent
Murder of strangers who are not enemies	Not more than 2 to 5 per cent	Not less than 95 per cent
Infliction of various bodily and other injuries on members of one's social group	Not more than 5 to 10 per cent	Not less than 90 per cent
Theft, larceny, robbery, forgery, and other crimes against property which have a clear-cut criminal character	Hardly more than 7 to 10 per cent	Hardly less than 90 to 93 per cent
Violation of various rules of strict honesty and fairness in pursuit of food, such as misuse of rationing cards, hoarding, and taking unfair advantage of others	From 20 to 99 per cent depending upon the nature of the violation	From 1 to 80 per cent
Violation of fundamental religious and moral principles	Hardly more than 10 to 20 per cent	From 80 to 90 per cent
Violation of less important religious, moral, juridical, conventional, and similar norms	From 50 to 99 per cent	From 1 to 50 per cent
Surrender or weakening of most of the aesthetic activities irreconcilable with food-seeking activities	From 50 to 99 per cent	From 1 to 50 per cent
Weakening of sex activities, especially, coitus	From 70 to 90 per cent during prolonged and intense starvation	From 1 to 30 per cent
Prostitution and other highly dishonorable sex activities	Hardly more than 10 per cent	Hardly less than 90 per cent

Source: Pitirim A. Sorokin, *Man and Society in Calamity* (New York: Penguin, 1942), 81.

Figure 10-1. *Steps in the Destruction Process*

			Machinery of Destruction			
			Civil Service	Army	Industry	Party
Steps of the Destruction Process	I	Definition				
		Expropriation				
		Concentration				
	II	Mobile killing operations				
		Deportations				
		Killing center operations				

Source: Raul Hilberg, *The Destruction of European Jews* (New York, 1961), 39.

step, Hilberg tracks the progressive concentration of Jews in two Polish ghettos in 1941 (see table 10-2).

These steps (i.e., definition, concentration, etc.) we now recognize as a repeating pattern in genocide. Further research is needed to see if these steps also pertain to communally based instances of crimes against humanity. Human rights analysts have suggested that when a government begins to identify people on the basis of communal differences (race, ethnicity, language, religion, tribe, and caste), a process may be set in motion that leads to various restrictions on mobility, serious assaults on life and property, and forced migration or violent death.[11] In the field of genocide scholarship, a noted component of early warning is the specification and segregation of particular identity groups.[12]

The graphical depiction of complex data in visually accessible formats has been pursued to good effect in the realm of demography and epidemiology, but these are mid-twentieth century developments. The applications developed for diseases include geographical map notations and time-series. Maps (such as Snow's) appear to have preceded time-series charts, which twentieth century analysts have imposed on the tabulated data methodically gathered by earlier (fifteenth through nineteenth century) observers.[13] Had Ignaz Semmelweis (a contemporary of Snow and the physician who uncovered the process by which puerperal fever was propagated and how it might be prevented) not left his data enmeshed in endlessly long and unreadable tables but instead had developed graphical charts, his crucial findings might

Table 10-2. *Densities in the Ghettos of Warsaw and Łódź*

	City of Warsaw, March 1941	*"Aryan" Warsaw*	*Ghetto of Warsaw*	*Ghetto of Łódź, September 1941*
Population	1,365,000	920,000	445,000	144,00
Area (square miles)	54.6	53.3	1.3	1.6
Rooms	284,912	223,617	61,295	25,000
Persons per room	4.8	4.1	7.2	5.8

Source: Raul Hilberg, *The Destruction of European Jews* (New York, 1961), 152.

have received a much earlier and more favorable hearing among his peers than they did.[14]

Epidemiological interest in the impact of war and crisis on human populations is a relatively recent development (apart from the work of visionaries such as Rudolf Virchow and Florence Nightingale).[15] However, familiarity with analysis and display of large data sets has allowed epidemiologists now engaged with war to advance our understanding of this impact considerably. The techniques are widely diffused throughout the public health community and these professionals, when at work in humanitarian crises, gather and supply the data that can then be robustly analyzed in terms of incidence, prevalence, and trends. These data are usually depicted as graphics of mortality or morbidity, or disease incidence rates across time. It is the compilation of these graphics over time that provides the basis for pattern recognition.

For example, the graphics from a landmark book, *Forced Migration and Mortality*, are presented below to show the refined U-shaped pattern of mortality experienced in flight to and settlement in refugee camps in response to famine.[16] This pattern (see figure 10-2) is created from data recorded during many particular crises, in which public health personnel noted increased deaths as exhausted, ill, and malnourished people reached the camps, and that mortality declined as suitable health and nutrition measures were introduced. This pattern, familiar throughout the humanitarian community, is used as a tool to monitor whether effective interventions have been delivered in an appropriate time frame.

Compare this standard U-shaped pattern to the graph in figure 10-3, an age-sex specific graph of mortality across time from the Katale camp in Zaire in 1994. The slow and ineffectual humanitarian response to a cholera outbreak among the hundreds of thousands of refugees from the Rwandan genocide contributed to this high mortality outcome. It is markedly diver-

Figure 10-2. *Model of Mortality Change in a Forced Migration Situation*

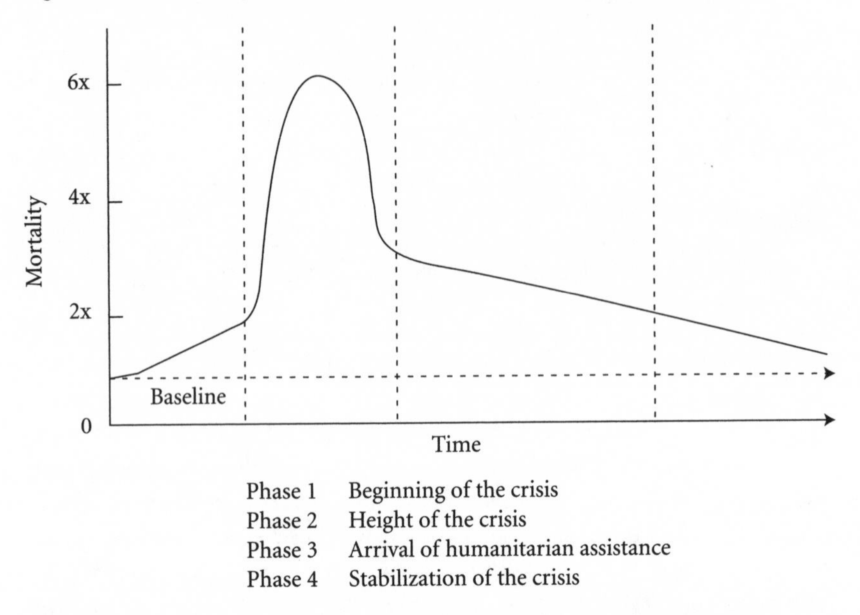

Source: National Research Council, *Forced Migration and Mortality* (Washington, D.C., 2001), 11.

gent from the age-specific death rate curves for stable populations in this part of Africa.[17]

These two graphics represent cumulative data sets, gathered from many observations over many years. They are, in fact, patterns of patterns. As such, these two graphs constitute adequate and robust depictions of recurrent demographic behaviors of populations in war and peace. Confronted with population mortality data from a new event, demographers, epidemiologists, and humanitarian authorities will compare the patterns captured in this new data set against the standard graphs of previously observed experiences of mortality and morbidity. Departures from these standard patterns do not mean that the new data are wrong but that they are unexpected—and warrant vigorous analysis and if need be further data collection for verification and explanation.

Key among these standard processes is attention to data quality, as well as quantity. In crisis areas, information is not prospectively or routinely gathered; documents or incidental data sets may be available, but the usual case in crisis settings is that whatever information one needs, one must gather

Figure 10-3. *Age-Specific Death Rates for Rwandan Refugees in Katale Camp, Zaire, July 17–August 5, 1994, and for Coale-Demeny Life Table "West" Level 12*

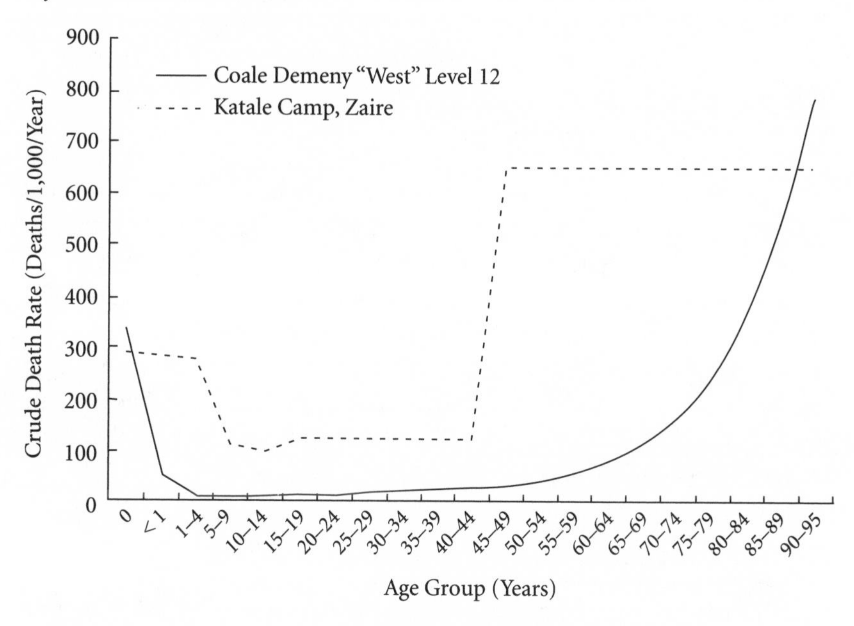

Source: National Research Council, *Forced Migration and Mortality* (Washington, D.C., 2001), 15.

at the time. First, one should obtain contextual information and initial hypotheses from informed observers in the community and from international stakeholders who have been in the region for some time. One should then gather data from many different sources, with the intent to triangulate among these sources, and move quickly to display the data in visual formats. These formats can then be used for intellectual and analytical provocation. Looking at the graphic or provisional pattern elicits further questions and forces a check and re-check of the accuracy and validity of the data that have been gathered. At the same time this examination enlists a search for possible explanations (hypotheses generation). Local observers may be prompted to inject into the discussion unexpected new sources of information relating to context or explanation. Repeating these steps iteratively winnows out serious flaws in data quality, adds further data quantity, and affirms major findings. This iterative process can result in rich data sets, whose descriptive and analytical power can best be expressed through visual patterns.

This process is ultimately probabilistic. Qualitative and quantitative data are gathered in a variety of ways. When they are arrayed in graphics and patterns, one can look for departures between what one has observed and what one might expect from previous instances (e.g., the patterns of received experience, such as standard age-adjusted mortality curves). Departures from the expected will spark questions and point to the need for new explanations. And so the process continues.

In this empirical and inductive approach to finding out about the world, what we seek—the meaning we apply to the endeavor—is never understood to be the "truth." That quest lies in other domains of inquiry. Nevertheless, people caught in war and disaster are confronted with and affected by a reality that the humanitarian and policy community seeks to understand. The successive steps outlined here help to develop a factual picture and interpretation through iterative analysis and pattern formation that seems, over time, to fit best with the mix of externalities and choices that define the outcomes of flight, shelter, disease, death, loss, suffering, and survival that characterize populations in crises.

Humanitarian Actors' Pattern Formation

In terms of data gathering and analysis, the relationship of humanitarian actors to information is distinct in many ways from that of social scientists. The data gathering task for humanitarians is more omnivorous, more based in real time, more tied to local input, more micro in geographic scope, and more limited in time frame. The data gathering is also problem-directed, aimed at uncovering issues that are already known to be vital aspects of threat or survival options for populations in crisis. In this sense, much of the effort to find data proceeds from mental patterns already held. We know that violent attacks on villages have been preceded or accompanied by systematic rape—has that been the experience in this new situation? Not knowing what to look for is, in these contexts, an error as grievous as not looking at all.

The data analysis is tethered more tightly to geographical and visual display, based on the assumption that people act in space as well as in time and on the need to grasp the data relatively quickly and comprehensively. Visual display permits that rapidity of data apprehension. Humanitarian actors value speed as well as accuracy and prize trenchant simplification. Pattern formation and pattern recognition provide ideal routes for direct understanding.

Patterns of events, a time series, patterns based within geographic maps, or patterns showing relationships in relation to other forms of relationships all furnish background understanding and context for the more particular set of interests that are the focus of the inquiry. Much of what we take to be knowledge or information is in the structure of "compared to what" or "what else is going on as well." Patterns are ideal for those who are concerned about departures from the usual state of affairs, because these departures will show up as sentinel events. The presence of these instances, outside the normal curve or pattern, evokes, first of all, attention, and then, depending on whether there is an immediate explanation, further question. Patterns—as opposed to lists of numbers or narrative accounts—allow us to see the full picture, as well as the details within it, literally at a glance. Patterns of events can also be displayed in ways that support discernment of trends through time, transmission or passage of phenomena across space, and variations in degrees of intensity or frequency.

A great range of information from different fields is applicable to pattern formation in crisis mapping settings. The different categories of interest include, for example:

—Geography, human and natural
—Demography, current and past trends
—Social and cultural variables
—Weather conditions and trends
—Agricultural and livestock impacts on land and water
—Market, trade, travel, and financial dynamics
—Fuel and transportation routes
—Weapons design, use, impacts
—Human behavior under various kinds of stress
—History of previous conflicts and responses
—Known behavior of assailants
—Recent seasonal and crisis migrations

From the humanitarian perspective, the patterns of interest that emerge from data relating to these issues will array along the dimensions listed below:

—Sense of geography, settlement, and land use in terms of steady state pressures and options for flight, exit, and hiding

—Changes in settlement and land use when residents are under acute or long-lasting attack

—Dynamics that infringe upon human security, international humanitarian law, and human rights

—Human behavior (individual and group)
  When at risk of or under attack;
  In the context of ethnic cleansing or genocide;
  In the context of fear or repression; and
  In the context of restricted movement
—Parameters, indicators, and escalation scenarios for
  Nation-state war fighting;
  Nation-state counter-insurgency war fighting;
  Sub-state war fighting; and
  War crimes, crimes against humanity (ethnic cleansing, mass killings), and genocide

Information organized along these lines can create a mental framework of alert systems for humanitarian aid personnel. Pattern formation serves to produce recognition heuristics and structures that help each of us to interpret phenomena quickly and usually accurately. These heuristics bear conscious attention, whenever possible, because they need to be updated and revised as new insights are obtained.

A recent article on improving humanitarian efforts to protect civilians in conflict settings included guidance that does not convey—but reflects—patterns of experience that seasoned aid personnel have developed.[18] Experts listed markers of community behavior that they knew had proved significant in many past operations and had proved sensitive to early degradations or improvements in civilian security (see table 10-3). Their effort was undertaken to prompt imagination and cognition; to support informed, natural observation; to guide newly arrived personnel; and to stimulate those who, through burn-out or fatigue, had ceased to take adequate notice of the perceptible nuanced shifts in their daily surroundings.

Methods for acquiring these data are varied, and the data may be subject to statistical analysis expressed as trend lines, scatter plot diagrams, as various detail levels of geo-spatial organization, or as qualitative associations and contextual understandings derived from inputs such as photographs or narratives that have been evaluated or tested by repetition through time.

Patterns can be expressed in two or three dimensions and be presented as static snapshots or across appropriate resolutions in time and space. A most important feature of pattern formation is that the data, to be robust and attentive to the kinds of issues we are concerned about, must be gathered or amassed from a rich array of sources. What is envisioned is that as the process of pattern formation and recognition matures, our capacity to identify a parsimonious set of highly relevant indicators will become increasingly more effective.

Table 10-3. *Examples of Potential Markers of Civilian Protection*

Commuting/Travel

Frequency and form of check-points, behavior of check-point staff, observed treatment of UN staff/INGO staff compared to local population

Driver behavior (anxiety on particular routes or at check-points; requests to transport persons other than staff; evasive response to questions about choice of routes)

Volume and type of traffic (time of day, type of cargo, reaction of civilians to passing military convoys)

Neighborhood/Community Appearance

Aggressive political slogans (graffiti, posters, official photographs)

Visible armed presence of police/militia/military (interaction with civilian population, treatment in bars and restaurants, behavior of soldiers on R&R; particular attention to GBV in all of these behaviors)

Weaponization of civilian population (people carrying guns and other weapons openly; guns, other weapons, and ammunition for sale in local markets; guns and other weapons in the homes of local staff)

Mobility of local population around community, by road, foot, to collect wood, water, herd animals, etc.

Existence of formal or informal curfews

Church/mosque/temple/school attendance decreased

Evidence of children playing outdoors at all

Farmers reluctant to travel to sell produce (crops not harvested, minimal road traffic, market days infrequent, and limited range of goods)

Social Interaction

Staff from local NGOs or administrative structures (teachers) not willing to be seen meeting with international humanitarian staff

Open hostility from local community manifested in verbal abuse, assaults, graffiti, reluctance to do business

Local staff or civilians prepared to discuss government/politics

Translators reluctant to translate certain questions or work with certain staff members (reflecting community tensions or security fears)

Staff reluctant to discuss certain issues on phone/via email

Local Media

Political type and content

Tone, biases, availability

Censorship

Local Bureaucracy

Contact with local officials (open and easily facilitated)

Permissions for programming (bribery; predictability; conflicting requirements from different government departments; attempts to manipulate or direct programming)

Source: Geoff Loane, Jennifer Leaning, Sara Schomig, Alexander van Tulleken, Kelli O'Laughlin, "Civilian Protection and Humanitarian Assistance—Report of the 2009 Civilian Protection Working Group," *Prehospital and Disaster Medicine,* XXIV (2009), 200.

Darfur: 2003–2006

As the conflict in Darfur began to attract international attention, a prominent feature of discussion among policymakers and humanitarians related to the dimensions of the war, its conduct, and the apparent targets of attack. Allegations of grave atrocities perpetrated by proxy soldiers (janjaweed) of the government of the Sudan began to surface, along with charges that their targets were black Africans from African tribes. Early observers in Darfur managed to sound the alarm, and Darfuri villagers, fleeing attacks on their homes and families, arrived as refugees in Chad and began to give riveting testimony about what had happened to them.

The need to obtain information about the conflict, including possible parameters of war crimes and specifics relating to the humanitarian needs of the affected population, loomed large at the onset of this war in early 2003 and continues to perplex the outside world. The government in Khartoum proved successful early on in restricting access, limiting information flows, and punishing local and international personnel who dared to counter the bland official denials and outright lies. How many people were dying and from what causes? Were their farms and villages being destroyed? Was there evidence of targeting of populations on the basis of defined characteristics? Were large numbers of women and young children being raped? What health and nutrition needs could be identified and how could food supplies be assessed over time?

Frustration with this profound information blockade, which hindered many forms of substantive and political response from the international community, propelled the quest for indirect means, methods, and technologies for finding out what was going on. How might people get in to report out? What means could people inside use to communicate to the outside? What indirect indicators or factors might be used to get at the questions of interest? How could we gain systematic knowledge from Chadian refugees? What could be learned from the air? Who was flying over the Sudan? What satellite information was already available, and how could more be acquired were there political will to do so?

The Darfuri crisis, more than any other in the last ten years, has cast into stark relief the capacity of an oppressive and rapacious state to block the light of independent scrutiny. The Sudan is not a small or isolated country, remote or meager in terms of international commerce, travel, or diplomatic engagement. Yet for almost eight years it has successfully prevented the compilation of a comprehensive and accurate account of how its war in Darfur has affected the nearly 8 million people of that region.

Interference with the usual information pathways led to a number of developments in pattern formation and crisis mapping.[19] Humanitarians first relied on familiar tactics to try to obtain reliable quantitative and qualitative information from the affected population through survey methods, questionnaires, and focus groups. The problems with these approaches were numerous. For example, access within Darfur was so uncertain, limited, and insecure that no adequate sampling system could be developed and adhered to for the time it would take to reach but a small number of people in a given affected area. Transport and terrain were similar hindrances to those trying to reach refugees in Chad and no group developed a sampling mode that permitted generalizations beyond the population of one refugee camp there. The government of the Sudan closely managed official visits from international authorities. The authorities' subsequent reports, transmitted in diplomatic understatement, reflected the constraints on independent ascertainment.

In the breach, a number of information-gathering techniques were honed or newly attempted. Human rights organizations and, to some extent, humanitarian organizations began to ask new questions relating to experiences of populations during their flight, since it became apparent from refugees' and internally displaced persons' testimonies that the struggle to escape and to survive in the punishing environment of Darfur and eastern Chad exacted a heavy toll. Photographs were used to convey context in the absence of witnesses or key informants. People who had re-congregated in marginally safer areas were asked to draw maps of their village and to recount what had happened to them. Major governments and international institutions also expanded their mapping capacities (often relying on satellite imagery) in an attempt to transmit a common understanding of current updates and share concerns regarding access, unreached populations, and food supplies. Within international civil society, all forms of existing information and communication technology (ICT), such as cell phones, and all remote sensing imagery in the public domain were leveraged to extract whatever findings might be relevant.

Maps

The influential maps of Darfur that the Humanitarian Information Unit of the U.S. State Department developed are familiar to all who have worked

Figure 10-4. *Eastern Chad and Darfur, Sudan: IDP/Refugee Camps and Confirmed Damaged/Destroyed Villages*

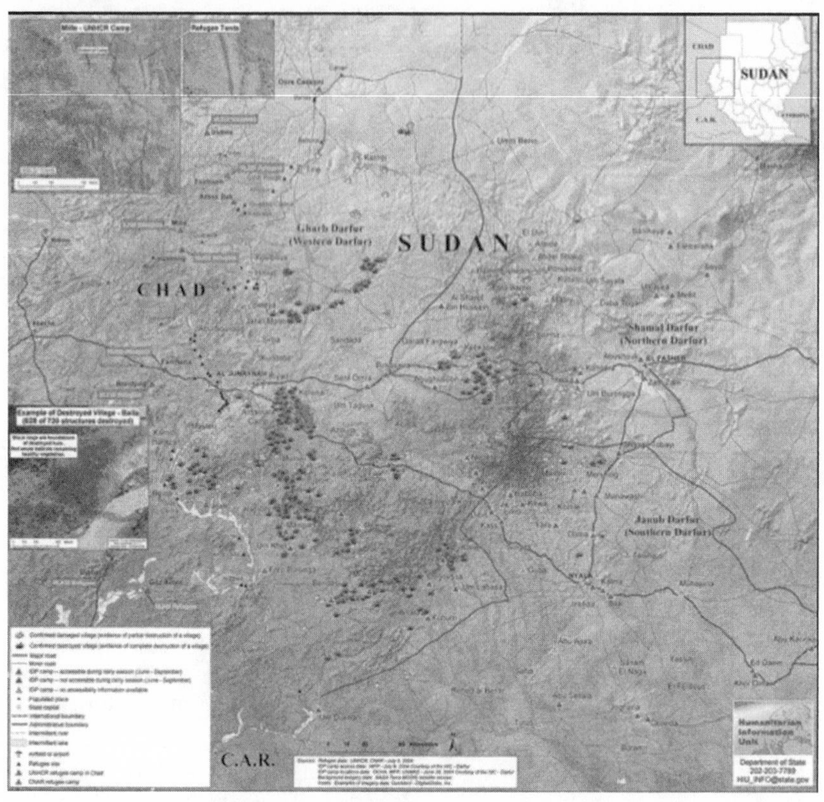

Source: Humanitarian Information Unit, 2007.

on the Darfuri conflict in the recent years. The example here illustrates the strengths of this graphic (geographical accuracy based on satellite imagery; topography, major roads, and seasonal aridity; some information on refugee camps in Chad; and updated visuals depicting the extensive assault on villages throughout Darfur). The political boundaries in the region are not clearly shown; nor is any attempt made to convey population density. What was striking about this map, when it appeared in its first iteration, were the flaming images of destroyed or partly destroyed villages. Analysts in the humanitarian and human rights community embraced these images and then struggled to make further interpretive use of them. Satellite images could portray geo-referenced locations and intensity of fires but could not

Figure 10-5. *Janjaweed Attack on Furawiya*

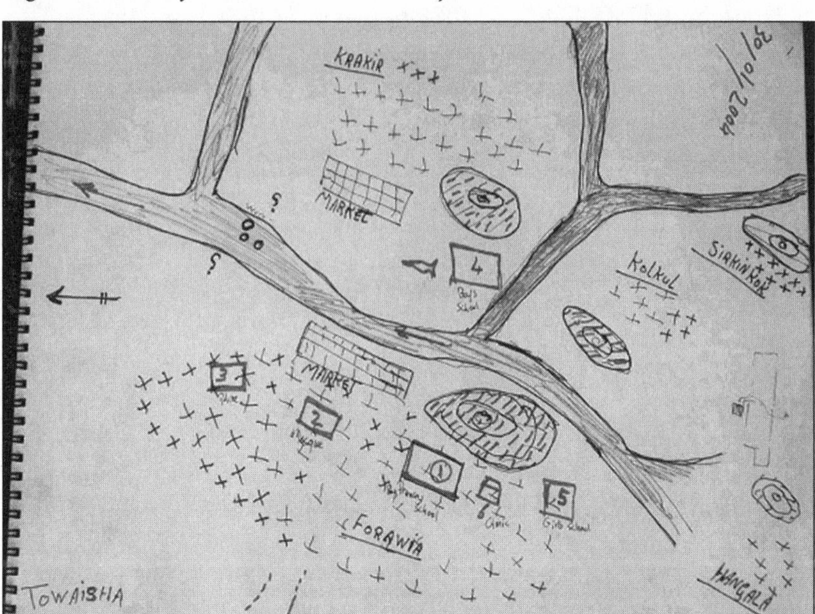

Source: Physicians for Human Rights, 2005.

provide information relating to the tribal or ethnic affiliation of the villages that had been attacked. It was known that people clustered in villages based on communal identity (tribes and clans of Arab or African Darfuris), but no data existed (in libraries, on old maps, or in documents or published literature from anthropologists or historians) regarding the geo-spatial coordinates of villages that had been studied in the past. Hence, it was impossible to use satellite imagery to make the case one way or the other relating to the communal dimensions of the conflict.

When talking with individuals or groups who may have been harmed, human rights investigators have found that the drawing of maps is among the most generative prods to memory and narrative. In virtually all cultures, local people can trace a map on the sand or a piece of paper of their village or local area; and they can superimpose on that map the direction of attack, the flight path that they took, the major sites of interest and value (storage, homes, markets, religious and other public areas, fields, stables, and pastures); and major and minor roads, paths, and sources of water. On that map they can also depict what was destroyed, the livestock killed or stolen, and the locations of killings and atrocities. As one person draws the map, the stories spill out, with others in the group adding details, pointing to areas on the map where the first narrator, the first cartographer, had not provided information or had not been a witness to events.

Clearly, human beings seem wired to tell stories in place as well as in time. In fact, it has proven useful when asking people about close sequences of events in time to ask them to draw a map, and to query them exactly about where they were in relation to each event being described. Invariably, prompted by a visual graphic, people become more precise in their chronologies and provide richer detail of what happened to them at a particular point in time. If this kind of mnemonic does not result in fuller information, one has grounds to question the psychological and cognitive status of the witness (perhaps traumatized, perhaps still deeply fearful) or the person's veracity. Shown on the previous page is a hand-drawn map—a page from the notebook of an investigator for Physicians for Human Rights, who in February 2005 gathered information from a group of male refugees in Chad about the details of the attack that drove them from their Darfur village of Furawiya. Several men participated in sketching and filling in the map as they recounted what happened at each site along the path of the janjaweed assault (tracked by the arrow).

Photographs

The role that photographs play in establishing the plausibility of an event, as relayed in verbal reports or news stories, has been extensively debated, with concerns raised about selection bias and other forms of subjectivity (and not including newer issues related to digital enhancement).[20] Yet from another perspective, photographs, when taken and interpreted with an informed eye, can yield important insights about the context in which the reported events are said to have occurred. What does it mean, in terms of daily experience, to say that the conflict in Darfur arose over disputes about dwindling resources? Why do women in particular have a difficult time escaping hot pursuit as they run into the bush after village attacks?

The photograph on the opposite page, taken on the Chad-Darfur border in May 2004, captures two camels in tow after a day out gathering firewood. Significant features of this photograph, when described by an informed observer, permit the elaboration of an argument relating to environmental resource constraints and environmental degradation in this region. Note that the camels are not carrying a full load. The paltry pile of firewood on each of the camels suggests a real scarcity of fuel. The shape and leaf formation of the

John Heffernan, Physicians for Human Rights

trees support that inference. It is early rainy season and leaves have sprouted, but the branches are tiny against a relatively heavy trunk and branch structure. The photograph has captured a feature that is common in deforested areas marked still by some element of social stability. People abide by a conservation etiquette: they will cut small amounts of wood from adolescent-size branches but leave the trunk and the early shoots alone so that each season there is still some wood to harvest. A third element in this photograph is harder to grasp as it relates to the condition of the soil. This terrain, when viewed at a distance and not traversed on foot, may look relatively unpopulated. Up close, however, the fine sandy soil is crisscrossed as far as the eye can see by numerous human and animal footprints. It is finely interspersed with the dust of animal dung. Already, in mid-2004, this land had reached its carrying capacity for human populations while the refugees from Darfur had barely begun to arrive there.

In the photograph on the next page, the four women fleeing an attack on their village are easy to spot and pick off, given the bleak terrain and lack of cover. A wider shot would have underscored this observation even further. But the vulnerability of these women derives in large measure from another factor, discernible at this resolution. Three of the four women are carrying at least one child.

It takes a great deal in most cultures struck by war or disaster for women to abandon their children. This generalization might well be supported by citation but it is so regularly affirmed in the experiences of humanitarian

Brian Steidle

actors that it is taken as a given. Sorokin, after exhaustive trawling of recorded experiences, reported that under 0.3 percent of people at the extreme edge of starvation resorted to cannibalism. That generalization forms the basis for pattern recognition. Similarly, this generalization (less academically substantiated) forms the basis for another pattern: The attachment of motherhood slows a woman down.

The information conveyed in this photograph not only supports that pattern but provides additional insight into why women are so particularly and consistently caught when the janjaweed go after them on horseback. They are of course not as physically strong or as fast as their male counterparts. But they also are always, or in many cases, encumbered by at least one child. In regions of relatively high fertility, a woman is very likely to be burdened by at least two of the following reproductive conditions: she may be pregnant, nursing an infant, carrying a baby who cannot yet walk, or holding the hand of a toddler. The physical concomitants of motherhood, as well as the psychological, make escape unlikely.

Alternative interpretations of these images could well challenge the contextual information gleaned from these photographs. That is the strength of the process of pattern formation. Hypotheses are generated, further information from many sources could and should be sought, and based on that further information, the hypotheses are refined. The point here is that the *kind* of hypothesis generated from these photographs is different from what one might develop upon reading a narrative text of environmental conditions in eastern Chad and Darfur (both areas known to be parts of the same diminishing ecosystem) or from a woman survivor who recounted what she and her sister had been through. Human beings choose to act or are acted upon in relation to their natural and lived environment. The verbal or textual account provides a linear subjectivity, with a focus on what is being reported; the photograph provides a contextual subjectivity, a visual panorama of the setting and circumstance in which the action is taking place. Robust pattern formation, in the context of conflict mapping, will need inputs from both categories. The effort is to situate every data point in the space and time from which it was apprehended.

Graphics

Graphics with quantitative content can employ images to differentiate among items and to convey relative size and proportionality. They can also communicate the meaning or value of these items in terms that are compelling because they are non-verbal. For example, in Darfur, families were reduced to half their size and lost large numbers of livestock in the attacks on their villages and the flights to Chad. Livestock are sources of wealth, food, and transport and are highly valued in all Darfuri communities. These losses were captured in a graphic in a Physicians for Human Rights (PHR) report, wherein the average number of survivors of each kind (humans by age and sex and animals by species) is depicted in a dark shade and the average number killed or missing is in lighter shades.[21] The cumulative impact is to show the force of numbers and the extinction of many members of the household that had grown up and lived in one land and now, attacked and dispersed, were forced to find their way in another.

The graphic developed for the PHR report on Darfur was influential in shaping the graphic for a *New York Times* cover story on the magnitude of deaths in the long-standing war in the Democratic Republic of the Congo.[22] The point conveyed in this graphic (see figure 10-4) is the large proportion of civilian deaths (women, children, and elderly) dying of causes secondary to the chronic instability and disruption wrought by years of war.

Both of these graphics were based on quantitative data, gathered and analyzed by careful epidemiological methods of sample surveys. Other ways to display these data (histograms, pie charts, and line plots) would have drained the social, psychological, and emotional meaning of these numbers. In war, perhaps more than in other circumstances, numbers tell only part of the story.

As graphics, numbers provide a pattern of what to look for in certain kinds of wars. Wars that involve an armed force deliberately targeting a subpopulation will result in massive human and material losses. Those conflicts among armed groups that persist for years in the same wide area and which

Figure 10-6. *Nonviolent Deaths in Congo's War Zone*

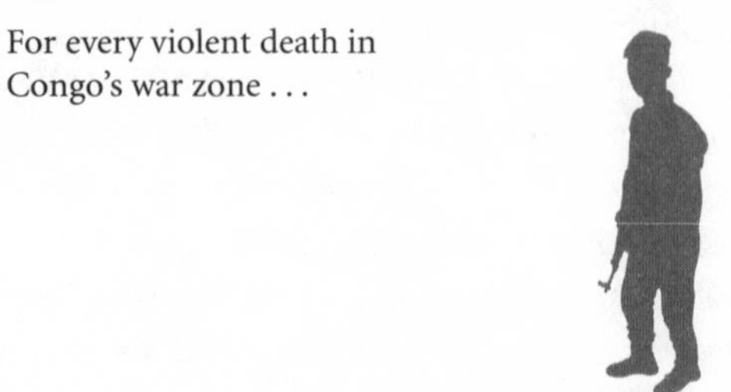

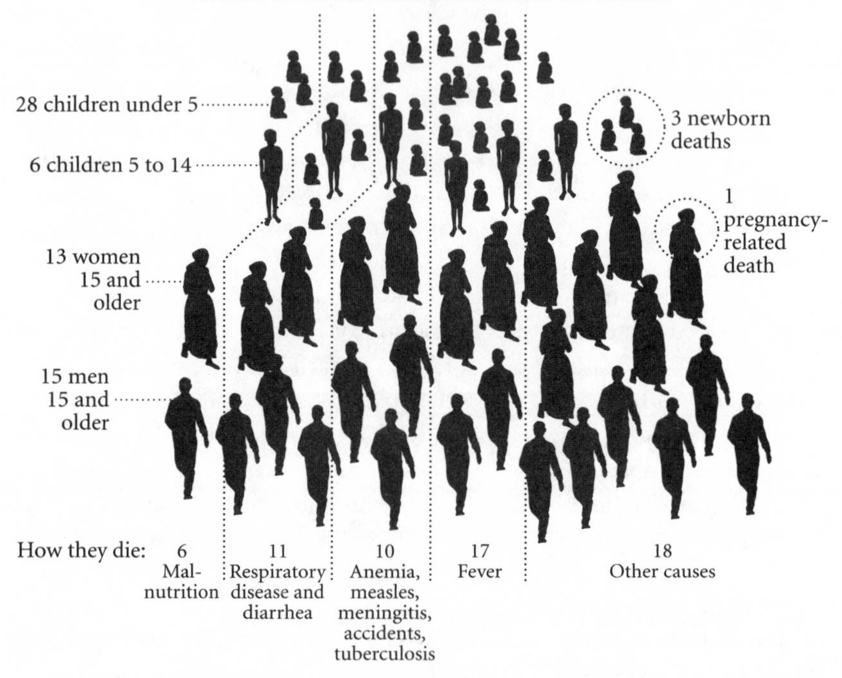

Source: © New York Times Graphics. Based on International Rescue Committee, printed in Marc Lacey, "Beyond the Bullets and Blades," *New York Times* (20 March 2005).

may also include targeting of civilian populations include a number of civilian deaths for every combatant killed.

Satellite Imagery

Flourishing possibilities to improve our understanding of a vast range of phenomena through remote sensing are now carrying over into the field of crisis mapping. Pattern formation and recognition are central tools for interpretation of satellite maps, although much that is seen is not yet sufficiently understood for stable and robust generalizations, even in military circles where this technology has been remarkably developed and long-deployed. In the case of Darfur, a creative use of satellite imaging and historical overlays of several bands, including infra-red, has demonstrated an increase in the vegetation that livestock have consumed in the areas of destruction and devastation.[23] Such independently derived observations validate refugee and humanitarian observers' reports of the slaughter or capture of animals at the time of attacks.

As satellite images become more available for general use (and historical data are now moving on line) the technological wings of the humanitarian community will begin to engage actively in the task of developing patterns relevant for early warning of mass atrocities.

Conclusion

Human beings and natural systems vary infinitely but general rules regarding their behavior and interactions are increasingly well understood. These generalities permit functional and essential simplifications to support the inductive process of acquiring knowledge and assessing situations. Pattern formation constitutes a creative means of developing candidate generalizations and pattern recognition provides a potent approach to simplification. Visualization in time and place fosters pattern development and hypothesis generation. Since data exist to generate patterns of almost infinite complexity and detail, human experience and contextual knowledge—plausibility of relationships and historical perspective—will always be needed to provide ongoing skeptical interrogation of presumptive patterns.

The quest for such means to organize and simplify information in the field of crisis early warning and early intervention is long-standing and urgent.[24] The capacity to generate patterns, when harnessed to the potential of emerging ICT and remote sensing technologies, presents the humanitarian and early warning communities with new assessment possibilities in real and actionable time frames. It has been often asserted that lack of political will rather than lack of information has constrained international policy development and response in the face of impending wide-scale mass atrocities, such as crimes against humanity. Accelerating advances in pattern formation linked to new technologies of ascertainment, display, and communication will, in the next several years, provide more opportunities to test that assertion. The aim among those pressing these advances is to make it much more difficult to say that in the face of information about mass atrocity crimes, we did not know enough soon enough to act decisively.

Notes

1. Susan C. Watkins, "The History of Graphics in Demography," *Studies in Visual Communication*, XI (1985), 2–21.

2. Gary King, Robert O. Keohane, and Sidney Verba, *Designing Social Inquiry: Scientific Inference in Qualitative Research* (Princeton, 1994).

3. Dallas English, "Geographical Epidemiology and Ecological Studies," in Paul Elliott, Jack Cuzick, Dallas English, and Richard Stern (eds.), *Geographical and Environmental Epidemiology: Methods for Small Area Studies* (Oxford, 1992), 3–13.

4. Carl W. Tyler Jr. and John M. Last, "Epidemiology," in John M. Last and Robert B. Wallace (eds.), *Public Health and Preventive Medicine* (Norwalk, 1992), 12.

5. Alexander H. Leighton, *Human Relations in a Changing World: Observations on the Use of the Social Sciences* (New York, 1946).

6. Donald J. Puchala, *Theory and History in International Relations* (New York, 2003).

7. Quincy Wright, *A Study of War* (Chicago, 1965). See also Richard E. Barringer, *Patterns in War* (Cambridge, MA, 1972), with an introduction by Quincy Wright. This second book is a heavily quantitative and model-based attempt to correlate 300 variables according to a theoretical model advanced by the author.

8. Edward R. Tufte, *The Visual Display of Quantitative Information* (Cheshire, CT, 1983), 53.

9. Pitirim A. Sorokin, *Man and Society in Calamity: The Effects of War, Revolution, Famine, Pestilence upon Human Mind, Behavior, Social Organization and Cultural Life* (New York, 1946).

10. Raul Hilberg, *The Destruction of the European Jews* (New York, 1967), v.

11. William Seltzer and Margo Anderson, "Using Population Data Systems to Target Vulnerable Population Subgroups and Individuals: Issues and Incidents," in Jana Asher, David Banks, and Fritz S. Scheuren (eds.), *Statistical Methods for Human Rights* (New York, 2008), 273–328.

12. Jennifer Leaning, "Identifying Precursors," in Carol Rittner, John K. Roth, and James M. Smith (eds.), *Will Genocide Ever End?* (St. Paul, MN, 2002), 117–122.

13. See, for instance, the absence of time-series figures in Creighton's magisterial two-volume history of British epidemics, Charles Creighton, *A History of Epidemics in Britain* (Cambridge, 1891 and 1896) 2v; or the time-series graphics of plague deaths developed by the twentieth century historian Carlos Cipolla on the basis of contemporary tabulated data from the 1630 epidemic in Italy, Carlo M. Cipolla, *Cristofano and the Plague: A Study in the History of Pubic Health in the Age of Galileo* (London, 1973), 66–75.

14. Herbert F. Spirer and Louise Spirer, "Death and Numbers: Semmelweis the Statistician," *Physicians for Social Responsibility Quarterly*, I (1991), 43–52.

15. Rudolf Virchow, "Report on the Typhus Epidemic in Upper Silesia," in L.J. Rather (ed.), *Collected Essays on Public Health and Epidemiology* (Canton, MA, 1985),

205–320. (This essay was first published in 1848.) Florence Nightingale, *Mortality in the British Army* (London, 1858), reprinted from the "Report of the Royal Commission Appointed to Enquire into the Regulations Affecting the Sanitary State of the Army," (1858), available at www.archive.org/details/mortalityofbriti00lond (accessed 21 February 2010).

16. Holly E. Reed and Charles B. Keely (eds.), *Forced Migration and Mortality* (Washington, D.C., 2001).

17. A. P. Davis, "Targeting the Vulnerable in Emergency Situations: Who Is Vulnerable?" *Lancet*, CCCXLVIII (1996), 868–871.

18. Geoffrey Loane, Jennifer Leaning, Sara Schomig, Alexander van Tulleken, and Kelli O'Laughlin, "Civilian Protection and Humanitarian Assistance—Report of the 2009 Civilian Protection Working Group," *Prehospital and Disaster Medicine* (July–August 2009), s197, available at http://pdm.medicine.wisc.edu/harvard_supplement/loane.pdf (accessed 23 February 2010).

19. Jennifer Leaning, "Diagnosing Genocide—The Case of Darfur," *New England Journal of Medicine*, CCCLI (2004), 735–738.

20. Susan Sontag, *On Photography* (New York, 2001).

21. Physicians for Human Rights, *Darfur, Assault on Survival. A Call for Security, Justice, and Restitution* (Cambridge, MA, 2006), 34.

22. Marc Lacey, "Beyond the Bullets and Blades," *New York Times* (20 March 2005); chart from International Rescue Committee, 1.

23. Russell Schimmer, "Tracking Genocide in Darfur: Population Displacement as Recorded by Remote Sensing," Genocide Studies Working Paper No. 36 (New Haven, 2008), available at www.yale.edu/gsp/gis-files/darfur/Tracking-Genocide-in-Darfur-by-Remote-Sensing_No.36.pdf (accessed 7 January 2010).

24. International Commission on Intervention and State Sovereignty, *The Responsibility to Protect* (Ottawa, 2001).

FRANK CHALK

11 *Monitoring African Governments' Domestic Media to Predict and Prevent Mass Atrocities: Opportunities and Obstacles*

Let me begin by posing an axiom: "Monitoring media can predict mass atrocities." While the axiom will not hold in every case, my experience confirms the usefulness of media monitoring for early warning. Governments and their agents usually organize mass atrocities, and one need not be a systems analyst to recognize that even dictators try to enlist the sympathy of their people with persuasive propaganda in order to commit crimes against humanity.

Hate Radio and the Rwandan Genocide

The story of Radio Télévision Libre des Mille Collines (RTLM)'s role in the Rwandan genocide of 1994 is among the best known cases in the sorry

The author would like to acknowledge the vital help he received at the start of his study of radio broadcasting from sociologist Kurt Jonassohn, his colleague and then co-director of the Montreal Institute for Genocide and Human Rights Studies (MIGS) at Concordia University, as well as the valuable research assistance provided for this chapter and his current work on radio broadcasting and mass-atrocity crimes by MIGS's graduate student fellow Erin Jesse and MIGS's interns Ryan Cronsberry, Maha El-Kadi, Chiara Fish, Inken Heldt, Laura Schuelke, Tara Tavender, and Scarlett Trazo. The outstanding research contributions of Danielle Kelton fully justified her listing as the co-author of his earlier work on Sudan broadcasting. Helen Scudding Sproul of the BBC Monitoring Service fulfilled every request for data with the enthusiasm and professional élan one expects from the BBC. Any errors of fact or interpretation are the author's alone. Short portions of this chapter were originally presented at the University of Western Ontario Conference on the Crisis in Darfur, 30 October 2005, London, Ontario, and a preliminary draft was presented at the workshop led by Robert Rotberg on Crimes against Humanity, Harvard Kennedy School of Government, Cambridge, Massachusetts, 4–6 December 2008.

history of hate propaganda since the end of Word War II.[1] Twenty-first century scholarship makes it clear that RTLM was not alone in whipping up the fear and hysteria so important to Hutu mass participation in the genocide—pressure from local leaders, the effects of long-standing disinformation from the government, and solidarity with Hutu neighbors played even more important roles than did the radio broadcasts.[2] But RTLM's hate radio facilitated the genocide, contributed to the authoritativeness of the leaders' orders to kill, and gave important early clues as to the intentions and thinking within the paranoid worlds of the genocidaires.[3]

Business and government leaders close to President Juvénal Habyarimana's wife's political circle, the *Akazu,* established RTLM in 1993 after the Arusha Peace Accords banned government-owned Radio Rwanda from broadcasting hate propaganda. RTLM's daily programming attracted unemployed youth to the Interhamwe militia, spread anti-Tutsi disinformation, disseminated the editorials of hate publications such as *Kangura* among the largely illiterate masses, and undermined trust in the United Nations Assistance Mission for Rwanda (UNAMIR), the UN military force in Rwanda.

Although the radio broadcasts advanced an extremist Hutu message, Western governments refused to fulfill UNAMIR commander General Roméo Dallaire's requests to supply him with radio jamming equipment or to support an operation to destroy RTLM's Kigali transmitter. White House lawyers argued that the United States' involvement in jamming RTLM would violate the First Amendment to the U.S. Constitution, protecting freedom of speech. U.S. Defense Department officials decided that flying a Commando Solo C-130, electronic warfare radio jamming aircraft over Rwanda would be too expensive and too dangerous. Voice of America (VOA) administrators in charge of VOA's francophone African service rejected broadcasts that would counter RTLM's disinformation, claiming that doing so would move VOA into the realm of propaganda.[4]

Western embassies often tuned into the French-language broadcasts of RTLM, but not its Kinyarwanda broadcasts; nor were these Kinyarwanda broadcasts thoroughly monitored, translated, and transcribed by Washington's once formidable Foreign Broadcast Information Service (FBIS) or by Caversham Park's BBC Monitoring Service.[5] This failure was unfortunate. The Kinyarwanda broadcasts were far more aggressive and much more virulent than the French-language broadcasts. In the 1990s, deep cuts to the budgets of FBIS and the BBC Monitoring Service had drastically reduced staff and monitoring capacity.

Alexander George and the Domestic News Broadcasts of Authoritarian Governments in Early Warning of Mass Atrocities

George, a political scientist, RAND corporation researcher, and strategist, was the first to distill the conclusion from research on propaganda during World War II that one of the surest indicators of an authoritarian government's intentions and future plans was the carefully crafted information it fed to its people in their native language.[6] Refining studies of the broadcasts of German radio during the war, George found that Propaganda Minister Joseph Goebbels and his aides had often prepared the German public for important changes in policy through anticipatory news releases and commentaries. He diagramed the relationships as follows:[7]

Situational Factor ← Elite Estimate ← Elite Expectation ← Elite Intention ← Propaganda Strategy ← Content or Policy

Goebbels' Ministry of Propaganda issued directives and guidelines, weekly and sometimes daily, which preceded new directions in Nazi policies and suggested stories designed to shape the public's response to them.[8] By these means, George argued, the Nazi elite minimized the probability of policy changes sparking a public backlash and signaled the response it strove to evoke among Germans when a prepared action was implemented. Reinforcing George's analysis, Herf's research on the transcripts of domestic German radio broadcasts and wall posters has shown that these mediums provided one of the earliest and most sustained indicators of Hitler's intention to annihilate the Jews of Europe.[9]

The Government of the Sudan's Response in the Media to International Pressure

George's conclusions led researchers at the Montreal Institute for Genocide and Human Rights Studies (MIGS) to mount a pilot project to study the role that monitoring African and other domestic government news broadcasts could play in early warning of the twenty-first century's most critical mass atrocity crimes—genocide, crimes against humanity, serious war crimes, and ethnic cleansing. In the chapter "Mass-Atrocity Crimes in Darfur and the Response of Government of Sudan Media to International Pressure," published in 2009, Danielle Kelton and I drew several practical conclusions from our study using government of Sudan (GOS) news broadcasts to anticipate Khartoum's policy directions. We noted

> from our analysis . . . that there are different patterns for the government's use of Sudan Radio, Sudan TV, and the Internet. The Government of Sudan uses Sudan TV and the websites of the Sudanese News Agency to anticipate policy changes and shape the reactions to them among Sudan's educated elite. The government acts as if it fears and respects the potential for political activism among educated Sudanese. Radio Sudan, on the other hand, addresses poor workers and farmers with little time for politics and anti-government activities. Radio Sudan rarely anticipates policy changes. Rather, it is largely a valuable tool for mobilizing participation in government-organized mass demonstrations by the poor in Sudan's largest cities, strengthening the government's claims that any attempt to insert UN troops for the enforcement of peace in Darfur would meet with massive resistance from the majority of Sudanese.[10]

Second, observing that GOS Radio had never detailed the content of the Southern Comprehensive Peace Agreement (CPA), we contended that the GOS had no intention of respecting the terms of the CPA:

> Unprepared by Sudan's government controlled media for the loss of revenue that would accompany any seriously implemented sharing of oil revenues with the south and the west, and schooled by the government media to regard southerners and Darfurians as fractious, disorganized, and backward interlopers in the serious work of governing Sudan, [ordinary] Arab northerners are unready for accommodation with the southern and western regions of the country which contribute the bulk of its revenues. This is the surest indication that the Government of Sudan has no intention of living with signed agreements pledging greater autonomy, revenue sharing, and an integrated defence force to the leaders of dissident movements in the south and the west. The international community will ignore this evidence at its peril. The struggle of the people in southern and western Sudan for greater autonomy, a fair share of oil revenues, and security from attack has only just begun.[11]

Our pilot study of GOS radio and other government media revealed that the Sudan's contemporary technologically diverse news environment was far more complex to monitor and analyze than Nazi Germany's narrower radio and print media-dominated environment in the 1940s. TV and Internet news media accessible primarily to the Sudanese northern political elite facilitates GOS efforts to target the most politically active part of the northern population, requiring us to prioritize these media sources for early warning purposes.[12]

Ugandan Government and Private Media in the Run-Up to Operation Lightning Thunder

Informed by these results, Laura Schuelke, MIGS's country desk officer for Uganda, and I worked on a retrospective study comparing Ugandan government and private media in the run-up to Operation Lightning Thunder, Uganda's military thrust into the Democratic Republic of the Congo (DRC) in 2008. Aimed at destroying important elements of Joseph Kony's Lord's Resistance Army and killing Kony, or forcing him to sign a peace agreement, the Ugandan government's brief military offensive introduced two policy firsts: 1) Uganda attacked Kony, rupturing the status quo after two years of peace negotiations and several Kony "no shows" at ceremonies organized to sign a peace accord between him and Uganda; and 2) Uganda coordinated its attack with the armed forces of the DRC and the government of Southern Sudan (GOSS), marking the first time the Ugandan Peoples Defence Forces (UPDF) had officially mounted a joint cross-border operation with two of Uganda's neighbors.[13]

Ugandan President Yoweri Museveni's government had comparatively more domestic support and international credibility, despite its obvious flaws, than did Omar al-Bashir's GOS.[14] Did a relatively popular government, such as Museveni's, use official government media to prepare the Ugandan public for its abandonment of the cease-fire with Kony and its multi-national armed expedition into the DRC, or, had the Ugandan government assumed that Kony was so hated by the Ugandan public that it would welcome, without any special preparation, the government's unprecedented moves, eliminating any need to prepare Ugandans via government-controlled news media?[15]

Schuelke concluded that Museveni's government made no sustained, overt use of the government media to prepare Ugandans for these important policy changes, although government spokespeople did point to possible retaliatory action against Kony by the GOSS; possible government leaks to the private media may have served the same purpose. Some five weeks before launching the cross-border attack, the privately owned *Daily Monitor* reported on the Ugandan army's preparations for an attack on Kony's camps in the DRC and one week prior to that attack, Ugandan government officials renewed their warnings to Kony that if he did not sign a peace accord there would be consequences.[16] Neither of these warnings met the test of a serious media campaign by the government of Uganda. Interestingly, comparing the behavior of the GOS and that of Uganda reveals that while the Sudan's more authoritarian government did use the media to prepare the public for changes in government policy, Uganda's less authoritarian government did not.

Open Source Information

The U.S. Intelligence Community "defines open source information as that information that is publicly available material that anyone can lawfully obtain by request, purchase, or observation."[17] Transcripts of broadcasts are just one part of "open source information (OSINT) produced by newspapers, journals, radio and television, and the Internet."[18] Following the recommendations of several government commissions and the Congress of the United States, in 2005 the director of national intelligence established a National Open Source Center (NOSC) under the management of the Central Intelligence Agency (CIA). The NOSC incorporated within it the Foreign Broadcast Information Service (FBIS), the information gathering agency that has monitored, transcribed, and translated into English foreign government radio news broadcasts for the U.S. government and private researchers since 1941.[19] As of late 2009, NOSC and the BBC Monitoring Service maintain the high level of cooperation and division of responsibilities that has characterized British and American information gathering since World War II.

What Media Monitors Look For

MIGS's country desk officers are expected to use the same historical research strategy that intelligence analysts employ when seeking to understand a country of interest.[20] They must first master the country file and acquire an in-depth knowledge of the country's history, national problems and interests, population and demographics, economy, and politics. Building on this foundation, the country desk officer is ready to study possible destabilizing forces; factions vying for power, influence, or control; non-governmental factions; and the government's responses to them.

Desk officers monitor government domestic news media for a wide variety of signs, but particularly focus their scrutiny and analyses on: 1) hate propaganda; 2) omissions of key information from news broadcasts; 3) evidence of increasing government control over the distribution of news; 4) the emergence of novel, participatory media vehicles known to penetrate deeply listeners' psyches; and 5) reports of people murdered on the basis of their ethnicity, nationality, race, religion, political affiliation, and social status. These five foci, briefly discussed below, are based on knowledge of the government media's role in the perpetration of mass atrocities in the Soviet Union, Nazi Germany, Indonesia, East Pakistan, Burundi, Cambodia, Rwanda, and Côte d'Ivoire.

Hate Propaganda

Hate propaganda that originates within a government and is disseminated via government-controlled media is a red flag that atrocity crimes are to come. Hate propaganda differs from normal criticism of opposition groups and it can take several forms: 1) It demonizes a group as "other" by characterizing its members as insects, rodents, snakes, dogs, weeds, or sub-humans; 2) It claims that members of the targeted group are involved in conspiracies to dominate the society; 3) It charges that members of the targeted group are plotting physically to annihilate pro-government groups once they achieve power; and 4) It exhorts the killing of members of the targeted group; it portrays the situation as a case of "kill or be killed."

Omissions of Key Information from News Broadcasts

Omitting a government's key responsibilities under its signed peace and conflict reduction agreements from government news broadcasts and other media are tell-tale indicators of forthcoming danger.[21] The government's rejection of news programs integral to bridge-building and reconciliation is another sign of its on-going hostility toward conflict resolution. Governments may also refuse to broadcast information essential to reunification of former child soldiers with their families or bar rebel forces from the air even after signing agreements pledging to integrate dissident politicians and demobilized fighters into their cabinets and armed forces.

Increasing Government Control over the Distribution of News

Whenever a government insists that all news broadcasts emanate from a central source under its control, thereby monopolizing the dissemination of the news, the door is opened to lethal abuses of the airwaves. This was the case in Indonesia under President Suharto from 1967 to 1998. News of the slaughter of alleged communists (1965) and of Indonesian operations in East Timor (1975 to 1998) originated from government-operated studios in Jakarta, despite the fact that Indonesia had dozens of commercial radio stations scattered from one end of the Indonesian archipelago to the other.

Novel, Participatory Media

Novel forms of communication are ideal mechanisms for disseminating hate propaganda. Talk radio, phone-in shows, and hot Zairois music, all new to Rwandan radio listeners, deepened the penetration of RTLM's hate propaganda and won a large listenership for its Kinyarwanda hate broadcasts. Valerie Bemeriki, RTLM's star radio journalist, modeled her broadcasting style on her favorite Belgian football announcers. Unlike the boring news broadcasters of Radio Rwanda, she sounded vivid, engaged, and interesting.[22]

Small-scale, Targeted Killings

Media reports of small-scale killings targeting victims on the basis of their membership in ethnic, national, racial, religious, political, and social groups are important warnings that larger-scale atrocity crimes may be in the offing. In the Rwandan case, many observers failed to see the emerging killing pattern in 1992–1993, wasting vital time needed to prepare appropriate soft and hard power interventions that would have saved thousands of lives.[23]

Where the U.S. and U.K. Governments are Needed to Deal with Problems of Monitoring Government News Media

This chapter argues that daily monitoring of open source news is vital to early warning to prevent genocide and crimes against humanity. The time has passed when serious intelligence analysts believe that it is only purloined secret information that leads to valuable operational conclusions. Such an out dated attitude, recalls Douglas Naquin, the current Director of the U.S. government's NOSC, has produced the impression that "'our business is stealing secrets.' Or 'our business is espionage.'" Contrary to these old assumptions, Naquin and other analysts contend that 90 percent of the intelligence information most useful to the U.S. government has always come from "open sources," that is, unclassified information drawn from "the Internet, databases, press, radio, television, video, geospatial data, photos and commercial imagery."[24]

Up until the early 1990s, the U.S. FBIS was the jewel in the open source crown, but the search for a "peace dividend" through budget retrenchment following the end of the Cold War, the growth of the Internet, and the coming to power of national leaders who were unfamiliar with the value of open sources ravaged the staff at FBIS. Naquin traces FBIS's downward spiral:

> The 1990s was not a good decade for FBIS. . . . Between 1993 and 2002, when I came in as director of FBIS, our staff was reduced almost in half. Also during that time period, we had to reduce a good percentage of our foreign national staff, people who had been with us around the world for 25- to 30-year careers.

In the aftermath of the Cold War, the staff of BBC Monitoring based at Caversham Park, on the outskirts of Reading, England, and BBC Monitoring's foreign staff suffered a similar fate for the same reasons.

The "peace dividend," resulting from the reduction in defense spending at the end of the Cold War, facilitated tax reductions but seriously reduced BBC Monitoring's and FBIS's coverage, which researchers had come to rely upon. One result of the lesser coverage is that several key problems confront researchers in the twenty-first century when they seek English translations of open source material. MIGS's initial, in-depth analyses of the domestic radio and TV news broadcasts of Sudanese government-operated stations were made possible by its annual subscriptions to BBC Monitoring, which records, transcribes, and translates GOS news programs and Friday night sermons from Arabic into English, posting them on its password-protected website within twenty-four hours. We now understand that the BBC's excellent coverage of the Sudan's media results from the British government's classification of the Sudan as a part of the Middle East.[25] Were it not for that conceptual judgment, Africa's largest country would probably have suffered the dismal fate to which BBC Monitoring consigns the rest of Africa.

A detailed set of priorities negotiated between BBC Monitoring and its principal government masters, primarily the Cabinet Office, advised by the Foreign and Commonwealth Office, the Defence Intelligence Staff, and other British intelligence agencies, largely drove BBC's broadcast surveillance operations for 2008–2009. These stakeholders as of late 2009 regard almost all of Africa as unworthy of the intensive monitoring that they devoted to Africa's media before the end of the Cold War.[26]

The BBC's "level one" countries—those designated to receive the highest level of monitoring—are the countries of the Middle East plus Afghanistan, China, Iran, North Korea, Pakistan and Russia. The "level two" countries in BBC Monitoring's hierarchy are Argentina, Belarus, the Former Yugoslav Republic of Macedonia (FYROM), India, Indonesia, Turkey, Ukraine, the countries of the Caucusus, Central Asia, and the Horn of Africa. In its report for 2007–2008, BBC announced that it had elevated five African countries—Ghana, Côte d'Ivoire, Malawi, Nigeria, and Zimbabwe—from level three to level two, but by any practical measure the actual coverage of government media in these African countries remains meager. Level three countries—those in the rest of Africa, Europe, Latin America, and Asia Pacific—receive the least coverage.

Along with the Sudan, MIGS's expanded its coverage to six other countries—the Democratic Republic of the Congo, Iran, Côte d'Ivoire, Rwanda, Uganda, and Zimbabwe—chosen because they topped our list of conflict states most likely, now or later, to become sites of genocides, crimes against humanity, war crimes, and ethnic cleansing. Since mid-July 2008, student interns or "country desk officers" from Concordia and McGill Universities have been posting their concise summaries of government radio and TV news broadcasts from these countries on MIGS's website.[27] BBC Monitoring's uneven and poor coverage of the African countries in which MIGS is particularly interested makes it difficult for us to identify indicators of future changes in government policies essential to early warning.[28] While we consult allAfrica.com to try to fill the information gaps, there is no real substitute for BBC Monitoring when it is truly on the job.[29]

The Case of Zimbabwe

BBC Monitoring's approach to gathering information about Zimbabwe offers some useful insights into the thinking of the executives of BBC Monitoring and the ministries that it serves. Responding helpfully to MIGS's complaints of inadequate coverage of Zimbabwe (especially during the days of massive political repression, systematic rape of women in townships that were perceived to be hostile toward Robert Mugabe, cholera epidemics caused by the breakdown of municipal utilities, and vigorous Zimbabwe government jamming [using transmitters and techniques imported from China] blotting out the broadcasts of independent radio stations such as the Zimbabwe Forum of Voice of America, the Voice of the People, SW Radio Africa, and Studio 7 of the Voice of America), BBC Monitoring pointed us to weekly media reports from the Media Monitoring Project of Zimbabwe (MMPZ), based in Harare and supported by the government of Norway.[30] The governments of Norway, the Netherlands, and the United States; as well as Article 19; the Open Society Initiative for Southern Africa; and the Communications Assistance Foundation fund MMPZ. While its reports are excellent, it rarely provides verbatim transcripts of government of Zimbabwe news broadcasts. Instead, its reports feature content analyses of the major media in Zimbabwe, contrasting the one-sided news stories appearing in government media with the less distorted treatment of the same topics in the independent commercial media.[31] Missing from MMPZ's reports are the raw data that MIGS needs—the transcripts of government news broadcasts or close summaries of such broadcasts that would provide evidence on which to base our own projections of future changes in government policies.

Where We Stand Today

The September 2001 al-Qaeda attacks on New York and Washington drew the 9/11 Commission and the Weapons of Mass Destruction Commission to highlight the importance of open source intelligence gathering. Both commissions called for devoting more resources to exploit open sources and for better coordination and dissemination of the information gathered by the U.S. government.[32] Seizing the opportunity to go beyond FBIS's traditional customers—the CIA and the Department of State—Naquin has set out to serve the entire intelligence community as well as the U.S. Department of Defense and the Department of Homeland Security. As of 2009, Naquin is trying to recoup FBIS's personnel losses from the 1990s. In 2007, he proposed importing staff from other government agencies, doubling the number of people employed at the Open Source Center over the next five years.[33] Coverage may be improving, but the tide is turning slowly. As of late 2009, neither the Open Source Center nor the BBC Monitoring Service has matched its outstanding coverage of the African government's media in the 1970s and the 1980s.

While the fundamental cause of this deficiency is the persistent shortage of personnel and funds, the problem has another important root—management's decision to concentrate on fewer countries and on fewer media outlets within those countries it does cover in order to compensate for its shortage of resources. Naquin rationalizes the decline in open source coverage, arguing, "No matter what resources the community has, it will never keep pace with the amount of data that is available." Proposing to substitute quality coverage for quantity, he declares, "We need to focus as much on asking the right question as on just trying to collect everything." In the past, he suggests, FBIS "often generated good products that were not seen by customers."[34] But quality information-collecting is by no means assured in Naquin's new model. To compensate for the massive budget cuts they suffered, BBC Monitoring and FBIS have increasingly turned to outside contractors to assist them with monitoring, transcribing and translating. Similar to BBC Monitoring, budget cuts have forced the U.S. Open Source Center to outsource much of its information-gathering and translation work to commercial companies, many of whose employees lack the expertise and the institutional memory of FBIS's former staff members. FBIS employs 700 independent contractors, while at the end of the 2007–2008 budget year, BBC Monitoring employed 234 independent contractors, who contributed 35 percent of the service's transcribed items.[35] *Private Eye*, the British satirical periodical, exaggerated wildly, but insightfully, the spirit of the cutbacks at BBC Monitoring when it reported in 2006 that "Caversham's budget has now been cut by £2m, losing 80 posts and ending the monitoring of radio broadcasts from boring places where nothing of interest happens—such as the former Soviet Union and the whole of Africa."[36]

The MIGS's country desk officers covering Côte d'Ivoire, the Democratic Republic of the Congo, Kenya, Libya, Rwanda, Somalia, and Zimbabwe are fighting an uphill battle in the face of surprisingly weak coverage of government news media in each of these countries. Every one of these countries has been gripped or may soon be gripped by mass political violence and atrocity crimes, and in every case BBC Monitoring and FBIS are unable to muster decent coverage.

BBC Monitoring supplied to MIGS an excellent BBC World Service Trust report on Kenya's vernacular hate media in the aftermath of the large-scale post-election violence in that country in December 2007; the report was provided in response to criticism of its failures in Kenyan coverage. The report was prepared with the help of local journalists, and media and human rights NGOs, and summarized the hate tactics of call-in show hosts on various vernacular radio stations. It also pointed to the failure of government media to facilitate democratic discourse during the crisis.[37] However, just as in the case of Zimbabwe, the report failed to include transcripts of the offending broadcasts, weakening the possibilities of using it for forward-looking research aimed at avoiding further political and communal violence. The BBC Monitoring Service maintains a monitoring station on the outskirts of Nairobi, but focused exclusively on Kenyan broadcasters using English or Kiswahili. Kenyan human rights groups and the United Nations Development Program hired firms to monitor the Kenyan media; not even those firms had more than a few transcripts, according to Somerville, who has written an important paper on violence and vernacular radio in Kenya.[38]

The whole approach of BBC is to supply information *after* the fact, when it is too late to prevent mass violence. The NGO analyses are far behind the curve of violence by the time the results are circulated.[39] Apathy and inadequate resources in the wake of retrenchments shape the weak performance of BBC Monitoring and FBIS. Their staffs should be augmented and their budgets replenished so that they can be reinvigorated, can contribute valuable data for early warnings of mass atrocities, and can assist in the prevention of such atrocities.

The Cost for Access to English Translations of Open Source Information

While BBC Monitoring's translated transcripts of African and Middle Eastern radio and TV broadcasts are available on-line to non-governmental researchers for an annual subscription fee, non-governmental researchers must access FBIS's transcripts through the more expensive World News Connection (WNC), a commercial service distributed by the National Technical Information Service of the U.S. Department of Commerce, now packaged as part of a commercial information service called Dialog. Since July 2008, ProQuest, a major provider of information databases to business and university libraries, has distributed Dialog and WNC.[40] ProQuest subscriptions are often expensive and their annual costs are usually beyond the means of university libraries and researchers.

The Thomson Corporation, which was the first commercial distributor of the WNC reports, advertised the WNC as "the only news service that allows you to take advantage of the intelligence gathering experience of OSC."[41] ProQuest now owns the commercial distribution rights to FBIS, but its relationship to the NOSC is not that of a public/private partnership in which the private partner finances improved service. ProQuest simply markets access to government-gathered data, which U.S. taxpayers already paid for. Any notion that the American NOSC and private distributors have significantly improved their coverage of African government radio and television news broadcasts is dispelled by checking the list of countries and media sources available through Dialog. The Dialog database offers the government news broadcasts of only seven African countries: Ghana, Kenya, Lesotho, Mozambique, Nigeria, Senegal, and Zambia.[42] On a continent where radio is still the chief purveyor of news to the majority of the population, such coverage is inadequate. And coverage of the print media is no better. To offer just one example, Dialog's coverage for Zimbabwe is limited to two newspapers, the *Financial Gazette* and *The Herald,* omitting stories from the *Chronicle,* the *Sunday News,* the *Sunday Mail,* the *Manica Post,* the *Zimbabwe Independent, The Standard,* and *The Zimbabwean.*

The Role of Civilian Observatories in Encouraging Governments to Implement the Principles of the Responsibility to Protect (R2P)

MIGS's radio monitoring project implements a philosophy of inclusive citizenship, bypassing government gatekeepers, and promoting a human rights-based global society by accessing foreign perspectives and widely disseminating summaries of otherwise inaccessible information to the educated public, especially those interested in preventing future mass atrocities. MIGS looks toward broadening public involvement in human rights activities and the rise of a new sense of volunteerism. MIGS country desk officers develop a sense of ownership over the data they summarize, taking on the role of citizen public policy advocates.

The American and British governments' actions to deepen their coverage of foreign media and make their translations freely available on the Internet would vastly improve ordinary citizens' access to what is written and broadcast in Africa, the Middle East, Asia, and Latin America. Country desk officers participating in the MIGS pilot project contribute to focusing Canadian and American government officials and legislators on advancing human rights internationally. Disseminating well-reasoned, balanced, and carefully documented early warnings of looming mass atrocities, especially when the political will to become involved is initially absent among the great powers and at the UN, the students increase the pressure on government leaders for thoughtful, timely action. Collaborating with NGOs, teachers, relief workers, and others who live in the affected areas, the students exercise countervailing power that challenges government analysts and serves as a catalyst for more widespread citizen reporting. This citizen-based, decentralized approach should contribute to mobilizing the will to intervene wisely, using soft power and, when necessary, deploying hard power to prevent future mass atrocities such as those committed in Rwanda and elsewhere. At their best, civilian observatories have the capacity to reinvigorate the application of R2P and contribute to an evidence-based, democratic global conversation.

Goals for the Future

We have identified two important issues for the future:

—British and American governments' insufficient monitoring and translation of African government radio and television news broadcasts

—Non-governmental researchers' limited access to translated African government news broadcasts and other news sources.

A recent report from the U.S. Congressional Research Service, which reviewed the George W. Bush administration's approach to open source intelligence, points out that "Congress also has broader options."[43] "A more radical approach," it observes:

> would be to establish an Open Source Agency completely outside the Intelligence Community (in addition to the existing Open Source Center). The goal would be to provide open source information not just to intelligence analysts but to all elements of the Federal Government including congressional committees. Such an entity could also be established in the Defense Department (outside of intelligence agencies) with special responsibilities for supporting multilateral operations involving a number of countries some of whom might not be intelligence partners of the United States.[44]

The utility of such an open source agency for multilateral cooperation leading to the enforcement of R2P is obvious. Not only could governments benefit from such an innovation; academic research institutes focused on the prevention of crimes against humanity and genocide would also gain improved access to valuable data, especially if the coverage of African states were broadened and deepened. As the CRS study points out,

> Proponents of this plan argue that open source information is essential for virtually all governmental functions but that the explosion of available information has not been matched by concerted efforts to acquire and analyze it. The goal would be to establish a center of expertise for the entire Federal Government *and to make available to the public free universal access to all unclassified information acquired through this initiative.*[45]

The attainment of such goals would, in my view, seriously enhance our ability to predict, identify, and document the intent to commit mass atrocity crimes. In democracies, equipping citizens' research observatories with information resources comparable to those of governments would encourage thoughtful and well-informed dialogues about early warning signs when large-scale atrocity crimes could still be prevented. Together with the work of responsible government agencies and international institutions, such observatories would help to discourage government decision-makers from postponing decisions and delaying actions essential to applying R2P in a timely and effective manner.

Notes

1. Also see Frank Chalk, "Hate Radio in Rwanda," in Howard Adelman and Astri Suhrke (eds.), *The Path of a Genocide: The Rwanda Crisis from Uganda to Zaire* (New York, 1999), 93–107; Frank Chalk, "Intervening to Prevent Genocidal Violence: The Role of the Media," in Allan Thompson (ed.), *The Media in the Rwanda Genocide* (Ottawa, 2007); see as well the essays by Alison Des Forges, Jean-Pierre Chretien, Marcel Kabanda, Mary Kimano, Charles Mironko, and Simone Monasebian, available at www.idrc.ca/rwandagenocide (accessed 27 January 2010); Aaron Karnell, "Role of Radio in the Genocide of Rwanda," unpub. PhD dissertation, College of Communications and Information Studies, University of Kentucky, 2003; International Criminal Tribunal for Rwanda (ICTR), *The Prosecutor versus Jean-Paul Akayesu,* ICTR–96–4–T, 1998, and subsequent appeal judgments.

2. See Darryl Ly, "Echoes of Violence: Considerations on Radio and Genocide in Rwanda," in Thompson (ed.), *The Media in the Rwanda Genocide*; Scott Straus, *The Order of Genocide: Race, Power, and the War in Rwanda* (Ithaca, 2006); Lee Ann Fujii, *Killing Neighbors: Webs of Violence in Rwanda* (Ithaca, 2009).

3. Ibid. See also Alison Des Forges, "The Radio: The Voice of the Campaign," in her *Leave None to Tell the Story: Genocide in Rwanda* (New York, 1999), available at www.hrw.org/legacy/reports/1999/rwanda/ (accessed 2 August 2009).

4. Interview between author and Lt. Col. Anthony Marley, Africa Bureau, Regional Affairs, U.S. Department of State, Washington, D.C. (20 April 1995). Also see the original U.S. policy documents supporting this interpretation on the web site of the National Security Archive, available at www.gwu.edu/~nsarchiv/NSAEBB/NSAEBB53/index.html (accessed 2 August 2009).

5. Author's research on RTLM transcripts (furnished by staff of the International Criminal Tribunal for Rwanda), FBIS printed transcripts, and BBC Monitoring On-Line Archive. Noted in Des Forges, *Leave None to Tell the Story* and Reporters sans frontières, *Les médias de la haine* (Paris, 1995).

6. Alexander George, "Prediction of Political Action by Means of Propaganda Analysis," *Public Opinion Quarterly*, XX (1956), 334–345; Alexander George, *Propaganda Analysis: A Study of Inferences Made from Nazi Propaganda in World War II* (Evanston, 1959).

7. George, *Propaganda Analysis*, 47.

8. Ibid., especially "A General Action Schema for Propaganda Analysis," 18–28 and "Prediction of an Elite's Major Actions," 131–170.

9. Jeffrey Herf, "The 'Jewish War': Goebbels and the Antisemitic Campaigns of the Nazi Propaganda Ministry," *Holocaust and Genocide Studies*, XIX (2005), 51–80. Herf's research revises the conventional wisdom in the field, shaped by Hannah Arendt and others, which held that little in the German media substantially revealed the ferocity or the timing of the Nazis' actual implementation of their genocidal

intentions toward European Jews. For a discussion of Arendt's early insights and change of position, see Herf, 54–55. Also see Herf's excellent book, *The Jewish Enemy: Nazi Propaganda during World II and the Holocaust* (Cambridge, MA, 2008).

10. Amanda F. Grzyb (ed.), *The World and Darfur: International Response to Crimes against Humanity in Western Sudan* (Montreal, 2009), 112–151.

11. Ibid.

12. Ibid.

13. Laura Schuelke, "Did the Ugandan Media Prepare the Population for Military Intervention in 'Operation Lightning Thunder' (14 December 2008–14 March 2009) in the DRCongo? Focus on Ugandan Radio Broadcasting, the *New Vision*, and the *Daily Monitor*," unpublished MIGS research report, 2009.

14. The Economist Intelligence Unit's Democracy Index for 2008 ranks Uganda 101st overall, while the Sudan ranks 146th. For Political Participation, on a 10 point scale, Uganda is at 3.89 points and the Sudan is at 1.67. For Electoral Participation and Pluralism, Uganda is at 4.33 and the Sudan is at 1.33. Democracy Index 2008 labels Uganda's government a "hybrid regime" and the Sudan's government "authoritarian." See "The Economist Intelligence Unit's Index of Democracy 2008," available at http://graphics.eiu.com/PDF/Democracy%20Index%202008.pdf (accessed 2 August 2009).

15. Ibid.

16. As early as November 12, 2008, the Ugandan government-owned *New Vision* featured Fortunate Ahimbisbwe's story, "GOSS [Government of South Sudan] to force LRA out of Sudan after November," warning that if Joseph Kony did not sign the final peace agreement by the end of November 2008, the GOSS would attack the Lord's Resistance Army. Schuelke, "Did the Ugandan Media Prepare the Population for Military Intervention." Also see *New Vision* online, (12 November 2008), available at www.newvision.co.ug/ (accessed 2 August 2009); Angelo Izama, "LRA attacks in DRC," *Daily Monitor* online (6 November 2008), available at www.monitor.co.ug/ (accessed 2 August 2009). The latter article reported that the Uganda People's Defence Forces had drawn up plans for a combined attack on the LRA together with the military forces of the DRC and the GOSS; Tabu Butagira, "UPDF ready to attack Kony," *Daily Monitor* online (1 December 2008); and Tabu Butagira and Risdel Kasasira, "Is UPDF About to Attack Kony's Congo Camps?" *Daily Monitor* online (7 December 2008).

17. Richard A. Best Jr. and Alfred Cumming, "Open Source Intelligence (OSINT): Issues for Congress," (2007), Order Code RL34270, 5–6, available at www.fas.org/sgp/crs/intel/RL34270.pdf (accessed 4 December 2008), citing Intelligence Community Directive Number 301 and P.L. 109–163, Sec. 931.

18. Ibid.

19. Ibid., 12.

20. See U.S. Department of the Army, "Open Source Intelligence," Field Manual Interim No. 2–22.9 (Washington, D.C., 2006), 4-6–4-7.

21. The refusal of Khartoum's news directors to include the terms of the Comprehensive Peace Agreement for South Sudan in its domestic, Arabic language radio broadcasts is such a warning of trouble to come.

22. See Frank Chalk, "Hate Radio in Rwanda," in Adelman and Suhrke (eds.), *The Path of a Genocide*, 93–107; interview between author and Valerie Bemeriki, Kigali Central Prison (March 2008).

23. On the importance of early logistical preparation for armed intervention, should it prove necessary, see Alan Kuperman, *The Limits of Humanitarian Intervention: Genocide in Rwanda* (Washington, D.C., 2001).

24. "Remarks by Doug Naquin," *CIRA (Central Intelligence Retirees' Association) Newsletter*, XXXII (2007), 3, available at www.fas.org/irp/eprint/naquin.pdf (accessed 2 August 2009).

25. Ibid.

26. BBC Monitoring, *A Year in Review: The World in Its Own Words, 2007–2008*, 6, available at www.monitor.bbc.co.uk/review08.pdf (accessed 4 December 2008).

27. See http://migs.concordia.ca/. We borrowed the term "country desk officer" from Professor David Crane's Impunity Watch project at the Syracuse University College of Law. See www.impunitywatch.net/impunity_watch_home/.

28. Ibid.

29. Ibid.

30. See Hansjoerg Biener, "Zimbabwe," Radio for Peace, Democracy and Human Rights, available at www.evrel.ewf.uni-erlangen.de/pesc/peaceradio-ZBW.html (accessed 4 December 2008); Media Monitoring Project of Zimbabwe, "Zimbabwe: Media Update Report, 3–9 November 08," (15 November 2008).

31. See AfDevInfo Organisation Record, available at www.afdevinfo.com/html reports/org/org_63385.html (accessed 4 December 2008). Robert Mugabe of Zimbabwe is a master coiner of hate labels. His party, ZANU-PF, casts its terroristic acts as "weeding out traitors." In February 1982, he characterized Joshua Nkomo and ZAPU, Nkomo's party, as "like a cobra in a house," concluding, "The only way to deal effectively with a snake is to strike and destroy its head." In 2008, ZANU-PF killers drove through the town of Buhera South, Zimbabwe, displaying the body of Chokuse Muphango on the back of a Mitsubishi 4 X 4 truck and proclaiming, "We have killed the dog." See "Joshua Nkomo's Letter," *Zimbabwe Metro* (7 June 1983), available at www.zimbabwe metro.com (accessed 22 November 2007); "Chris McGreal, "Choose Mugabe or Face a Bullet," *Zimbabwe Times* (18 June 2008), available at www.thezimbabwetimes.com (accessed 2 August 2009), cited in Clapperton Chakanetsa Mavhunga, "The Mobile Workshop: Mobility, Technology, and Human-Animal Interaction in Gonarezhou (National Park), 1850–Present," unpub. Ph.D. dissertation, University of Michigan, 2008, 406–408, available at http://deepblue.lib.umich.edu/bitstream/2027.42/61738/1/mavhungc_1.pdf (accessed 2 August 2009).

32. See *The 9/11 Commission Report*, available at www.9-11commission.gov/report/911Report.pdf and the Report of the International Weapons of Mass

Destruction Commission, *Weapons of Terror*, available at www.wmdcommission.org (both accessed 2 August 2009).

33. Reported in Robert Ackerman, "Intelligence Center Mines Open Sources," *SIGNAL Magazine* (March 2006), available at www.afcea.org/signal/articlesanmviewer.asp?a=1102&print=yes (accessed 2 August 2009).

34. Ibid.

35. Wikipedia, "Foreign Broadcast Information Service," available at http://en.wikipedia.org/wiki/Foreign_Broadcast_Information_Service (accessed 4 December 2008). BBC Monitoring, *A Year in Review*, 9.

36. *Private Eye*, No. 1150, (2006), as quoted on Cryptome, available at http://cryptome.org/bbc-osc.htm (accessed 14 August 2008).

37. BBC World Service Trust, "The Kenyan 2007 Elections and Their Aftermath: The Role of the Media and Communication," Policy Briefing No. 1 (London, 2008), available at http://downloads.bbc.co.uk/worldservice/trust/pdf/kenya_policy_briefing_08.pdf (accessed 2 August 2009).

38. Keith Somerville, "Kenya: Violence, Hate Speech and Vernacular Radio," MIGS Occasional Paper, (Montreal, 2009), available at http://migs.concordia.ca/papers.html.

39. In the case of Kenya, the BBC Trust report appeared four months after the crisis erupted.

40. "ProQuest Acquires Dialog," (1 July 2008), available at www.proquest.com/en-US/aboutus/ pressroom/08/20080701.shtml (accessed 4 December 2008).

41. World News Connection, available at http://wnc.dialog.com/ (accessed 4 December 2008).

42. "Sources Included in World News Connection (WNC), Dialog File 985," (2003), available at http://support.dialog.com/searchaids/dialog/pdf/file985_sources.pdf (accessed 4 December 2008).

43. CRS, "Open Source Intelligence (OSINT)," 20.

44. Ibid., 20–21.

45. Ibid. Emphasis added.

Contributors

Claire Applegarth holds a Master in Public Policy degree from Harvard Kennedy School, where she concentrated on international security policy. Her Policy Analysis Exercise, co-written with Andrew Block, presented an action plan on the Responsibility to Protect to the United Kingdom's Foreign and Commonwealth Office. In the summer of 2008, Applegarth was a Council of Women World Leaders Fellow in the Office of the Foreign Minister of Liberia. Prior to the Kennedy School, she served as a Research Analyst at the consultancy DFI International and as a Herbert Scoville Jr. Peace Fellow at the Arms Control Association. She has also interned at the Center for Strategic and International Studies and the United Nations Institute for Disarmament Research.

Andrew Block holds a Master in Public Policy degree from Harvard Kennedy School, where he and Claire Applegarth co-authored an action plan on the Responsibility to Protect for the United Kingdom Foreign and Commonwealth Office. Block has served as Policy Director for prominent U.S. House and Senate campaigns. He has worked with the Department of State at the American embassy in Lusaka, Zambia, where he coordinated the U.S. Ambassador's grant-making program and researched contemporary African political affairs.

Frank Chalk is Professor of History and Director of the Montreal Institute for Genocide and Human Rights Studies at Concordia University (MIGS). He is the co-author, with Kurt Jonassohn, of *The History and Sociology of Genocide: Analyses and Case Studies* (1990). Other publications include "Hate Radio in Rwanda," in Howard Adelman and Astri Suhrke (eds.),

The Path of a Genocide: The Rwanda Crisis from Uganda to Zaire (1999), and "Radio Broadcasting in the Incitement and Interdiction of Gross Violations of Human Rights, including Genocide," in Roger W. Smith (ed.), *Genocide: Essays toward Understanding, Early Warning, and Prevention* (1999). Together with Dinah Shelton, Howard Adelman, Alexander Kiss, and William Schabas, he edited the three-volume *Encyclopedia of Genocide and Crimes against Humanity* (2004). More recent publications include "Le Service hongrois de la BBC et le sauvetage des juifs de Hongrie" in Jacques Sémelin, Claire Andrieu, Sarah Gensburger (eds.), *La résistance aux génocides, De la pluralité des actes de sauvetage* (2008) (English version, *The Resistance to Genocide: The Plurality of Acts of Rescue*, 2010), and, with Danielle Kelton, "Mass Atrocity Crimes in Darfur and the Response of Government of Sudan Media to International Pressure," in Amanda F. Grzyb (ed.), *The World and Darfur: International Response to Crimes against Humanity in Western Sudan* (2009). With General Roméo Dallaire, Chalk co-directed a major MIGS research project in Canada and the United States which led to the publication of *Mobilizing the Will to Intervene: Leadership and Action to Prevent Mass Atrocities* (2009). He is also a researcher and cluster leader in the Concordia research project on "Life Stories of Montrealers Displaced by War, Genocide, and Other Human Rights Violations," a five-year project funded by the Social Science and Humanities Research Council of Canada. Chalk served as President of the International Association of Genocide Scholars (1999–2001), and is a past president of the Canadian Association of African Studies. In 2000–2001, Chalk was a Fellow of the Center for Advanced Holocaust Studies at the U.S. Holocaust Memorial Museum in Washington, D.C. From 1975 to 1976, he was a Fulbright professor of history at the University of Ibadan, Nigeria.

David M. Crane has been Professor of Practice at Syracuse University College of Law since 2006. In 2005, he was a Distinguished Visiting Professor. From 2002–2005 he was the founding Chief Prosecutor of the Special Court for Sierra Leone, appointed to that position by the Secretary-General of the United Nations. Crane served for more than thirty years in the federal government of the United States, during which time he was appointed to the Senior Executive Service of the United States in 1997. For his service to humanity, Case Western Reserve University in Ohio awarded him an honorary Doctor of Laws degree in 2008. Prior to his departure from West Africa in 2005, Crane was made an honorary Paramount Chief by the Civil Society Organizations of Sierra Leone.

Richard J. Goldstone was a Distinguished Visitor from the Judiciary at Georgetown University Law Center in 2010. From 1994 to 2003 he was a Justice of the Constitutional Court of South Africa, while also serving as the Chief Prosecutor of the United Nations (UN) International Criminal Tribunals for the former Yugoslavia and Rwanda from 1994–1996. He was also the chairperson of the International Independent Inquiry on Kosovo, which Swedish Prime Minister Goran Persson established. He is chairperson emeritus of the Human Rights Institute of the International Bar Association. He is an Honorary Bencher of the Inner Temple, London, an Honorary Fellow of St. John's College, Cambridge, and an Honorary Member of the Association of the Bar of New York. Goldstone is a Foreign Member of the American Academy of Arts and Sciences and serves on a number of boards, including the Human Rights Institute of South Africa, Physicians for Human Rights, the International Center for Transitional Justice, and the Center for Economic and Social Rights, and has served as a member of the International Group of Advisers of the International Committee of the Red Cross and the committee, chaired by Paul A. Volcker, appointed by the Secretary-General of the UN to investigate allegations regarding the Iraq Oil for Food Program. In 2005, he was awarded the Thomas J. Dodd Prize in International Justice and Human Rights jointly with the UN High Commissioner for Human Rights, Louise Arbour. In 2009, he received a MacArthur Foundation Award for International Justice. He holds Honorary Doctorate of Law degrees from seventeen universities and is a fellow of the Weatherhead Center for International Affairs at Harvard University.

Don Hubert is Associate Professor of Public and International Affairs at the University of Ottawa and a Senior Associate at the Global Center for the Responsibility to Protect at the City University of New York. For nearly a decade, he led policy development on Canada's human security agenda at the Department of Foreign Affairs, including responsibility for small arms proliferation, natural resources linked to armed conflict, the "responsibility to protect," and corporate social responsibility. He served as Deputy to the Chair of the Kimberley Process in 2004 and was a consultant for the International Commission on Intervention and State Sovereignty in 2000. He is currently completing *Human Security: Global Politics and the Human Costs of War* (forthcoming). His publications include "The Landmine Ban: A Case Study in Humanitarian Advocacy" (2000); "The Responsibility to Protect: Supplementary Volume of the International Commission on Intervention and State Sovereignty," with Thomas Weiss (2001); and *Human*

Security and the New Diplomacy: Protecting People, Promoting Peace, with Rob McRae (2001).

Sarah E. Kreps is Assistant Professor of Government at Cornell University. She is the author of *Coalitions of Convenience? United States Military Interventions after the Cold War* (forthcoming) and a number of articles on issues of international cooperation, nuclear proliferation, and international peacekeeping. She previously held fellowships at Harvard Kennedy School's Belfer Center for Science and International Affairs and the Miller Center for Public Affairs at the University of Virginia. Between 1999 and 2003, Kreps served as an active duty officer in the United States Air Force, where she was a program manager for intelligence, surveillance, and reconnaissance systems and a foreign area officer for European and sub-Saharan African Affairs.

Dan Kuwali is Deputy Director of Legal Services in the Malawi Defence Force. He is also the Managing Consultant of the law firm, K.D. Freeman & Associates. He is a correspondent for the *Yearbook of International Humanitarian Law* and Adjunct Assistant Professor and Course Director of International Humanitarian Law at Lund University, Sweden. He was a Fellow at the Carr Center for Human Rights Policy, Harvard Kennedy School. He served as Division Legal Advisor with the United Nations Mission in the Democratic Republic of the Congo. Kuwali has been a Marie Curie Researcher at the Grotius Centre of International Legal Studies in The Hague, and Guest Researcher at the Nordic African Institute.

Jennifer Leaning is Director of the Harvard Francois Xavier Bagnoud (FXB) Center for Health and Human Rights. An expert in public health and rights-based responses to humanitarian crises, Leaning is the FXB Professor of the Practice of Health and Human Rights at Harvard School of Public Health and Associate Professor of Medicine at Harvard Medical School. Prior to her current appointment, Leaning served for five years as co-director of the Harvard Humanitarian Initiative. From 1999 to 2005, Leaning directed the Program on Humanitarian Crises and Human Rights at the FXB Center. During the 1980s and 1990s, Leaning held progressively responsible roles in medical management at Harvard Community Health Plan and worked clinically in emergency medicine at Brigham and Women's Hospital. She has served on the boards of Physicians for Human Rights, Physicians for Social Responsibility, and Oxfam America and is a member of the Board of Directors of the Humane Society of the United States and the Massachusetts Bay

Chapter of the American Red Cross. She is on the editorial boards of several journals and a member of the Board of Syndics at Harvard University Press. The author of many academic articles, she has also edited *Humanitarian Crises: The Medical and Public Health Response* (1999).

Edward C. Luck is Senior Vice President for Research and Programs at the International Peace Institute and Special Adviser to the United Nations (UN) Secretary-General, for whom he primarily focuses on responsibility to protect issues. He is currently on public service leave as Professor of Practice in International and Public Affairs at the School of International and Public Affairs, Columbia University, where he remains Director of the Center on International Organization. A past president and CEO of the UN Association of the USA, he has served the UN in a variety of capacities, taught at Princeton University and Sciences-Po (Paris), and founded a research center co-sponsored by the New York University School of Law and Princeton's Woodrow Wilson School. Among his books are *United Nations Security Council: Practice and Promise*, with Michael Doyle (2006); *International Law and Organization: Closing the Compliance Gap* (2004); and *Mixed Messages: American Politics and International Organization, 1919–1999* (1999).

Robert I. Rotberg is Director, Program on Intrastate Conflict and Conflict Resolution, Harvard Kennedy School, and President, World Peace Foundation. He was Professor of Political Science and History, MIT; Academic Vice President, Tufts University; and President, Lafayette College. He is the author and editor of numerous books and articles on U.S. foreign policy, Africa, Asia, and the Caribbean, most recently *Corruption, Global Security, and World Order* (2009), *China into Africa: Trade, Aid, and Influence* (2008), *Worst of the Worst: Dealing with Repressive and Rogue Nations* (2007), *Building a New Afghanistan* (2007), *A Leadership for Peace: How Edwin Ginn Tried to Change the World* (2006), *Battling Terrorism in the Horn of Africa* (2005), *When States Fail: Causes and Consequences* (2004), *State Failure and State Weakness in a Time of Terror* (2003), *Ending Autocracy, Enabling Democracy: The Tribulations of Southern Africa 1960–2000* (2002), *Peacekeeping and Peace Enforcement in Africa: Methods of Conflict Prevention* (2001), and *Truth v. Justice: The Morality of Truth Commissions* (2000).

Sarah Sewall teaches international affairs at Harvard Kennedy School, where she also directs the Program on National Security and Human Rights in the Carr Center for Human Rights Policy. She led the Obama Transition's

National Security Agency Review process in 2008. During the Clinton Administration, Sewall served as the first Deputy Assistant Secretary of Defense for Peacekeeping and Humanitarian Assistance. From 1983–1996, she served as Senior Foreign Policy Advisor to Senate Majority Leader George J. Mitchell on the Democratic Policy Committee and the Senate Arms Control Observer Group. Before joining Harvard, Sewall was at the American Academy of Arts and Sciences, where she edited *The United States and the International Criminal Court* (2002). Her more recent publications include the introduction to the University of Chicago edition of the *U.S. Army and Marine Corps Counterinsurgency Manual* (2007) and, with John White, *Parameters of Partnership: U.S. Civil-Military Relations in the 21st Century* (2009). She is a member of the U.S. Department of Defense's Defense Policy Board Advisory Committee and the Center for Naval Analyses Defense Advisory Committee.

Index

The World Peace Foundation

The World Peace Foundation was created in 1910 by the imagination and fortune of Edwin Ginn, the Boston publisher, to encourage international peace and cooperation. The Foundation seeks to advance the cause of world peace through study, analysis, and the advocacy of wise action. As an operating, not a grant-giving foundation, it provides financial support only for projects that it has initiated itself. In its early years, the Foundation focused its attention on building the peacekeeping capacity of the League of Nations, and then on the development of world order through the United Nations. The Foundation established and nurtured the premier scholarly journal in its field, *International Organization.* Since 1993, the Foundation has examined the causes and cures of intrastate conflict. The peace of the world in these decades has been disturbed primarily by outbreaks of vicious ethnic, religious, linguistic, and intercommunal antagonism within divided countries. Part of the task of the Foundation is to resolve conflicts as well as to study them. The Foundation's work in Congo, Cyprus, Burma, Sri Lanka, Haiti, the Sudan, Zimbabwe, and all of Africa has resolution of conflict as its goal. The Foundation has sponsored a detailed study of negotiating the end of deadly conflict within and between states. It is also engaged in an analysis of the successes and failures of African leadership.

Harvard Kennedy School Program on Intrastate Conflict, Conflict Prevention, and Conflict Resolution

On July 1, 1999, the Program on Intrastate Conflict, Conflict Prevention, and Conflict Resolution was established in the Belfer Center at the Harvard Kennedy School as a result of an association between the Center and the World Peace Foundation. The Program analyzes the causes of ethnic, religious, and other intercommunal conflict and seeks to identify practical ways to prevent and limit such conflict. It is concerned with measuring good governance, the consequences of the global proliferation of small arms, the failure and vulnerability of weak states, failed states and rogue states, UN peace building reform, with peace building and peace enforcement capabilities in Africa, conflict resolution in war-torn countries, the role of good leadership in Africa, China's influence in Africa, assessing crimes against humanity, and the role of truth commissions in conflict prevention and conflict resolution.

The Brookings Institution

The Brookings Institution is a private nonprofit organization devoted to research, education, and publication on important issues of domestic and foreign policy. Its principal purpose is to bring the highest quality independent research and analysis to bear on current and emerging policy problems. Interpretations or conclusions in Brookings publications should be understood to be solely those of the authors.